**EDITORIAL RESEARCH REPORTS ON**

# POLITICAL

# INSTABILITY

# ABROAD

Timely Reports to Keep
Journalists, Scholars and the Public
Abreast of Developing Issues, Events and Trends

**Published by Congressional Quarterly, Inc.**

**1414 22nd Street N.W.**

**Washington, D.C. 20037**

## About the Cover

*The cover was designed by Art Director Howard Chapman who, assisted by staff artist Richard Pottern, provided many of the graphics in this book.*

PRINTED IN THE UNITED STATES OF AMERICA, AUGUST 1976

**Editor, Hoyt Gimlin**
**Editorial Assistant, Jeanne D. Heise**
**Production Manager, I. D. Fuller**

**Library of Congress Cataloging in Publication Data**
Main entry under title:

Editorial research reports on political instability abroad.

Bibliography: p.
Includes index.
1. World politics—1975-1985—Addresses, essays, lectures. I. Congressional Quarterly, Inc. II. Title: Political instability abroad.
D849.E34      327′.09′047      76-22177
ISBN 0-87187-096-7

# Contents

# Contents

# Foreword

If it is ever possible to characterize something so vast and complex as the world political order, a good argument can be made for the word "instability." Political instability reaches all continents today—nations in the industrial West as well as those carved out of the former colonial empires in Asia and Africa. Western Europe nervously watches native communism's performance at the ballot box in Italy, the potentially volatile loosening of controls in Spain, and still another act in Portugal's revolutionary drama. Even in England, the mother of Parliaments, serious thought is directed at the nation's ability to withstand still further economic calamities without rending the social fabric.

Nor has the Communist bloc been spared unrest and turmoil. The restiveness of Eastern Europe was the ghost at the banquet when the 25th Soviet Communist Party Congress met in Moscow in February. Even seemingly monolithic China has been subjected to political traumas that suggest Chairman Mao's succession remains unsettled.

Interestingly, the issues causing political unrest today are often unrelated to matters of East-West doctrinal belief. Strident nationalism, race and religion—as old-fashioned as those causes may sound—underlie much of the strife. Nationalism is a key element in Third World demands for economic parity with the West and it is present on both sides in the Panama Canal dispute. In southern Africa, the threat of racial war dominates all other concerns. In Northern Ireland, Cyprus, Lebanon, Israel, the Philippines and a host of other places, there are religious roots to conflict or unrest.

All the while, world arms sales rise and confidence dwindles in the ability of the United Nations to bring about internationally minded agreements. The 10 reports composing this book portray various areas of conflict, concern and political instability—and they attempt to suggest some possibilities for accommodation.

Hoyt Gimlin
Editor

August 1976
Washington, D.C.

# WORLD ARMS SALES

by

John Hamer

May 7
1 9 7 6

# WORLD ARMS SALES

E VERY NATION wants arms. Nearly all of the world's countries have some kind of military forces, and most are trying constantly to expand and improve them. The United States, the Soviet Union and other major nations manufacture and maintain their own vast arsenals. But small or poor nations must obtain their armaments from others—primarily from the large, industrial nations that produce and sell weapons. The international trade in arms has become one of the world's fastest-growing global businesses in recent years. But today there is rising concern about the sheer volume of the world arms trade, and an intensifying debate over what can or should be done to limit or control the worldwide traffic in armaments.

It is a complex debate, with many thorny questions and few easy answers. It gives rise to questions such as these: Does every nation have a sovereign right to arm and defend itself? Is it wise or moral for strong nations to arm weak nations? Do military forces help to preserve the peace or tend to trigger wars? Should arms be sold to both sides in areas of conflict? Who should decide how much weaponry is sufficient—buyers or suppliers? Do arms sales win friends and allies, or will the purchased weapons someday be used against their makers or their makers' allies? If one industrial nation stops selling arms, will other developed nations step in to meet the demand?

These are questions that clearly nag the leaders of the principal arms-exporting nations—the United States, the Soviet Union, France, Britain, Czechoslovakia, China, Poland, Canada and West Germany *(see box, p. 8)*—as well as the Third World of Asian, African and Latin American nations that have become the principal arms importers. The questions must have occurred to leaders of the rapidly developing nations that already have or soon will have the capacity to export arms—Israel, Brazil, India, South Africa, Argentina, Iran, Egypt, Pakistan, Singapore, South Korea and Jordan, among others.[1]

To a great degree, the global arms trade today is a wide open and highly competitive market. Many observers see striking

---

[1] See "Controlling the International Arms Trade," United Nations Association of the United States of America, UNA-USA National Policy Panel on Conventional Arms Control, April 1976, p. 7.

similarities to the early 1900s, when arms salesmen gained a reputation as "merchants of death." The arms dealers of those days were immortalized in George Bernard Shaw's *Major Barbara* (1905) by the character called Undershaft, whose creed was "to give arms to all men who offer an honest price for them without respect of persons or principles...to capitalist and socialist, to Protestant and Catholic, to burglar and policeman, to black man, white man and yellow man, to all sorts and conditions, all nationalities, all faiths, all follies, all causes and all crimes."

In many ways, Undershaft's philosophy still prevails. According to the U.S. Arms Control and Disarmament Agency, the estimated value of worldwide transfers of conventional arms exceeded $8.4-billion in 1974, the latest year for which complete figures are available.[2] The term "transfers" includes not only arms sold but also those provided as military aid. A further complexity in terminology is the Department of Defense reference to arms "orders," which are items contracted for but not actually delivered *(see p. 5)*. The Arms Control Agency uses the term "arms" to include weapons and ammunition, support equipment and spare parts, but not training, services or construction.

From 1950 to 1975, about 41 per cent of all American military exports were weapons and ammunition, 18 per cent supporting equipment, 17 per cent spare parts and 24 per cent training, services and construction. The agency said world military expenditures rose to $315-billion in 1974, up from $280-billion in 1973 and $160-billion in 1965, in terms of current dollars. The estimated spending on military materials worldwide in 1974 represented about 6 per cent of the value of all goods and services produced that year.

Though comparisons are difficult to make, there is general agreement among experts that Russia's defense expenditures recently have been greater than America's.[3] But as of 1974, according to the agency, the United States remained the world's leading arms dealer. However, "I think 1975 will show the Soviets ahead" in arms sales when total figures for that year are compiled, agency Director Fred C. Ikle said on April 1. He attributed this to Soviet sales in Africa and the Middle East.

---

[2] This was well above the $5.3-billion in arms transfers in 1965, although it was down from the 1973 peak of $9.4-billion. See "World Military Expenditures and Arms Transfers, 1965-1974," ACDA, March 31, 1976, p. 3. For U.S. figures, the agency said it used official trade statistics compiled by the Census Bureau and information provided by the Department of Defense. To estimate foreign arms transfers, it used "a variety of methods...which reflected careful analysis of all available sources of data, including foreign trade statistics..., estimates produced by contract research specialists, and information appearing in U.N. reports, the press, and secondary sources."

[3] By $10-billion a year, according to the unofficial but authoritative International Institute for Strategic Studies in London, as reported in its survey of "The Military Balance, 1975-76." For background, see "American Global Strategy," *E.R.R.*, 1976 Vol. I, pp. 87-104.

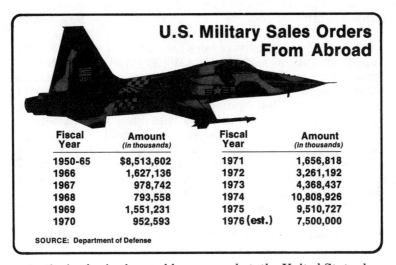

## U.S. Military Sales Orders From Abroad

| Fiscal Year | Amount (In thousands) | Fiscal Year | Amount (In thousands) |
|---|---|---|---|
| 1950-65 | $8,513,602 | 1971 | 1,656,818 |
| 1966 | 1,627,136 | 1972 | 3,261,192 |
| 1967 | 978,742 | 1973 | 4,368,437 |
| 1968 | 793,558 | 1974 | 10,808,926 |
| 1969 | 1,551,231 | 1975 | 9,510,727 |
| 1970 | 952,593 | 1976 (est.) | 7,500,000 |

SOURCE: Department of Defense

As the leader in the world arms market, the United States has set the pace and tone of the global trade since World War II.[4] During the last decade, there has been a complete reversal of traditional American arms policy. The United States in the past simply gave its allies, friends and prospective friends large quantities of armaments—in outright grants or on favorable credit—as part of its overall military aid and security assistance programs. However, in the 1970s the policy has changed to stress cash and credit sales to a far greater degree. To some extent this is the result of the Nixon Doctrine, which pledged that the United States would help developing nations become self-sufficient without interfering in their internal affairs. It is also the result of the conflict in the Middle East, where the United States has sold great quantities of weapons to Israel, and of the rapid rise in world oil prices, which gave Persian Gulf countries enormous amounts of money to spend on arms.[5]

But this policy has developed in a short period of time without much publicity or public debate. For many years U.S. arms sales abroad seldom topped $1-billion annually, but in the early 1970s they began to climb rapidly and in 1974 foreign military sales orders, including both cash and credit transactions, reached $10.8-billion *(see above)*, surpassing the total of arms sales in the 1950-65 period. While the Pentagon was becoming a salesman, commercial dealers were increasing their share of the market. Commercial sales deliveries, which the State Department approves by issuing export licenses, were expected to more than triple in fiscal year 1976 to reach $2.1-billion.[6]

[4] See "International Arms Sales," *E.R.R.*, 1970 Vol. II, pp. 647-666.

[5] See "Persian Gulf Oil," *E.R.R.*, 1973 Vol. I, pp. 231-248, and "Resurgent Iran," *E.R.R.*, 1974 Vol. I, pp. 305-322.

[6] The licenses are required by the Mutual Security Act of 1954. See *Congressional Quarterly Weekly Report*, Dec. 20, 1975, pp. 2817-2819.

Under the foreign military sales program the Defense Department oversees arms sales, and the Military Assistance Advisory Groups overseas *(see box, p. 341)* act as sales agents. Foreign countries in the market for U.S. weapons contract directly with the Pentagon, which then supplies the armaments from existing stockpiles or handles transactions with the private American company manufacturing the new equipment. The foreign nations pay the Pentagon the purchase price plus a pro-rata share of the weapons research and development costs and a 2 per cent management fee. If sales are made through commercial channels, the State Department's export licenses permit the arms shipments to go abroad. More than 16,000 licenses were issued in fiscal year 1974. If credit is needed for arms purchases, it is generally arranged by the U.S. government or obtained through private sources with a government guarantee.

American arms sales abroad have become so widespread, *The Washington Post* commented editorially on Nov. 28, 1975, that they "now may constitute the principal way by which the United States relates to most nations of the world." If so, this has occurred largely without the knowledge or approval of the American public. According to a Louis Harris Survey released the previous March, Americans opposed U.S. military aid to foreign countries and U.S. arms sales abroad by sizable margins.[7] By a majority of almost 4 to 1, the persons who were questioned said they believed that America's supplying of arms worsened its relations with other countries and encouraged dictators to use military power against their own people.

### U.S. Government's Justification of Its Policy

The White House, the Defense Department and the State Department offer several reasons for continued U.S. arms sales abroad. These can be summed up as an argument that arms sales are an essential tool of U.S. foreign policy and a vital means of exercising U.S. influence overseas. The State Department said in a "Current Policy" statement issued in 1975: "The United States is, for many countries, the supplier of choice. Our products are preferred because they are of high quality. Our hardware is well-designed, well-made, and dependable. Our supporting systems—training and logistics—are second to none. Of equal importance, many nations want to buy from us because they want to be associated with the United States on other matters of mutual interest, and they may wish to avoid relations with other exporting countries whose intentions are open to question."[8] There are several additional elements to the

---

[7] By a ratio of 65 to 22 on aid and 53 to 35 on sales.

[8] "U.S. Foreign Military Sales," The Department of State, Bureau of Public Affairs, Office of Media Services, Current Policy No. 4, July 1975.

government's rationale for arms sales abroad. They include political, economic and social concerns, such as:

*Political influence.* By selling arms, the United States can exert pressure on the internal politics and national policies of recipient countries.

*Conflict control.* The United States can exercise control over regional arms races and alter the outcome of conflicts by allowing or refusing sales or by withholding spare parts, ammunition and maintenance.

*Balance of payments.* Arms sales abroad helped the United States to move from an international trade deficit in 1974 to a surplus in 1975.[9] Trade is a major element in the overall balance of payments between this country and others.

*Employment.* Industry officials estimate that for every $1-billion in U.S. arms sales abroad, more than 30,000 American jobs are directly created and 60,000 other jobs are provided in related enterprises.

*Taxpayer savings.* The switch from grants to sales saves American taxpayers the cost of supplying foreign nations with free arms, and it adds millions to the U.S. Treasury in corporate and individual income taxes.

*Unit-cost savings.* Adding foreign sales to contracts with U.S. military forces allows American arms manufacturers to lower the per-unit cost, helps pay for research and development, and in some cases makes it possible for the United States to produce for its own use weapons it otherwise could not afford.

*Stockpile reduction.* Foreign sales allow the United States to reduce large stocks of surplus and outdated military equipment and possibly to make a profit at the same time.

*Competition preemption.* By becoming the dominant arms supplier to foreign nations, the United States can preempt sales offered by other nations, particularly the Soviet Union and Communist-bloc countries.

*Government destablization.* In some cases, the United States may wish to use arms sales—open or clandestine—to help opposition groups, to encourage disorder and to help overthrow unfriendly foreign governments.

## Counter Arguments by Arms Trade Critics

For virtually every argument for continued foreign arms sales there is an opposing argument. First of all, critics of the weapons trade dispute the contention that arms sales constitute an effective foreign policy tool. They point out that in numerous countries U.S. arms sales and military aid have yielded this

---

[9] See "U.S. Balance of Payments Developments Fourth Quarter and Year 1975," *Survey of Current Business,* March 1976, pp. 30-52.

**Arms Transfers of Major Suppliers, 1965-1974**
*(in billions of current dollars)*

| Country | Amount | Country | Amount |
|---------|--------|---------|--------|
| United States | 31.6 | China | 2.2 |
| Soviet Union | 18.8 | Poland | 1.2 |
| France | 2.8 | Canada | 1.2 |
| United Kingdom | 2.1 | West Germany | 1.2 |
| Czechoslovakia | 1.3 | All others | 2.1 |

**World Total 64.5**

SOURCE: U.S. Arms Control and Disarmament Agency

country little long-term influence.[10] Moreover, conflicts have erupted in many parts of the world in which both sides used American-made weapons—specifically between Jordan and Israel in 1973, between India and Pakistan in 1971, and on Cyprus between Turkish troops and Greek Cypriots in 1974.

In some parts of the world, U.S. arms sales seem to have fueled regional arms races. When one nation buys costly new military equipment, its neighbors and rivals may feel compelled to keep pace. This clearly has occurred in Latin America, where Chile and Peru have kept up an arms race for many years. The principle of controlling conflicts by refusing sales or withholding parts or services would apply only if the United States were the world's exclusive arms dealer. Instead it is only one of many nations willing to sell and maintain military goods. In practice, if a conflict breaks out there often is pressure on the United States to supply even more arms—as was the case in Ethiopia.[11]

There are several examples of arms sales tending to increase American commitments abroad rather than decrease them. Critics of arms sales foresee "the tail wagging the dog." Eugene LaRocque, a retired admiral who directs the Center for Defense Information in Washington, D.C., has said: "Arms sales constitute the first step toward a U.S. commitment to the government of the purchasing country. Shipments of U.S. weapons are normally followed by U.S. soldiers, sailors, and airmen, as well as civilian technicians who are required to train the new owners of the equipment."

Sales of increasingly sophisticated military equipment almost inevitably raise the stakes of any potential conflict. Moreover, sales to military dictators are likely to stir anti-American

---

[10] This argument is made, among others, by Fred Kaplan in "Still the Merchants of Death," *The Progressive*, March 1976, p. 22.

[11] See "Ethiopia in Turmoil," *E.R.R.*, 1974 Vol. II, p. 922.

feelings among the local populace. This was particularly true in Greece where the downfall of the ruling military junta in 1974 brought forth public denunciations of the United States. Raymond Smith, chairman of a State Department "open forum" panel on arms, has said that arms sales "are a positive indication to the recipient and its opponents that suppliers would prefer the recipient in power."[12] There is also the prospect that ruling regimes will be overthrown and the American-supplied military equipment will fall into the hands of those opposed to the United States.

The prime example of this was South Vietnam, and the possibility exists in numerous other countries. It is argued that if the United States does not sell arms, other nations—especially the Soviet Union—will step in to meet the demand. George Kennan, a former U.S. ambassador to Russia, disputes this argument: "If we stop selling arms the Russians will probably not sell them, because they don't want to waste the money. They have people over there saying, 'If we don't do it, the Americans will.' "[13] Other countries might continue selling arms even if the superpowers do not, but arms-control advocates say that little serious effort has been made to reach a limitation agreement *(see p. 16)*.

## Growing Sales by Other Industrial Countries

The Soviet Union, where all arms exports are controlled by the Kremlin, has for decades shipped large quantities of weapons to Warsaw Pact nations,[14] North Korea and North Vietnam. And the Russians have become the principal suppliers of many Third World nations, offering low prices and liberal credit. Until Cairo's recent break with Moscow, Egypt was the chief recipient of Soviet arms, followed by India. Both received tanks, MIG fighter-bombers and ground-based anti-aircraft missiles. The Soviet AK-47 automatic rifle, widely regarded as the world's best combat rifle, also has been a big seller worldwide.[15]

For many years France and Britain have vied for third place among the world's arms dealers, their principal markets being the Middle East, Latin America and former African colonies. The French recently have pulled ahead; in 1974 they sold $3-billion in war materials to some 80 nations. Their best-selling products are the Mirage supersonic fighter, AMX tanks, Alouette helicopters and Exocet anti-ship missiles. France's arms industry, employing some 270,000 people, is considered vital to the national economy. The French government strongly sup-

---

[12] Quoted by Kaplan, *op. cit.*, p. 25.
[13] Quoted by Kaplan, *op. cit.*, p. 23.
[14] Bulgaria, Czechoslovakia, East Germany, Hungary, Poland, Rumania and Russia. The Pact, signed in Warsaw in 1955, is a mutual assistance treaty that is the Communist bloc's counterpart to the North Atlantic Treaty Organization in the West.
[15] See "The Arms Dealers: Guns for All," *Time*, March 3, 1975.

ports the overseas arms sales effort, allowing military officers to act as salesmen and annually printing a sales catalogue describing products available. The yearly Paris Air Show is aimed at promoting French products, and the French government also keeps a large permanent weapons exhibition on display near Versailles.

Britain's arms industry also has become important to the national economy, with overseas sales more than doubling since 1965. The British sell frigates, submarines, patrol boats and tanks, among other weapons. The British embassies in Washington, Paris, Bonn, Ottawa and Canberra have special sections to deal with arms sales, and the British have converted a transport ship into a floating arms exhibit for display around the globe. A comprehensive sales catalogue is published twice a year. West Germany exports submarines, Leopard tanks, and entire munitions factories. Italy sells helicopters, frigates, tanks and the famous Beretta pistol. Sweden and Switzerland supposedly ban arms sales to nations at war or in areas of tension, but the Swedes sell Saab aircraft worldwide and the Swiss specialize in anti-aircraft weapons.

Among the Eastern European nations, Czechoslovakia long has been a major arms dealer; the famous Bren gun and the Skoda Works howitzer were among the most popular combat weapons of pre-World War II years. The Czechs also are widely regarded as perhaps the most ruthless arms salesmen. Their government-sponsored company, Omnipol, will sell arms to terrorists, guerrillas or almost anyone else who can pay the price. Poland is a major outlet for the Warsaw Pact's surplus tanks, many of them originally made in the Soviet Union. Details of China's sales are difficult to obtain, but Peking is known to have supplied weapons to North Vietnam, North Korea, Pakistan and several revolutionary groups in Africa.

---

# Heritage of Munitions Merchants

---

THE GLOBAL arms trade today is still saddled with the reputation of the turn-of-the-century "merchants of death" who sold weapons to all sides in any conflict, and were even suspected of encouraging wars to win new markets. Despite exaggerations, the "death merchant" stereotype did have some basis in reality. Sir Basil Zaharoff (1850-1936), sometimes called "the mystery man of Europe," was the archetypal international arms salesman who helped give the trade its bad name. "Bribing, cheating, lying fluently in eight languages and playing upon nations' fears of their neighbors, Zaharoff—as chief salesman for Britain's Vickers company—amassed a huge fortune by selling weapons to both sides in the Boer War, Balkan conflicts and World War I," said *Time* magazine.[16] However, Zaharoff was honored in his day by governments that believed he was serving their national interests—he was knighted by the British and decorated by the French.

---

> *"The United States has become the Krupp of the world."*
>
> Rep. Philip H. Hayes (D Ind.)

---

Zaharoff had an American counterpart in Frank Bannerman, whose New York firm first sold surplus Civil War guns, bullets, swords and cannonballs, then graduated to cannons, cartridges and Gatling guns after the Spanish-American War. Bannerman also sold a wide range of exotic weapons such as crossbows, lances and blow-guns, as well as uniforms, buttons, helmets, flags, saddles and knapsacks. "Francis Bannerman Sons...billed itself—correctly, no doubt—as 'the largest dealer in the world in military goods,'" Joseph E. Persico wrote in a recent historical account. "The firm advertised its wares in a profusely illustrated catalogue that military men the world over valued as a standard reference work. The catalogue spelled out the terms of sale in what Bannerman called The Golden Rule in Action: 'First you pay your money, then you get your goods.' In short, cash on the gun barrel and no questions asked."[17]

In the 1920s and 1930s, the belief became widespread that the private manufacture and sale of arms had been responsible for World War I, and cries arose to control the trade. There came such investigations as the 1934 Senate Munitions Inquiry—the Nye Committee[18]—and in Britain, the 1936 Royal Commission on the Private Manufacture of and Trading in Arms.[19] "Both investigations unearthed an enormous number of unsavory practices: bribery, collusive bidding, profiteering, the violation of arms embargoes, illegal financial transactions, the production of shoddy equipment and even sales to the enemy," George Thayer wrote in *The War Business* (1969).

---

[16] March 3, 1975.
[17] "The Great Gun Merchant," *American Heritage,* August 1974, p. 53.
[18] Sen. Gerald P. Nye (R N.D. 1925-45) was chairman.
[19] Colin S. Gray, "What Is Good for General Motors..." *Journal of the Royal United Services Institute for Defense Studies,* June 1972, p. 36.

A League of Nations commission also investigated private arms manufacturing and a vote by the full League to abolish the practice received overwhelming support but no definite results. The commission report found that armament firms had fomented war scares, bribed officials, spread false expenditure reports to stimulate arms buying, sought to control newspapers, organized international arms rings and conducted monopolistic practices.[20]

## Changes in the Market After World War II

Despite such efforts, the world arms trade continued between the two world wars. But it was changed drastically by World War II and by the Cold War that followed. Through the Lend-Lease Act and other legislation, the United States gave vast quantities of arms and supplies to its allies during the war, and in the post-war years America continued to distribute arms to contain the threat of communism. The Truman Doctrine in 1947, the establishment of the North Atlantic Treaty Organization and passage of the Mutual Defense Assistance Act in 1949, the Mutual Security Acts of 1951 and 1954, the formation of the Southeast Asia Treaty Organization in 1954, and the Foreign Assistance Act of 1961 all tended to increase U.S. military aid, through both grants and sales.[21]

During the first years after World War II, the United States and Britain gave away most of their obsolete military equipment to friendly nations. But by the mid-1950s it became evident that many recipient countries were economically capable of purchasing arms. About the same time, the Soviet Union entered the world arms trade in a significant way. "Pressure was soon brought to bear, first in Washington and later in London, to *sell* military equipment (both obsolete and new) in order to recoup as much as possible of the high research, development, production and operating costs of the weapons," Thayer wrote. "As other countries entered the arms trade it occurred to them as well that selling arms was a convenient and lucrative method of bringing in hard currencies." Communist bloc countries, seeking to increase their influence, felt compelled to compete with the West in the world arms market.

When President Kennedy took office in 1961, the goals of the foreign military sales program changed. Secretary of Defense Robert S. McNamara realized that continued overseas deployment of U.S. troops and equipment would lead to a balance-of-payments deficit, so he tried to persuade American allies to start purchasing U.S. weapons in substantial quantities. "At first, the Pentagon's export drive was directed at the most advanced and

[20] John Stanley and Maurice Pearton, *The International Trade in Arms* (1972).

[21] For background, see chapters on "Foreign Policy" and "National Security Policy" in Congressional Quarterly's *Congress and the Nation 1945-1964*, Vol. I (1965).

| Largest U.S. Foreign Military Sales by Country (fiscal year 1974) | | | |
|---|---|---|---|
| Country | Amount (in millions) | Country | Amount (in millions) |
| Iran | $3,800 | West Germany | 218 |
| Israel | 2,100 | Spain | 148 |
| Saudi Arabia | 588 | Canada | 94 |
| Greece | 435 | Taiwan | 88 |

SOURCE: Department of Defense

prosperous nations of Western Europe, as well as Japan, Canada and Australia," Michael T. Klare wrote in *The Progressive*. "As the 1960s progressed, however, the market for American military products in the developed nations began to shrink and the Pentagon began to encourage substantial arms purchases by Third World nations that had become dependent upon the United States for economic and military aid."[22]

McNamara set up a system of loans and credits that enabled even poor nations to buy U.S. arms. They included low-interest, long-term credit sales; loans secured from private U.S. lenders and backed by government guarantees; direct cash sales by the Pentagon; direct commercial sales by U.S. firms; licensed overseas production of U.S. weapons by foreign firms or governments; and so-called "third country" arrangements in which American arms bought by one country were transferred to another country. "Spurred by these programs," Klare wrote, "Third World governments bought U.S. arms worth $1.2-billion during the last years of the McNamara era, a substantial increase indeed over the $431-million spent in the preceding 15 years."

### Federal Procedures to Review Arms Sales

Over the years, the U.S. government has developed a structured review process to pass on all requests for military equipment and services by other nations and on all proposals to sell arms overseas. The normal review body for arms transfers that involve appropriated federal funds is the Security Assistance Program Review Committee, whose chairman is the Under Secretary of State for security assistance, currently Carlyle E. Maw. The committee includes representatives from the departments of State, Defense and Treasury, the Office of Management and Budget, the National Security Council, the Agency for International Development, and the Arms Control and Disarmament Agency. This committee reviews both the amount and nature of the proposed transfer.

---

[22] "The Pentagon Bleeds the Third World," *The Progressive*, June 1974, p. 22.

In· cases of government or commercial cash sales, the procedures vary somewhat. All of these sales are reviewed under State Department policy guidelines. The department's pertinent regional bureau (such as Bureau of African Affairs) and the Bureau of Politico-Military Affairs are both involved, and in important sales the President or the Secretary of State may make the final decision. The State Department said in its "Current Policy" statement of July 1975: "Although the views of Defense Department officials are fully taken into account in the decision-making process, it should be emphasized that the Defense Department does not make policy with respect to military sales or transfers." The document went on to say: "Procedures in and of themselves, of course, cannot insure that sales, or any other activity, support the national interest. Decisions are made by men, not organizational and staffing arrangements."

---

# New Controversies in Arms Trade

---

I N RECENT MONTHS the world arms market has been embroiled in a new controversy over revelations that bribery, payoffs, kickbacks and other corruption apparently have become common practice among arms sellers and buyers worldwide. Hints of the scandals surfaced during the Watergate investigations, and in February the Senate Subcommittee on Multinational Corporations presented evidence that Lockheed Aircraft Corporation, seeking to increase overseas arms sales, had paid bribes that may have reached the highest levels of the Japanese government and the Dutch royal family. Lockheed now stands accused of paying bribes in at least 15 countries, and the continuing U.S. investigations and parliamentary inquiries abroad may have a major and lasting effect on the way weapons are bought and sold in the future.

In the Netherlands, Queen Juliana's husband, Prince Bernhard, was accused of accepting more than $1-million from Lockheed since 1960 in connection with its efforts to sell F-104 Starfighters and later L-1011 TriStarjets. When asked to deny the charges at a press conference, Bernhard replied: "I cannot say that, I will not say it, I am standing above such things."[23] In Japan, Lockheed has admitted paying more than $7-million since 1958 to Yoshio Kodama, a powerful right-wing figure, for his help in promoting sales of the F-104, L-1011, the C-130 Hercules cargo plane and the P-3C Orion anti-submarine

---

[23] Quoted in *Newsweek*, Feb. 23, 1976.

plane. The disclosures have turned into a major political scandal in Japan because of the possibility that much of the money was funneled to high-ranking government officials in the ruling Liberal Democratic Party.

But Lockheed clearly was not alone in paying foreign officials to win arms contracts over the past several years. Similar charges have been leveled at Boeing, McDonnell Douglas, Northrop, Rockwell International, United Technologies and several other American arms or aircraft manufacturers. In March, Boeing officials admitted paying $70-million in "commission payments" to sales agents and subcontractors all over the world in the past five years, but denied that any of the payments were illegal.

President Ford on March 31 set up a 10-member Cabinet-level task force, headed by Secretary of Commerce Elliot L. Richardson to investigate corporate payments overseas. The Securities and Exchange Commission is investigating at least 85 companies, and the Internal Revenue Service has assigned some 300 agents to search corporate record books to determine if any tax laws were broken.

## Ethical Problem Involved in Old Traditions

Many Europeans cannot understand the American concern over arms-sale payments abroad. *The Economist,* the prestigious London weekly, has argued in several articles that the uproar about bribery is naive, and that any realistic international businessman must regard payoffs as part of the process of bridging two cultures.

Anthony Sampson, who is writing a book on the arms manufacturers, wrote in *New York* magazine: "Where, after all, does bribing begin and end? What is the real distinction between social corruption—the lavish dinner party, the pot of caviar—and the passing of money into secret bank accounts?"

> But the problem with bribery [Sampson continued] is that it very easily escalates among rivals so that it ends with a huge advantage to whichever company is the richest and most ruthless. And whatever justification might be put forward for allowing bribery in other industries, the arms business is a very special, and very dangerous, case.... But the commercial incentive to export remains very powerful and is becoming increasingly so. The bribe is not merely a means of persuading a foreign government to favor one company against another. Quite often it is an inducement to a government to buy arms that it does not really need or want.[24]

---

[24] "Lockheed's Foreign Policy: Who, in the End, Corrupted Whom?" *New York,* March 15, 1976, p. 58.

Indeed, as the arms market has expanded, pressure has mounted from many sides to make sales that must be regarded as questionable. "The arsenals of many developing nations," according to Gen. J. N. Chaudhuri, former chief of staff for India's army, "have tanks too heavy for the local bridges, aircraft without enough pilots and warships that cannot put out to sea."[25] The military elite often plays a central role in the formation of new governments, and they usually want to bolster their forces for prestige purposes as well as to protect their positions. Asked what Peru would do with a shipment of surplus U.S. Navy destroyers, an unidentified Latin American specialist at the State Department said: "They sail them in naval parades."[26]

In the light of recent revelations, it appears possible that the boom in the world arms trade during the 1970s may have been a creation of weapons manufacturers so eager to make sales that they would willingly grease the palms of agents, officials or anyone else who could help them close a deal. Bribes may have stimulated the appetite of developing nations to acquire armaments, often at the expense of food, housing, education and health-care programs. "The arguments of the arms companies is always that if they do not sell the arms, someone else will," Sampson wrote, "and that it is hopeless to frustrate the ambitions of young nations. But the Lockheed-Northrop documents provide some evidence that the companies, with their persistent bribing and lobbying, are themselves creating the new atmosphere of military ambition..."

## Prospects for Greater Oversight and Control

Proposals for limiting the world arms trade arouse fierce emotions on all sides. Idealists call for voluntary multilateral reductions by arms sellers and buyers, while cynics maintain that it is hopeless even to consider controls because no nation will relinquish the right to arm itself. In between the two extremes, however, are many who believe that it may be possible to regulate world arms sales to some degree if it is done carefully and equitably. There is some precedent: the Antarctic has been declared a weapons-free zone, and the United States and other arms-sellers restrict sales of such weapons as shoulder-fired anti-aircraft missiles because of the possibility they might end up in the hands of terrorists.

But on the whole, efforts since World War II to limit the international flow of conventional arms have met with little success. The Tripartite Declaration of 1950, in which the United States, France and Britain pledged to limit sales to Middle Eastern countries, fell apart after four years when the French decided to

---

[25] Quoted in *Time*, March 3, 1975, p. 41.
[26] Quoted by Fred Kaplan, *The Progressive*, March 1976, p. 24.

sell tanks and planes to Israel. The United States has tried writing an "end-use clause" into arms contracts whereby the recipient agrees not to sell the arms to a third party without U.S. permission, but this often has been circumvented. Embargoes to nations in volatile areas seldom have worked either. France sold weapons to South Africa, Pakistan, India and Latin America when no other suppliers would. Judging from the limited success of the Strategic Arms Limitation talks, it is debatable whether meaningful controls over conventional arms can be achieved. Jean-Jacques Servan-Schreiber, publisher of the French newspaper *L'Express*, has suggested that France will sell even nuclear weapons before too long.[27]

The U.S. government, while giving lip service to the general idea of controls at the United Nations and at the Conference of the Committee on Disarmament in Geneva, generally has taken the position that little can be done. "The control problem is further complicated by the proliferation of supply sources and the growing economic importance of arms exports for the supplier countries," a State Department publication stated last year. "As a result no one country can control the world arms flow to any significant degree."[28]

Indeed, much of the opposition to conventional arms controls comes from the purchasing nations. They maintain—with some justification—that it is unfair and discriminatory for the developed nations to call for arms-sales cutbacks when they are unwilling to reduce their own large domestic military expenditures. Moreover, if the arms trade was reduced it is likely that many developing nations would step up their own arms-production capability.

Even so, there has been some regional action toward limiting conventional arms races. In December 1974, eight Latin American countries[29] signed the Declaration of Ayacucho, expressing their desire to create "conditions which will make possible the effective limitation of armaments and put an end to their acquisition for purposes of war."

As for the arms producers, Sen. John C. Culver (D Iowa), in a letter to Secretary of State Henry A. Kissinger that was signed by more than 100 other members of Congress, proposed last October the convening of an international conference of major producing nations "to seek some rational control and coordination of what now seems to be pathological competition in foreign military sales."[30] Sen. Edward M. Kennedy (D Mass.), one of the

---

[27] *Time*, March 3, 1975, p. 44.

[28] "World Arms Trade," Bureau of Public Affairs, Department of State, July 1975.

[29] Argentina, Bolivia, Chile, Colombia, Ecuador, Panama, Peru and Venezuela.

[30] Text of letter reprinted in the *Congressional Record*, Dec. 3, 1975, p. S 20962. The letter was dated Oct. 31, 1975.

signers, has said: "We are told that it we do not sell arms other nations will do so, yet we have never tried to get common agreement. We have never asked the British, French, the Scandinavian countries, as well as the Soviet Union, whether they are interested in any kind of moratorium."[31]

In response to the Culver letter, Kissinger wrote: "I am directing that a full-scale review of possible limitations on the traffic in conventional arms be undertaken with a view toward making recommendations as to what further actions might most usefully be taken."[32] Kissinger already had ordered a "National Security Study Memorandum" prepared on U.S. arms transfer policy. Those working on the memorandum "are reportedly arguing that there is a pressing need for greater regulation of the chaotic arms trade," Judith Miller reported in *The Progressive*. "There is also, apparently, a greater recognition that the current unofficial policy of 'the more the merrier' may eventually conflict with other foreign policy goals."[33]

On the problem of corporate bribery, numerous U.S. companies are drawing up ethics or conduct codes in response to the recent wave of scandals. Some undoubtedly are only making public-relations gestures, but others appear genuinely concerned about setting effective guidelines. The Ford administration has proposed to the international Organization for Economic Cooperation and Development, the United Nations Commission on Transnational Corporations, and the General Agreement on Tariffs and Trade that some kind of international code of business conduct be considered. In Congress, the chairman of the Senate Banking, Housing and Urban Affairs Committee William Proxmire (D Wis.), said he expects to complete action by early June on a bill to ban bribery of foreign officials by American corporations and require companies to report to the Securities and Exchange Commission payments of more than $1,000 to any foreign official, political party or negotiating agent.[34]

But the most far-reaching congressional action came in the fiscal 1976 foreign aid bill, which drastically revised the U.S. military sales program and gave Congress much broader authority to review and veto foreign arms sales proposed by the Pentagon or by private firms. The measure would require the President to submit to Congress all proposed sales of defense

---

[31] Quoted by Richard D. Lyons, *The New York Times*, Oct. 19, 1975.
[32] Text of letter reprinted in the *Congressional Record*, Dec. 3, 1975, p. S 20963.
[33] "Alarm Over Arms Sales," *The Progressive*, December 1975, p. 7.
[34] For details, see *Congressional Quarterly Weekly Report*, April 24, 1976, p. 969. The United States and its major industrial trading partners in early April agreed on an 11-page draft code of "guidelines for multinational enterprises." It forbids, but does not punish, bribery of foreign officials by multinational corporations. It will be proposed for adoption at a ministerial meeting of the Organization for Economic Cooperation and Development in Paris in June.

## Military Assistance Advisory Groups

America's foreign military sales programs overseas, as well as grant aid and military training programs, are supervised by Military Assistance Advisory Groups, commonly known as MAAGs. They were originally established after World War II to administer grants and help strengthen Western alliances, but in recent years have become chiefly arms sales agents, according to critics.

A report to Congress by the General Accounting Office in October 1975, "Assessment of Overseas Advisory Efforts of the U.S. Security Assistance Program," questioned the need for MAAGs in many countries and recommended that some be eliminated. "In 1974, advisory efforts concentrated mostly on providing assistance to upper military echelons of the host country in force-structure planning and logistics, principally as a means of facilitating military sales," the report said. Today there are about 1,600 military personnel assigned to more than 40 MAAGs overseas, with administrative costs of the program exceeding $85-million annually.

equipment totaling more than $7-million, or sales of equipment or services costing $25-million or more. Congress would then have 30 days to reject the proposed sale by passing a joint resolution of disapproval. The bill also would impose a $9-billion annual ceiling on combined government and commercial sales abroad.[35]

## Relationship of Arms to National Sovereignty

Whatever procedural arrangements are devised to oversee, publicize or regulate the world arms trade, however, it is unlikely that the flow of arms ever can be shut off completely. "The plain fact seems to be that arms transfers are rooted in the international system of sovereign states itself, and, while the one continues, the other can hardly stop," John Stanley and Maurice Pearton wrote in *The International Trade in Arms* (1972). "Although it is an ambiguous concept, 'national sovereignty' is universally recognized to confer the right to self-defense."

The problem of world arms sales, then, seems to be a problem inherent with nation-states. "Commentators, both journalists and well-meaning academic investigators, should confront the fact that there are few villains in the arms trade," wrote Dr. Colin S. Gray of the Canadian Institute of International Affairs. "The arms trade is flourishing not because of the nefarious influence of any latter-day merchants of death, but because the use of force is an ever-present reality in the current international system." When nations no longer feel the need to resort to force, the world arms trade no doubt will cease.

---

[35] President Ford May veto the bill, however. For details, see *Congressional Quarterly Weekly Report*, April 24, 1976, p. 935.

# Selected Bibliography

## Books

Barnaby, Frank and Ronald Huisken, *Arms Uncontrolled*, Stockholm International Peace Research Institute, Harvard University Press, 1975.

Sellers, Robert C. (ed.), *Armed Forces of the World*, Praeger Publishers, 1971.

Stanley, John and Maurice Pearton, *The International Trade in Arms*, Praeger Publishers, 1972.

Thayer, George, *The War Business*, Simon and Schuster, 1969.

## Articles

"America on Top Among World's Arms Peddlers," *U.S. News & World Report*, Jan. 13, 1975.

"Bribery: A Shocker in U.S., But a Tradition Overseas," *U.S. News & World Report*, April 12, 1976.

Gray, Colin S., "What Is Good for General Motors..." *Journal of the Royal United Services for Defense Studies*, June 1972.

Kaplan, Fred, "Still the Merchants of Death," *The Progressive*, March 1976.

Klare, Michael T., "The Pentagon Bleeds the Third World," *The Progressive*, June 1974.

Karnow, Stanley, "Weapons for Sale," *The New Republic*, March 23, 1974.

"Payoffs: The Growing Scandal," *Newsweek*, Feb. 23, 1976.

Sampson, Anthony, "Lockheed's Foreign Policy: Who, in the End, Corrupted Whom?" *New York*, March 15, 1976.

Sivard, Ruth Leger, "Let Them Eat Bullets!" *Bulletin of the Atomic Scientists*, April 1975.

Szulc, Tad, "Kickback—Corrupting U.S. Arms Sales," *The New Republic*, April 17, 1976.

"The Arms Dealers: Guns for All," *Time*, March 3, 1975.

## Studies and Reports

Arms Control and Disarmament Agency, "The International Transfer of Conventional Arms," a report to Congress, April 12, 1974.

—"World Military Expenditures and Arms Transfers 1965-1974," March 1976.

Arms Control Association, "Arms Control Today" newsletter, selected issues.

Center for Defense Information, "The Defense Monitor" newsletter, selected issues.

Editorial Research Reports, "International Arms Sales," 1970 Vol. II, p. 647.

International Defense Business, "International Arms Trade: Exports, U.S. Foreign Military Sales 1950-1973," June 30, 1975.

International Institute for Strategic Studies, London, "The Military Balance 1975-1976," 1975.

United Nations Association of the United States of America, "Controlling the International Arms Trade," UNA-USA Policy Panel on Conventional Arms Control, April 1976.

# WESTERN EUROPEAN COMMUNISM

## by

## Yorick Blumenfeld

**Apr. 23
1 9 7 6**

# WESTERN EUROPEAN COMMUNISM

THE CONCERTED EFFORTS of the Communist parties of Western Europe to attain power peacefully through the electoral process may become one of the major political dramas of the 1970s. Many Western European Communists profess the benign nature of their Marxism and assert their independence from the Soviet Union. Nonetheless, their actions hold promises and threats for both Moscow and Washington. The United States fears the prospect of Communists gaining control of the governments of longtime North Atlantic Treaty Organization (Nato) allies. The Soviet Union fears the development of independent and liberalized Communist parties that could strongly influence discontented Soviet satellite governments in Eastern Europe.[1]

Two elections in the days and months ahead could tell much about the future trend of communism in Western Europe. On April 25, in Portugal's first national legislative elections in nearly 50 years, the Communists are expected to fare badly because of general disapproval of their efforts last fall to create a revolutionary state by force (see p. 24). But in Italy, where the governing Christian Democratic Party probably will resign soon and is expected to call for elections in June, the Communists easily could become the largest party in the government (see p. 25).

If the Russians feel threatened by a communism that is democratic, the United States feels threatened by a Europe that could turn Marxist. Speaking to the American Society of Newspaper Editors in Washington, D.C., on April 13, Secretary of State Henry A. Kissinger said: "I believe the advent of Communists in Western European countries is likely to produce a sequence of events in which other European countries will also be tempted to move in the same direction." This enunciation of what is, in effect, a "domino theory" for Europe was among Kissinger's most forceful statements yet on the dangers he sees for the Atlantic alliance.

---

[1] Journalist Pete Hamill went so far as to predict in *The Village Voice*, March 29, 1976, that "the Americans and the Russians will almost certainly join forces to try to crush this new form of communism, which threatens the basic assumptions of both superpowers."

23

But although those were Kissinger's bluntest public remarks this year, in early April the press obtained copies of a non-verbatim summary of statements he made in London last December to a group of American ambassadors posted in Europe. At that meeting, Kissinger said that if the Communists gained power in Western Europe the Atlantic alliance "could not survive" and the United States would be "alone and isolated."[2]

On April 18, *Pravda,* the official Communist Party newspaper, charged that the United States was interfering in the internal affairs of Western European countries by warning them about Communist participation in their governments. *Pravda* contended that this was a violation of the Helsinki agreement signed by the United States, the Soviet Union and 33 other countries at the European security conference last year. The charges appeared to be aimed at Kissinger's recent remarks.

Along with expressions of alarm, top American officials including President Gerald R. Ford and Nato commander Gen. Alexander M. Haig also have issued warnings against European acceptance of Communists. But these comments, clearly aimed at bolstering resistance to Communist initiatives, may have had the opposite effect. Across the continent journalists, politicians and diplomats have indicated that Europeans resent American intervention in their domestic affairs.

Moreover, the Communist encroachment varies from country to country and to a large extent reflects local conditions in Europe. To deal with the Communists as a united bloc simply is not realistic. Zbigniew Brzezinski, director of the Research Institute on Communist Affairs at Columbia University, told a group of reporters at the National Press Club, March 26: "We should not exclude our ability to talk with all elements of the spectrum of governments. Our dialogue with the Soviet Union is essential; it has to be continued and it has to be extended. We have slighted the Western European Communists. While the evolution of communism in Western Europe is in the right direction, it is still in a very early phase."

## Failure of Communists in Portugal

ALTHOUGH COMMUNISTS have made inroads in many European countries *(see map),* Portugal, France, Italy and Spain have been most deeply affected. In Portugal, where the Communist Party tried to capture power by revolution last fall, the party secretary, Alvaro Cunhal, is trying to dissociate

---

[2] As reported in *The New York Times,* April 7, 1976.

**Communists in Western Europe**

Party Members and Per cent
of Communists in Parliament

FINLAND
47,000 (20%)

NORWAY

North
Sea

IRELAND

DENMARK
7,750 (3.3%)

SWEDEN
17,000 (8%)

BRITAIN
30,000 (none)

Atlantic
Ocean

NETH.

BELGIUM
10,000 (2.3%)

FRANCE
275,000 (15%)

W.
GERMANY

SWITZ.

PORTUGAL

SPAIN

French Chamber of Deputies, Paris

Mediterranean
Sea

ITALY
1,700,000 (29%)

AFRICA

GREECE

TURKEY

himself from the extremists and to mend his fences with the Socialists. The April 25 elections are to be followed on June 27 by the selection of a chief of state, replacing the current provisional president.

The situation in Portugal illustrates the danger of trying to describe Western European communism in simplistic terms, however. Of the 14 parties offering candidates in this campaign, eight—mostly minor parties— claim to be to the left of the Communists. Polls quoted in the weekly newspaper *Expresso* recently indicated that the Socialists and left-of-center Popular Democrats each were likely to gain about 30 per cent of the votes, the conservative Social Democratic Center Party about 25 per cent, and the Communists about 10-12 per cent. If this division does occur, no party can rule without forming a coalition. Perhaps the most important finding of the polls, however, was the fact that 50 per cent of those questioned said they still had not decided which party they would support.[3]

### Communist Involvement in Violent Overthrow

What happened in Portugal between May 1974 and December 1975 represented the first time since the end of World War II that Communists had tried to take over a Western European state by revolutionary means. The Communists and their sympathizers in the Armed Forces Movement began to push the country down the revolutionary path in the spring of 1975,

---

[3] *The Christian Science Monitor*, April 5, 1976.

following an aborted plot of the right wing. The extreme left wing seized control of the country's ailing economy and the Portuguese Communist Party tried to disrupt the administrative functioning of the government. Most communication media, including the newspapers, the radio stations and the state television, were seized by the Communists. As the old structures in Portugal began to buckle, fears arose that a possible alliance between the Communists and the extremists in the Armed Forces Movement would end up in a Communist military dictatorship.

In November 1975, the political crisis was brought to a head when the Communists used huge masses of workers to blockade the presidential palace and the National Assembly. The workers demanded the dismissal of the cabinet and the formation of a left-wing revolutionary government. The government of Prime Minister Jose Pinheiro de Azevedo "suspended" its functioning because it no longer had "the minimum conditions needed to govern." However, rather than oust the government, the 18-member revolutionary council, which held supreme power, removed General Otelo de Carvalho from his command of the military. This caused a virtual mutiny within the left-wing military units in Lisbon, but won support in the north of Portugal.

On Nov. 25 paratroops seized the air force's regional command headquarters and air bases. Lisbon's military police and several other units declared their support for the paratroops. However, soldiers loyal to the government recovered the posts and the rebellion was crushed. The army and navy were purged of 100 senior leftist commanders, including the chief of staff. The Communists issued a communiqué saying that "the forces of the left would commit a serious error in overestimating their own forces and in trying any desperate act."

### Basis for Victory of Portuguese Moderates

After the attempted coup in November, the moderate elements in Portugal were capable of quickly consolidating their position. Mario Soares, the Socialist leader, said on Nov. 30 that the Communists had been defeated on four fronts in Portugal: in the national elections on April 25, 1975, where they had received only 12.5 per cent of the vote as opposed to 38 per cent for the Socialists and 26.5 per cent for the Popular Democrats; in the street demonstrations when the people realized that they had to be ready to fight for freedom; in the large trade unions, where the Socialists were able to win most of the elections; and in the armed forces.[4]

Although the Socialists, the Popular Democrats and the Com-

---

[4] See William Pfaff, "Post-Marxist Europe," *The New Yorker*, Jan. 12, 1976, p. 80.

munists still are represented in the provisional government on a "four-two-one" basis, the balance of power has shifted dramatically since November. The government has handed back many of the farms, the factories, and the mass media to their former owners. In the army, which has been cut from 210,000 to 57,000 soldiers, most of the leftist officers have been purged.

Francisco Sa Carneiro, the leader of the Popular Democrats, is steadily gaining in popularity. He is trying to turn the election campaign in April into a fight between those whom he calls "Marxists" and those whom he calls "real social democrats." The conservative Social Democratic Center party, under Freitas de Amaral, which won only 7 per cent of the vote a year ago, now may gain a quarter of the electorate. Indeed, the Socialist leader Soares is finding that his past willingness to work with the Communists could turn to his disadvantage.[5]

## Reassessment of Communist Role in Portugal

To many observers, the Communist leader Alvaro Cunhal, who spent 14 years in exile in Moscow and Prague, is a Stalinist

hard-liner trying to repeat the 1917 Russian Revolution in Portugal. But circumstances seem to have dictated much of the line followed by Cunhal since he returned to Portugal on April 30, 1974. The Portuguese Communist Party, which had prepared itself for revolution through nearly 50 years of clandestine activity, quickly stepped in to fill the ideological and organizational vacuum which existed after the downfall of the old regime.[6]

**Alvaro Cunhal**

At first Cunhal was all reason and moderation. "Our enemies proclaim that Communists threaten small businesses...the truth is that Communists defend, not only the interests of the working class and the peasantry, but all classes and middle layers. Small farmers, small industrialists, small businessmen—all these can look to us Communists as the true defenders of their legitimate interests."[7] When the provisional government was formed, Cunhal wrote that the Communists wanted "a broad coalition of social and political forces, whose program does not envisage profound reforms of the socio-economic structure."

---

[5] See "Coming in from the Cold," *The Economist,* March 6, 1976.
[6] See Dan Griffin and Laurence Stern, "The Portuguese Connection," *Ramparts,* May 1974, p. 44.
[7] Alvaro Cunhal, *Pela Revolucao Democratica e Nacional* (1975), p. 213.

The Communists fared badly in the April 1975 elections, Cunhal claimed, because the people still were laboring under the burden of anti-Communist prejudice and were denied "the freedom to think." Cunhal made it clear that "electoralism" had no meaning for Communists.[8] However, Cunhal also began to feel increasing pressure from the Maoists and the radicals to his left. The MRPP (Reorganizing Movement of the Proletariat Party), a Maoist group, attacked the Communists for moving too slowly.

Last year's Stalinist shock tactics, while furtively encouraged by Moscow, were rapidly disowned by the other Communist leaders in Western Europe. The Italian and French Communists argued that Cunhal failed because his effort to seek power disproportionate to his popular support only could have worked with the direct support of the Red Army. Now it is widely predicted that a defeat of Cunhal's hard line at the polls on April 25 could end his party's alignment with the Soviet Union. "The Portuguese Communist Party will have to take a democratic line," said Soares, "like the Italian Communist Party." But it may be a long time before the Portuguese people can believe that the Communists are ready to abide by the rules of democracy.

---

# Emergence of European Communism

---

IT HAS BEEN recognized for some time that international communism is no longer a monolithic organization with a single center of authority or a single orthodox doctrine. Indeed, throughout its development the Communist movement has been plagued by schisms over the best way to reach the classless society. The facade of unanimity that has been the hallmark of Soviet communism was the creation of Stalin, who wished to bolster what he considered an isolated and beleaguered movement. That such unity was illusory was illustrated clearly when Marshal Tito of Yugoslavia first split from Moscow in 1948, openly defying Stalin's authority.

### Early Disputes Over Definitions of Marxism

When Marx set up the Workingmen's International Association in London on Sept. 28, 1864, later to be known as the First International, he drew up a program to unite the individual left-wing contingents into one movement. Marx intentionally kept the door open to such diverse groups as the British trade union-

---

[8] Tony Cliff, "Portugal at the Crossroads," *International Socialism*, September 1975, p. 12.

ists, French Proudhonists,[9] Polish anarchists, and Belgian radicals. The association sought, in the words of Marx, "to afford a central medium of communication and cooperation" for the European working class. However, the internal disputes over organizational control between the factions were such that the First International had to be dissolved in 1876.[10]

The Second International, founded in Paris in 1889 to promote proletarian unity, also embraced contending strains of radical thought. The right wing, the so-called "revisionists" led by Eduard Bernstein, believed in the possibility of a progressive improvement of working-class conditions within the framework of capitalist society. Bernstein, like his contemporary successors in France and Italy, looked toward the time when this peaceful, evolutionary process would succeed in replacing capitalism with socialism.

---

*"...[T]he ideological struggle of the Second International still is being fought by the Communists and Socialists in Western Europe."*

---

The centrists of the Second International, while sharply criticizing the revisionists for failing to recognize the validity of Marx's theories, also believed in a civilized and democratic process of evolution. Since progress toward socialism was inevitable, there was no need for revolutionary tactics, they argued. The left wing of the Second International, which included such Russians as Lenin, rejected any collaboration with the liberal elements in a capitalist society and demanded its violent overthrow. Although the Second International fell apart under the pressures of World War I, the ideological struggle of the Second International still is being fought by the Communists and Socialists in Western Europe.

For Karl Marx, it was axiomatic that the victory of socialism would be brought about by the industrial proletariat of the most advanced economies of the West. Lenin broke with this concept by seizing power in backward Russia. Lenin formed the Third International in January 1919, calling upon revolutionaries from 38 Communist groups to send delegates to Russia. The new body was a highly elitist and hierarchical structure which abandoned any pretense of democratic form.

---

[9] Pierre J. Proudhon (1809-1865) was a French radical theorist who fought for the rights of workers and believed in the moral responsibility of the individual.

[10] See "World Communist Summit," *E.R.R.*, 1969 Vol. I, p. 400.

On the eve of the 1917 Revolution, the Bolsheviks still were affirming their own devotion to parliamentary government. Lenin quickly dropped his democratic platform when he assumed power, proclaiming that any tactics were morally permissible in the war against the bourgeoisie. He described as "infantile" those party members who insisted on principled revolutionary positions. For many workers in Western Europe, as well as for most socialist intellectuals, communism as developed by Lenin and implemented by Stalin filled them with revulsion. They rejected a communism which guaranteed every freedom under a Communist constitution, but which repudiated every article in practice. Gradually the Europeans began to work out a form of communism that would reflect more closely their own national aspirations.

## Development of Different Roads to Communism

The Yugoslav defiance of Soviet authority, which broke into the open in June 1948, provided the first alternative to Soviet communism in a generation. Marshal Tito, while retaining his Marxist beliefs, rejected the Soviet brand of dictatorship. Nikita Khrushchev, as Stalin's successor, reluctantly came to accept that there were different roads to socialism and that these also implied divergent kinds of socialism. No longer was the Soviet brand of socialism a "model" which had to be accepted by the Chinese, the Yugoslavs, or the Western European Communists.

The Italian Communist Party, in existence since 1921, always was based on ideological and economic premises different from those of Stalinist Russia. The intellectual leader of the party, Antonio Gramsci (1891-1937), believed that Marxism was more a methodology than a dogma. He saw no contradiction in a Catholic being a Communist. Today the Italian Communists make much of the fact that Gramsci refashioned the Leninist concept of the "dictatorship of the proletariat" into what he called the "hegemony of the working class."

Gramsci's successor, Palmiro Togliatti (1893-1964), who helped build his party into the largest Communist party in the West, also insisted on greater independence from Moscow. It was Togliatti who first proposed a system of "polycentric" Communist parties. His idea was to grant individual, national units complete autonomy. Togliatti's guidelines for Italy's Communist Party were that it was to come to power by constitutional means, that it was to be a mass party rather than a restricted revolutionary "vanguard," that it should be free of anti-clericalism, and that it should seek its own way toward communism.[11]

---

[11] "Italy's Communists," *The Economist*, Feb. 28, 1976, pp. 53-60.

The French Communist Party's recent commitment to democracy is much more suspect than that of the Italians. The French Communist Party remained loyal to Moscow through the excesses of Stalin, the crises of Hungary and Poland and all the contradictions of Khrushchev. However, in May 1968 the French Communist Party made clear it no longer sought to play a revolutionary role in national politics. Individual members of the French Communist Party even looked toward Alexander Dubcek's reforms in Prague with hope. Then, with the Soviet invasion of Czechoslovakia in August 1968, the French Communists split with Moscow for the first time in history. "The armed intervention in Czechoslovakia seems to us neither justified nor in conformity with our internal law," wrote one party member in *L'Humanité*, the Paris Communist daily. Moscow was able to crush the "revisionists" in Prague with tanks, but the drive for democratic socialism grew elsewhere.

## Moscow's Reactions to New European Parties

Through the centuries the Russians traditionally have been hostile to and suspicious of all forms of Western ideology. Marxism's triumph in 1917 did not alter this situation. Seen from the Kremlin, the increasing power and prestige of the Western Communist parties spells a potential new crisis for the hierarchical and dictatorial Soviet system. The Kremlin is faced with heresies even more extreme than Dubcek's.

Last November Vadim Zagladin, a Soviet Central Committee member in charge of Moscow's dealings with Western Communist parties, warned against new "electoral preoccupations" in France and Italy. Zagladin said that the wrong kind of alliance with non-Communist parties could cause the Western Communists to lose their identity as well as their "revolutionary" character. "Questionable strategems never produce stable results," Zagladin said. In obvious reference to events in Portugal, the Kremlin emphasized that although a "popular majority" is an essential component of Leninist revolutionary strategy, for Leninists "this majority is not arithmetical but political."

While the Western Communists attacked their Portuguese comrades for failing to accept the "arithmetical" result of the April 25, 1975, elections, Moscow has been restrained in its support.[12] The Soviet response to the French, Italian and Spanish parties thus far has been indirect. Victor Zorza, the Soviet-affairs analyst, has said that the Kremlin sees the new "democratic communism" as a greater menace to the Soviet

---

[12] A document allegedly described as top secret and signed by Boris Ponomaryov, a ranking member of the Politburo, in October 1974, set out a five-point plan for action for the takeover of power by the Western Communist parties.

system than any political threat posed by Western capitalists.[13]

At the 25th Party Congress in Moscow in late February, representatives of the Italian, British and Spanish parties dared to stand up to the Soviet leaders. They claimed they not only had the right to ignore Moscow's directives, but also to decide for themselves what was the best way to develop communism in their respective countries. Georges Marchais, the French leader, boycotted the Congress. And Enrico Berlinguer, the Italian party leader, told the Congress that the Italians were committed to building a society that would guarantee all individual and collective liberties, including religious freedom and freedom for the arts and sciences. His speech was censored heavily by the Soviet press.

## Coalition Governments in Popular Front Era

Although there is great concern both in Western Europe and the United States about actual Communist participation or control of the Italian or French governments, such participation would not be an entirely new experience. The "popular front" movements in Europe of the 1930s were widespread coalitions of the parties of the left. The Socialists, left-wing Radicals and Communists had opposed each other rigorously until 1935. Indeed, there existed no doctrinal links between them. Then, at the Seventh Congress of the Comintern, in July 1935, Moscow reversed its former directives. The Socialist and liberal movements, denounced in 1928 as "social fascists," were now proclaimed to be desirable allies in the common struggle against fascism.

After the street demonstrations in Paris in February 1936, which united all the hitherto dissonant parties of the left, the French Socialists, Radicals and Communists joined forces to win an overwhelming electoral triumph. However, Prime Minister Leon Blum (1872-1950) was careful not to include any Communists in his Popular Front government which took office on June 4, 1936. Blum's hope was to achieve a legal and peaceful social revolution, somewhat analogous to the American New Deal. But there were serious handicaps. As a party the Socialists never before had held power and had no experience of ministerial responsibility. Participation in government long had been contrary to socialist principles.[14]

Blum had a majority in the Chamber of Deputies only if the three parties of the left held together. The Communists wanted to push Blum further and faster than he had intended to go. Immediately after the election, France was hit by a series of

---

[13] Victor Zorza, "West Europe's Communists," *The Washington Post*, Nov. 27, 1975.
[14] See Norah Lofts and Margery Weiner, *Eternal France* (1968), p. 291.

strikes which included the occupation of factories by the workers. Blum quickly agreed to give the workers a 40-hour week, holidays with pay, and the right of collective bargaining. He reorganized the Bank of France and proposed the nationalization of major industries.[15]

The Communist Party called on the workers to end the occupation of the plants. However, the economic situation continued to deteriorate. With the devaluation of the French franc in September 1936 and mounting unemployment, the Socialists split between those who felt the Popular Front had gone too far and those who held it had to push for more reforms. Opposition to Blum's fiscal measures finally forced his resignation in 1937. It is significant, in the context of the French Communist Party's contemporary efforts, that Maurice Thorez (1900-1964), who was then the party secretary, urged his comrades to drop the clenched fist salute in favor of the outstretched hand, praised the Roman Catholic hierarchy, and sang the *Marseillaise* with greater gusto than the *Internationale*.

## Postwar Leftist Coalitions in France and Italy

The second phase of cooperation between the Communist parties and the Western European governments occurred at the end of World War II. Once again, the Communists conveniently forgot the traditional slogans about collaborating with the "class enemy" and joined governments led by "bourgeois parties." When Pierre Mendes France greeted General De Gaulle in Paris in 1944, he said: "So, general, now you are the head of the Popular Front." But as De Gaulle subsequently was to write in his memoirs, Maurice Thorez and his party did indeed "serve the public interest" at this moment in French history.[16]

In the French referendum of Oct. 21, 1945, the Communists emerged as the single largest party in France, having received 26.2 per cent as opposed to 23.4 per cent for the Socialists. When De Gaulle formed his first government, in November 1945, there were four Communists in his cabinet. If the Russians meddled at all in French affairs, it was to push Thorez into supporting a government they thought would help Russia. It was only in May 1947, after the Communists had voted against the government on a motion of confidence, that the Socialist Prime Minister, Paul Ramadier, dismissed the Communist ministers. Thereafter, the French Communists were to be political outcasts.[17]

In Italy, much the same pattern developed. When Palmiro Togliatti returned from Moscow in March 1944, he set forth the so-called "Salerno Policy" which called for the broadest possible

---

[15] Andre Maurois, *A History of France* (1949), p. 488.

[16] Charles de Gaulle, *Memoires de Guerre*, Vol. III (1956), p. 101.

[17] Anthony Hartley, *Gaullism* (1971), p. 90.

union against fascism. "I am ready to participate in government even with the King," said Togliatti. The Italian Communists took the portfolios of Finance, Justice, and Agriculture in the government set up in December 1945 by the Christian Democrats. A year later the Italian Socialist and Communist parties agreed on a unity of action pact. However, the behavior of Thorez and Togliatti was too similar to leave any doubt that they were carrying out Stalin's directives.

# Alternatives for Western Communists

THERE IS extensive debate over whether the new course adopted by the Western European Communists is merely a change of tactics or whether it is a profound and genuine transformation. French Minister of Justice Jean Lecanuet, for example, suggested in February that the Communists were "changing their mask but not their skin." Lecanuet added that "If they came to power, their mask would drop." Clearly there are reasons for such doubts.

Because the Communists for so long have proclaimed that any tactics are morally permissible in the war against the bourgeoisie, many Western observers regard the new "democratic communism" as a Machiavellian deception. Others note that while the French and Italian Communists may be sincere in their affirmations, they attach completely different Marxist meanings to such concepts as freedom and democracy. Even Eric Heffer, a left-wing British Labor Member of Parliament, has said that declarations by Western Communist parties that they accept democratic ideas must be suspect while the Soviet Union still imprisons its dissidents and publicly boasts of the guaranteed freedoms of its constitution. In the countries that have become Communist since 1917 there is no political opposition or cultural freedom.[18]

The rapid transformation of some Communist parties has been dictated by political circumstance, not by a voluntary change of will. Olivier Todd, an editor of *Nouvel Observateur*, suggests that the leaders of all the European Communist parties are terrified at the idea of a Social Democratic Western Europe. The Communists have feared that the electoral gains of the Socialists have been made at their expense and that the hard, Stalinist line was not to the liking of the working class. Such a tactical shift would explain why, in the long list of freedoms set

---

[18] See Daniel Seligman, "Communists in Democratic Clothing," *Fortune*, March 1976, p. 117.

## Communist Unity Conference?

Since 1974 the Soviet Union has been pushing the idea of a "unity" conference of Communist parties from Eastern and Western Europe. A drafting commission has been meeting to plan the conference for about 15 months.

However, at the Bulgarian Communist Congress this spring, there were signs that the Soviets may have decided to forget the whole thing. Bulgarian leader Todor Zhivkov, one of the original sponsors, hardly mentioned the proposed European conference. And the Soviet Politburo delegate, Fyodor Kulakov, said nothing at all about it.

Instead, the idea of a "world conference" of Communist parties was suggested. "Conditions are at hand," Zhivkov said. The Soviets may believe that at a world conference, the liberal Western European Communists might be outnumbered and overpowered.

Eric Bourne wrote in *The Christian Science Monitor*, April 6, 1976: "The [European] conference may still take place. But, after all the public exposures of an ideological disagreement that could become as significant as the Tito-Stalin clash of 1948, the Russians clearly have lost interest in it."

out in the declaration of Nov. 18, 1975, by the first secretaries of the French and Italian Communist parties, there was no mention of any kind of economic freedom. How free a society can be within a totalitarian economy remains a matter of conjecture.

## Historic Compromise Sought by Italian Party

Italy not only has the largest Communist Party in Western Europe, with 1.7 million members, but the Italian Communist Party is also the nearest to becoming a governing force through the democratic process. It is a target they missed by 2 per cent last June when they extended their so-called "Red Belt" across northern and central Italy. The Communists now control 40 of the 94 provinces, are the single largest party in all the major cities north of Rome, and have become known for their generally honest, capable, and stable local administrations.[19]

Although the Communists may emerge as victors in the next election, there is nothing in the Italian Constitution requiring that the largest party form the new government. The Communists appear in no hurry and Enrico Berlinguer's rhetoric does not suggest that he would want to run a coalition limited to Socialists and Communists. Berlinguer has stressed that a Popular Front type of government, even with a majority, would polarize the nation. He claims he does not want to split Italy into two hostile camps.[20]

[19] See Peter Nichols, "On the Italian Crisis," *Foreign Affairs,* spring 1976, p. 518.
[20] See "Italy's Threatened Democracy," *E.R.R.*, 1975 Vol. I, pp. 1-20.

**Enrico Berlinguer**

The Italian Communist Party's positions are startlingly different from those of the Soviet Union. The Italians believe that only within the framework of advanced capitalism is it possible to build both a socialist and a democratic society. To attain socialism one must not destroy but cooperate with the existing democratic institutions. Berlinguer claims that he neither wants to "seize power" in the name of the working class nor does he want further nationalization of an economy already 70 per cent state-controlled.

Even the conservative London *Economist* wrote last January, "Perhaps Italy requires a part-Communist government just in order to achieve that reinvigoration of other parties." Should the Communists join a government, they will not have an easy time of it. The United States has threatened economic sanctions and possible expulsion from Nato, while the powerful Catholic Church solemnly proclaimed last December that it was impossible to be a Marxist and a Christian at the same time. Catholic opposition to the Communist stand on such issues as abortion and divorce undoubtedly will mount.

### Radical French Deviation from Stalinist Line

The French Communist Party, which suffered from a thoroughly Stalinist and mediocre leadership until the early 1970s, has been trying frantically to refurbish its image, with mixed results. Arthur Schlesinger Jr. wrote in *The Wall Street Journal*, April 2, 1976: "The French Communist Party is a collection of hacks with no serious claim to responsibility." At the Party Congress in Paris on Feb. 7, Georges Marchais said his aim was to achieve "socialism in French colors." The failure of Marchais to show up at the 25th Soviet Party Congress in Moscow in February was seen as a particularly significant move on the part of the French to dissociate themselves from the Kremlin's fold.

Marchais believes that it no longer can be a Communist objective to take over power with a bare majority. He says that the present economic crisis "offers unprecedented possibilities" to win over a "vast majority of the people." With half a million members and a record influx of 93,873 new card carriers last year, the French party is all set for a "leap forward," Marchais said.

However, the electoral alliance between the Communists and the Socialists remains fragile. At the cantonal elections held in mid-March, the Socialists emerged with 26.5 per cent of the vote compared with 23 per cent for the Communists. Marchais criticized the Socialists for violating an agreement to back Communist candidates in the run-offs. However, the Socialist-Communist alliance captured more than half of the 1,800 seats at stake at the cantonal level and its hope is to win a majority in the next parliamentary elections in 1978.

The basic lack of democracy in the French Communist Party remains a sore point. On Jan. 7, 1976, Marchais first suggested in a radio interview that Lenin's phrase "dictatorship of the proletariat" might have outlived its purpose. It was too reminiscent of Hitler, Mussolini, Salazar and Franco, he said. Within a month and despite the misgivings of the older members, who were given a perfunctory hearing at best, the majority of 1,600 delegates at the Party Congress endorsed a new line.[21] This was parting company not with Stalin but with Lenin. Non-Communist observers wondered whether a policy abandoned so precipitously might not be revived just as easily.[22]

**Georges Marchais**

## New Initiatives by Other European Communists

There are 23 Communist parties in Europe west of the Elbe, with just over 2 million members out of a total population of 377 million people. This is not an impressive total. Nor is there any indication that the Communists have increased their overall electoral strength over the past 30 years. Only in Portugal, Iceland and Finland are Communists currently represented in government. On the other hand, in Spain the Communist Party is still illegal and working underground,[23] while in the United Kingdom the party has tried to follow a more subtle strategy of working through the trade union movement.

The Communist Party in Britain has only 32,000 members—about half of the total it had during World War II. It has no members in Parliament and controls no local council. In

[21] See Ronald Tiersky, "French Communism in 1976," *Problems of Communism*, January-February 1976, pp. 20-47.
[22] John Ardagh, "The War Within the French Left," *New Society*, Feb. 19, 1976, p. 375.
[23] See "Threatened Spanish Succession," *E.R.R.*, 1974 Vol. I, pp. 385-402.

an effort to revamp the party, its retiring secretary-general, John Gollan, issued a 20,000-word article in the January issue of *Marxism Today* in which he firmly dissociated the British Communist Party from Moscow. Attacking Leonid Brezhnev's assertion that banned Russian writers deserved only scorn, Gollan wrote: "The public, in order to express scorn or praise, must be able to know the work in question."

In Finland, the 50,000 members of the Finnish Communist Party are split between a "majority" supporting the chairman, Aarne Saarinen, and a "minority" who frequently have been called "Stalinists." When Saarinen joined a left-center government coalition last November, the minority strongly condemned the move. However, both factions maintain a slavish loyalty to Moscow. President Kekkonen of Finland believes that his country can solve its serious economic problems only if the Communists, who polled a fifth of the vote in last year's national elections, participate in the government.[24]

Spain's 22,000 Communists-in-exile, who are supported by a number of secret members in Spain, remain a largely unknown factor. Their secretary, Santiago Carrillo, who lives in Paris, is the most moderate of all of Europe's Communist leaders. He even describes his party as the only "centrist" force in Spain. Carillo has been harshly critical of the Soviet Union on such issues as Czechoslovakia and has maintained contacts with Peking. In 1970 the Russians decided to launch a counter-party, the Spanish Workers Communist Party (PCDE) headed by the Moscow-based Enrique Lister, in order to weaken the revisionist and libertarian movement of Carillo.

### Dilemma for Western Democratic Governments

An understanding of the new Communist movements is necessary if there is to be any agreement as to how the Western democracies are to handle them. Mark Farland wrote recently in *The Observer* that the idea of a "reformist" communism is as familiar to the American people as "the dark side of the moon." The very notion of an anti-Soviet communism is almost heretical. While there is recognition that both Tito and Mao are very different Communists from Brezhnev, there remains a reluctance to accept the independence of the Western European parties. A teaser frequently posed is: "Would a French Communist ever take up arms against the Soviet Union?"[25]

Henry Brandon, the Washington correspondent for the London *Sunday Times*, suggested that while Kissinger recognized

---

[24] The Finnish Communists hold the ministries of transport, labor, housing and education. See Mark Arnold-Foster, "The Red Map of Europe," *The Guardian*, Feb. 16, 1976.
[25] C.L. Sulzberger, "Does National Marxism Exist?" *The New York Times*, March 10, 1976.

that the Italian and French Communists have come a long way from being instruments of Soviet policy, he still has the "greatest reservations over how the Communist parties would act when sharing power or how they would buttress their position once in power." Kissinger is concerned that the inclusion of Communists in the governments of France or Italy would change the entire character of the European-American relationship. It is assumed, for example, that while the Communists would not urge their countries to pull out of Nato, they would join in setting up budget priorities which would damage Nato's efforts to preserve the overall balance of power.

Speaking in Paris on March 22, Vice President Nelson A. Rockefeller asserted that the United States would have to review its relationship with any Western European government that included Communists. However, it is generally thought in Europe that such remarks are counter-productive. Flora Lewis reported in *The New York Times,* April 4, 1976, that "the United States campaign against Communist participation had only irritated the whole range of public opinion in Europe."

While the Western European Communists currently are seeking "bourgeois" allies and taking an independent line, there can be no guarantee that the French or Italian parties always would remain distant from Moscow. A change in leadership easily could push that party—and if in power the country that it ruled—back into Russian arms. Socialist writer Jean-François Revel has turned the debate into a national best-seller in France. Revel maintains in *The Totalitarian Temptation* (1976) that Socialists are committing suicide by working with the Communists. He argues that one cannot expect the Communists to turn into law-abiding Socialists. Revel rejects the notion that bringing Communists into Western governments might speed their conversion from revolutionary outsiders to evolutionary insiders.

An American attempt to keep the Communists out of office could provoke a popular backlash against the United States. Even Washington agrees that it has no right to block from office a party freely elected by the voters. So complex and so contradictory is this dilemma that most observers think the Atlantic democracies must give immediate priority to deciding and implementing their policies toward Communist participation in Western European governments.

# Selected Bibliography

## Books

Cunhal, Alvaro, *Pela Revolucao Democratica e Nacional*, Portuguese Communist Party, 1975.

Maurois, André, *A History of France*, Jonathan Cape, 1949.

McInnes, Neil, *The Communist Parties of Western Europe*, Royal Institute of International Affairs, 1975.

Revel, Jean-François, *The Totalitarian Temptation*, Paris, 1976.

## Articles

Ardagh, John, "The War Within the French Left," *New Society*, Feb. 19, 1976.

Bartoli, Edgardo, "The Road to Power: The Italian Communist Party and the Church," *Survey*, autumn 1975.

Fallaci, Oriana, "Disintegrating Portugal: An Interview with Mario Soares," *The New York Review of Books*, Nov. 13, 1975.

Goldsborough, James, "The Changing Image of Europe's Communists," *International Herald Tribune* (Paris), Jan. 28, 1976.

Griffin, Dan and Laurence Stern, "The Portuguese Connection," *Ramparts*, May 1975, p. 41.

Hamill, Pete, "A New Communism Haunts the Kremlin," *The Village Voice*, March 29, 1976.

"Italy's Communists," *The Economist*, Feb. 28, 1976.

Nichols, Peter, "On the Italian Crisis," *Foreign Affairs*, April 1976.

Pfaff, William, "Post-Marxist Europe," *The New Yorker*, Jan. 12, 1976.

Pick, Hella, "Communists Call for Broad Front to Gain Democratic Power," *The Guardian*, Nov. 18, 1975.

Pines, Burton, "Red Star Over Europe," *Time*, March 15, 1976.

Schwarz, Walter, "The Thin Red Line of Democracy," *The Guardian*, Jan. 13, 1976.

Szulc, Tad, "How Gloom Muddled Kissinger's Portugal Policy," *The Washington Star*, Dec. 7, 1975.

Willey, Fay, "The White Menace," *Newsweek*, Feb. 2, 1976.

Seligman, Daniel, "Communism's Crisis of Authority," *Fortune*, February 1976 (second of a three-part series).

## Studies and Reports

Cliff, Tony, *Portugal at the Crossroads*, published by International Socialism, September 1975.

Editorial Research Reports, "Italy's Threatened Democracy," 1975 Vol. I, p. 14; "Soviet Options: 25th Party Congress," 1976 Vol. I, p. 127.

# Soviet Options: 25th Party Congress

by

## Yorick Blumenfeld

**Feb. 20**
**1 9 7 6**

# SOVIET OPTIONS: 25th PARTY CONGRESS

T HE POLISHED facade that is presented to the world by Soviet communism at its party congresses rarely reflects the actual state of conditions in world communism, in Russia generally or in the Kremlin. And that is expected to be the case when the 25th Congress, the first in five years, convenes in Moscow on Feb. 24 to hail the unity and progress achieved under the past dozen years of leadership provided by the sometimes-ailing party leader, Leonid I. Brezhnev.

Soviet-affairs specialists throughout the world will be searching for clues to pending change or continuance of the existing order—for any inkling of disagreement on such fundamental and diverse issues as détente, strategic arms control, political succession to Brezhnev, restiveness among Communist parties in western Europe, the continuing war of words with China, and economic problems facing the Soviet Union. Difficult choices, both on goals and tactics, are inevitable in what Professor Zbigniew Brzezinski of Columbia University has called the "transition to the post-Brezhnev era."

It was Brezhnev who, at the last party congress in 1971, pushed for détente and cooperation with the United States as the way to obtain the credits and technology necessary to modernize Russia. There is evidence that uncertainty has now developed in the Kremlin as to what this policy actually means for the Soviet Union. Tensions arising between those favoring an extension of détente and those pushing for a resumption of international revolutionary militancy remain barely submerged. Indeed, there are signs that the "activists" in the Kremlin, feeling that Russia has gained as much as it can from détente, prefer to take a much tougher position in regard to the West. Moscow's support of the pro-Soviet forces in Angola reflects this attitude.

Victor Zorza, the Washington-based writer on Soviet affairs, has said he sees indications of a shift in the Kremlin to a harder line. He regards the stress being placed on heavy industry in Russia, the continuing Soviet arms build-up, and Moscow's renewed emphasis on helping the world's "national liberation movements" as signs of change. The outcome of Secretary of State Henry A. Kissinger's visit to Moscow in January indicated that little progress had been made in persuading Russia to end its intervention in Angola.

At the same time, the continued debates on the numerical limitations on strategic arms have been cited as evidence of Brezhnev's unwillingness to choose between opposing sides in the Kremlin. The rejection of western proposals for troop and nuclear reductions in central Europe seemed to indicate that on some issues the hard-liners held the upper hand. In all likelihood, it will be Brezhnev himself, in his keynote speech to the 25th Congress, who will indicate whether a major Soviet policy shift is in the making and whether a summit meeting will take place with President Ford in 1976 or will await the outcome of the presidential election.[1]

## Question of Brezhnev's Health and Succession

There has been persistent speculation since 1974 that the Soviet leader would probably announce his voluntary retirement at the 25th Congress. Brezhnev's long absences from public view in early 1975 were widely interpreted as a sign of bad health. *The Washington Post* said that U.S. intelligence specialists were "virtually convinced" that Brezhnev had "a form of cancer, probably leukemia."[2] The Soviet news agency, *Tass*, attributed Brezhnev's seclusion to flu. But speculation persisted. *The New York Times* noted, June 13, that according to unconfirmed reports circulating in Moscow Brezhnev had been undergoing throat surgery for some problem, possibly caused by a stroke.

But except for health, which remains a closely guarded secret, there is no apparent reason to expect Brezhnev, at age 69, to step down. Indeed, Brezhnev, who has now run the Soviet Union longer than anyone except Stalin, would appear to be politically stronger than ever.[3] Over the past decade there have been only minor changes in the ruling Politburo. The three leaders who were reported to have opposed his policy of détente—Pyotr Chelest, Genady Voronov and Alexander Shelepin—have all been replaced by figures who are sympathetic to his point of view. Shelepin, the secret police chief who was reputed to have had ambitions to succeed Brezhnev, was dropped from power in April 1975.

Edward Crankshaw, a veteran observer of the Soviet scene, has suggested that Brezhnev is solidly entrenched because he

---

[1] President Ford indicated in an interview published in *The Christian Science Monitor*, Feb. 9, 1976, that he thought a new arms control agreement—and a visit by Brezhnev—was possible by summer.

[2] Published in the *Post*, Jan. 7, 1975. The Central Intelligence Agency promptly said such reports were baseless.

[3] "Kremlin Succession," *E.R.R.* 1969 Vol. II, pp. 897-916.

**The likely issues...**

**Brezhnev Succession ● Future of Detente ● Strategic Arms ● Trouble With China ● Economic Problems**

"very accurately represents a strong consensus position."[4] Crankshaw maintained that it is no longer of much importance who holds the reins of power because the pressures of geopolitics, economics and internal social factors dictate the general policy line. "The future will be a continuation of the present," Crankshaw wrote.

## European Communism's Challenge to Moscow

For the past three years the Soviet Communist Party and its closest allies have been trying to organize a pan-European conference and a world Communist conference[5] but Moscow's persistent claim to ideological leadership has blocked the progress of planning sessions. Brezhnev originally hoped a European conference would offer timely proof that Moscow was the sole guardian and interpreter of Communist truths. But his efforts have so far produced only disarray in world communism.

---

[4] Edward Crankshaw, "Consensus in Russia," *The New York Times Magazine*, Nov. 30, 1975, p. 15.

[5] See Kevin Devlin's "The Interparty Drama," *Problems of Communism*, August 1975, p. 18.

Although a European conference may eventually take place, the preliminary meetings have been fruitless. In October 1975, a meeting of delegates from 27 European Communist parties in East Berlin failed to produce an agenda. The basic split was between the pro-Soviet majority and the independent-minded minority led by Yugoslavs, Italians and Spaniards. Russians, East Germans and Czechs feared unpleasant repercussions within their own parties if the conference was too permissive.

At another meeting the next month, the parties decided to replace the concept of Moscow-led proletarian internationalism with calls for all "democratic, progressive and peace-loving forces" to join with the Communist parties in the fight for a better world. But even this attempt to appease the dissident groups failed to make headway. At yet another meeting in December to discuss a draft declaration, agreement again was beyond reach. Hela Pick of the British *Guardian* quoted a delegate as saying: "Just about the only proposition on which all the European Communist parties can wholeheartedly agree is that they subscribe to Marxism."[6]

While the Kremlin was at odds over the compromising policies of the French and Italian Communist parties, Enrico Berlinguer, the leader of the Italian Communist Party, emphasized that it was quite "beyond the bounds of reality" to believe that communism could be established in western Europe in the same way as it had developed in Asia and eastern Europe. Such assertions of independence on the part of European Communist parties were unprecedented. A trend towards constitutional, rather than revolutionary, communism could become as significant as China's break with the Soviet Union in the 1960s. Moscow seems always to have regarded the Communist parties in western Europe as a greater political and ideological threat than the capitalist or democratic governments they seek to replace.

### Status of Talks on Strategic Arms Limitations

The Kremlin has blown hot and cold on the issue of strategic arms limitations. The first stage of arms-limitation talks between the United States and Russia—SALT I—resulted in the signing of two pacts in Moscow, May 26, 1972, by Brezhnev and President Nixon. One was the Treaty on the Limitation of Anti-Ballistic Missile Systems, and the other was technically an executive agreement placing a numerical freeze on U.S. and Soviet offensive missile launchers for five years at roughly the existing levels. Under a complex set of formulas, Russia could achieve a lead of 2,359 to 1,710 in offensive missiles but the United States would retain a sizable lead, about 3 to 1, in warheads. Long-range bombers were not included in the agreement.

---

[6] *Guardian,* Dec. 19, 1975.

## Major Events Since Stalin's Death

| | |
|---|---|
| March 5, 1953 | Stalin dies |
| March 21, 1953 | Khrushchev elected First Secretary |
| February 1956 | Khrushchev condemns Stalinism |
| October-November 1956 | Soviet troops put down rebellion in Hungary |
| March 27, 1958 | Khrushchev elected Premier |
| September 1959 | Khrushchev visits United States |
| October 1962 | Cuban missile crisis |
| July 25, 1963 | Nuclear test-ban treaty signed |
| Oct. 14-15, 1964 | Khrushchev deposed; Brezhnev and Kosygin assume leadership |
| November 1964 | Chou En-lai visits Moscow |
| August 1968 | Russians invade Czechoslovakia |
| March 1969 | Armed clashes on China's border |
| May 1972 | President Nixon visits Moscow |
| July 1972 | Egypt expels Soviet military men |
| June 1973 | Brezhnev visits United States |
| October 1973 | Russia backs Arabs in Israeli war |
| Aug. 1, 1975 | European security pact signed |

The second stage of arms-limitation negotiations was initiated the following November and appeared headed for ratification two years later when Brezhnev and President Ford reached a tentative agreement at their meeting in Vladivostok, on Nov. 24, 1974. The Vladivostok guidelines provided for an exact "equivalence" between the United States and Russia on the number of strategic weapons through 1885.

However, the negotiations to limit the number of delivery vehicles eventually bogged down, as was signaled by the repeated postponement of a Brezhnev visit to the United States in 1975. Although each country had agreed to limit itself to 2.400 long-range missiles and bombers, trouble soon arose over whether and how to include two new weapons. They were the American "cruise" missile, now in an advanced state of development, and the Russian Backfire bomber, of which about 50 are in service, according to U.S. military information.

Initially both sides agreed that the two weapons should not be counted among the 2,400 missiles or bombers. When it was discovered that the Backfire could carry two air-to-surface missiles and by in-flight refueling fly distances of 7,000 miles or more, the United States began to insist that the Backfire was a long-range bomber and should be counted. Russia has balked at doing so, although it appeared to yield some ground during Kissinger's trip to Moscow in January 1976. As for cruise missiles, he proposed that the United States would agree to count them among the 1,320 missiles (out of the 2,400 total) which could be

47

armed with multiple warheads. The cruise missile, armed with nuclear or conventional explosives, could be launched from the air or sea and guided to a target with a high degree of accuracy.

Stopping in Brussels on Jan. 23 to report to ministers of the North Atlantic Treaty Organization on his Moscow talks, Kissinger said that "some significant progress" had been made toward reaching a compromise formula. However, the Secretary of State emphasized that any proposal to alter the ceiling would have to be seen in the context of several other elements in détente before a final agreement could be signed. The present interim agreement is scheduled to expire in October 1977.

Ronald Reagan, Ford's Republican challenger for the 1976 Republican presidential nomination, said "Its [the cruise missile's] significance should not be underestimated, for it could reverse our 25-year dependence on nuclear weapons for security." For the Russians, he continued. "this weapon poses a frightening problem. They've just managed, with enormous effort and sacrifice, to achieve something like nuclear strategic parity with the U.S.—and here we come up with a new weapon that could force them into a major new effort to keep up."[7]

# Kremlin Debate on Domestic Policy

ONE OF THE most important functions of the 25th Party Congress is to provide the Soviet leadership an occasion to evaluate the domestic situation. Ever since Stalin's time, economic failures or other shortcomings have been concealed behind Communist rhetoric and spurious statistics. Indeed, whenever the Kremlin faced serious internal difficulties, every effort was made to hold the line and to give the world the appearance of stability. Nevertheless, despite all the official formulations and propaganda, a party congress can indicate dramatic shifts of national policy.

At the 10th Party Congress in 1921 Lenin unveiled his New Economic Policy, temporarily restoring a measure of private enterprise in Russia. At the 15th Congress, Stalin took full control of party power by purging Leon Trotsky. In 1956, at the 20th Congress, Nikita Khrushchev made his famous "secret speech" in which he denounced the excesses of Stalinism and signaled the beginning of a period of relative liberalization in the Soviet Union.

---

[7] Speech delivered Feb. 10 at Exeter, N.H.; excerpts printed in *The Wall Street Journal,* Feb. 13.

## Role of the Soviet Party Congress

The party congress is, theoretically, the highest authority in Soviet communism. Party statutes require a congress to be held every five years to make policy and give direction. In reality, the role of the congress is to approve the policies set by the party leaders and give these policies an air of legitimacy. It is also a forum for assessing achievements and describing future tasks.

Daniel Seligman, writing in *Fortune,*[*] has described a party congress as, "first of all, a quasi-religious ceremony punctuated by repeated affirmations of the party's dedication to its Marxist-Leninist faith." He continues to say that the serious business which actually goes on is frequently lost to non-Communist observers, "who are apt to be put off by the crudeness and mendacity of many official formulations, and who thus tend to view the congresses as mere exercises in propaganda."

The party congress, again in theory, directly represents today a membership of about 15 million, or about 6 per cent of the Russian population. More than that, it speaks to, and sometimes for, Communist parties in some or all of the 92 countries of the world where they are found.

In terms of the Soviet Union, the Congress elects the Central Committee to conduct its work between five-year sessions. The committee must meet every six months. It, in turn, forms a Political Bureau (Politburo) to carry on the work between committee sessions—and herein resides the real power. The Politburo consists of the top leadership and is the effective policy-making organ. A Secretariat (Brezhnev is First Secretary) provides day-to-day executive and administrative direction to the entire party.

*January 1976 issue

Today the Soviet leadership is faced with deficiencies in agriculture and a lag in the planned rate of economic growth. An unusually hot summer and scant rainfall east of the Urals caused the 1975 Russian harvest to be the most disastrous in over a decade. Although the Kremlin did not issue precise figures, the chairman of the Supreme Soviet's Budget and Planning Commission, Grigory Vashchenko, released percentage estimates which enabled western statisticians to deduce that the grain harvest was perhaps as low as 133 million tons. The state plan had set a goal of 215 million tons. Once again, a failure in agriculture has raised questions about the Soviet Union's ability to feed its 255 million people[8] adequately.

When Brezhnev took over from Khrushchev in 1964, he tried to boost production by spending more rubbles for farm

---

[8] Mid-1975 estimate by the Population Reference Bureau, Inc., Washington, D.C.

mechanization and fertilizer. But, western observers have pointed out, the root of the trouble has been that farmers have never had sufficient incentives to produce under the many different collectivization plans. Moreover, it is reported that all too often the farm managers have been ignorant and idle.

In the early 1970s when a Politburo member, Gennady Voronov, proposed to loosen the collective system sufficiently to allow small groups of peasants to organize their own work and to make a profit, he was expelled from office. The built-in bias in the system against any Lenin-style New Economic Policy in agriculture runs very deep. Brezhnev has planned another series of immensely costly investments in agriculture in 1976 which are unlikely to correct the inefficiencies.

A significant portion of the grain crop—from perhaps 10 to 25 per cent of the total—is written off annually because of post-harvest losses due to such things as inadequate storage and theft. Shortages occur and Russia is forced time and again to buy grain on the world market. America has been a prime supplier of Russia's grain needs since 1972.[9] President Ford said in January 1976 that since the preceding summer, Russia had purchased 9.8 million metric tons of grain from the United States. He indicated that the amount might have been greater except for a temporary hold being placed on new sales until a new long-term agreement could be worked out so as not to disrupt the American food market.[10] A new agreement assures that Russia will purchase at least six million tons of American corn and wheat each year for the next five years.

The Kremlin fears the consequences of another poor harvest. There are signs that some of Russia's winter wheat crop has been badly damaged by lack of snow cover. If the spring crop is also less than normal, Russia will be faced with a huge grain deficit. Even the Kremlin cannot afford to continue the massive purchases of grain from abroad without encountering internal repercussions. Brezhnev put his personal prestige behind an improvement in agriculture when he came to power and a dozen years of his stewardship have not provided the desired results.

### Modest Objectives of Newest Five-Year Plan

The Supreme Soviet acknowledged Dec. 2, 1975, that the harvest failure would mean much slower economic growth in 1976. Nikolai K. Baibakov, chairman of the State Planning Committee, set the economic growth rate at a modest 4.3 per cent. He cited a failure to complete new plants according to schedule, low

[9] See "World Grain Trade," *E.R.R.*, 1973 Vol. II, pp. 711-732. See also "The Soviet Economy is Not Immune" by Marshall I. Goldman in *Foreign Policy*, winter 1975-76, pp. 75-85.

[10] Speech to the American Farm Bureau Federation, St. Louis, Jan. 5, 1976.

## Past Soviet Communist Party Congresses

| No. | Date | Place | Major Events |
|-----|------|-------|--------------|
| 1 | 1898 | Minsk | Nine socialists meet secretly and issue a declaration of Marxist principles |
| 2 | 1903 | Brussels | 57 delegates adopt Bolshevik faction's party rules |
| 3 | 1905 | London | Bolshevik faction informally organizes, opposing Menshevik faction |
| 4 | 1906 | Stockholm | Bolsheviks and Mensheviks attempt to unify |
| 5 | 1907 | London | Lenin and Bolsheviks strengthen their hold on the party organization |
| 6 | 1917 | Petrograd | At secret meeting, Stalin gives important opening speech |
| 7 | 1918 | Petrograd | Ratification of Treaty of Brest-Litovsk ending Russian role in World War I |
| 8 | 1919 | Moscow | Peasant delegates express murmurs of rebellion |
| 9 | 1920 | Moscow | Further peasant and worker unrest |
| 10 | 1921 | Moscow | Lenin unveils New Economic Policy, temporarily restoring a measure of private enterprise |
| 11 | 1922 | Moscow | Stalin elected a member of the Secretariat and given title of General Secretary |
| 12 | 1923 | Moscow | Lenin, ill, unable to participate |
| 13 | 1924 | Moscow | First Congress held after Lenin's death |
| 14 | 1925 | Moscow | Kamanev challenges Stalin's credentials as supreme leader of party |
| 15 | 1927 | Moscow | Stalin takes control of the party |
| 16 | 1929 | Moscow | Principles of crash industrialization and collectivization adopted |
| 17 | 1934 | Moscow | Stalin hints of policy of agreement with Germany |
| 18 | 1939 | Moscow | Stalin creates an entirely new party structure, completely consolidating his rule |
| 19 | 1952 | Moscow | Word "Bolshevik" officially dropped from the party's title |
| 20 | 1956 | Moscow | Khrushchev denounces excesses of Stalinism |
| 21 | 1959 | Moscow | Khrushchev announces Russian military superiority over U.S. |
| 22 | 1961 | Moscow | Stalin's emblamed body removed from Lenin Mausoleum; all ideological restraint on scientific research lifted |
| 23 | 1966 | Moscow | Congress calls for world Communist unity in the face of Communist Chinese efforts to split the international movement |
| 24 | 1971 | Moscow | Congress endorses an improved consumer economy and détente |

productivity, poor management, and grain imports. Priority is to be given to agricultural output.

When Brezhnev signed his name to the Ninth Five-Year Plan in 1971, consumer goods came first, ahead of industrial investment. But in December 1975, the draft proposal of the Tenth Five-Year Plan (1976-80) reverted to the old order of priorities. Heavy industry is due to grow faster (between 38 and 42 per cent) than consumer goods' production (30 per cent) during the next five years. Consumer industries have been told, however, to increase the assortment and improve the quality of the goods. The plan is due for adoption by the 25th Party Congress.

The guidelines for 1976-1980 point to lower growth rates in nearly every key economic sector except foreign trade and the production of such raw materials as grain, oil and natural gas. The volume of foreign trade is to rise by 30 to 35 per cent during this time. Western experts believe that this means the Soviet Union will run up record deficits in its trade with hard-currency nations. It is believed that Russia made large sales of gold and diamonds in 1975 to offset a $5 billion deficit. Alec Nove, an expert in Soviet economics, has said that although the new plan is "comparatively modest," it can be fulfilled only if there is a large increase in labor productivity and if there is much greater efficiency in the use of available resources.[11]

## Need for More Economic Cooperation With West

The party congress in 1971 decided that the improvement of living standards in the Soviet Union required a foreign policy based on cooperation with the United States in order to bring American credits and technology to the rescue of Russian industry. Despite a big increase in trade with capitalist countries, help from the West was not forthcoming on the scale the Kremlin had hoped for. The U.S. Congress set a ceiling of $75-million a year on government-backed export credits to Russia. The 1972 Soviet-American trade expansion agreement was later cancelled by Moscow after Congress, in approving the Foreign Trade Act of 1974, made the lowering of U.S. trade barriers contingent upon Soviet willingness to let more Russian Jews and dissidents emigrate.

Sen. Henry M. Jackson (D Wash.), the author of that provision and the leading congressional critic of détente, observed late in 1975: "The Soviets are in real difficulty.... They need scientific help. They need technological help. They need managerial help. You name it—they need it. But what is it that they're proposing

―――――――
[11] Alex Nove, "Modest Targets in Russia's Five Year Plan," *The Times* of London, Jan. 5, 1976. See also *Soviet Life* (official English-language publication distributed in the United States) dated March 1976, pp. 2-3.

to offer us?"[12] On the part of the Russians there was a continuing reluctance to become more dependent on western political good will than was absolutely necessary. Premier Aleksei Kosygin declared in Moscow in June 1975 that the Soviet Union, by cultivating "mutually advantageous economic ties" with the capitalist countries, was helping to promote a more stable political relationship between East and West. However, he said that the "discriminatory character of American trade laws" had hindered the expansion of such ties.

There is a strong argument that Moscow needs trade. The recession in western countries crimped Soviet exports, notably timber and minerals, which dropped both in volume and price value during 1975. The cost of imported western technology continued to rise steeply. Raw materials, which make up most of Russia's exports to capitalist countries, are especially vulnerable to economic misfortunes in the industrial West.

## Continued Increase in Soviet Military Strength

The Soviet economy continues to underwrite a huge armaments industry. There have been a great number of reports, especially from American foes of détente, about spectacular rises in Soviet defense spending and capabilities during the past decade. While there is general agreement that Soviet defense spending has been rising, it is acknowledged that these expenditures are difficult to estimate in dollar values.

Soviet pricing policies are different from those in western countries. The published defense figure is generally viewed by western analysts as a barometer of East-West relations, but it does not reflect all Soviet military outlays. The nuclear weapons program, for instance, is believed to be paid out of the science budget. The 1976 allocation for Soviet military spending has been announced at 1.4 billion rubles, the same as in 1975. The U.S. defense budget for fiscal year 1977, which President Ford sent to Congress in January, requests $100.1-billion, $9-billion more than in fiscal 1976.

Acknowledging the difficulties involved in comparing American and Soviet defense expenditures, the London-based International Institute for Strategic Studies reported in its survey of "The Military Balance, 1975-76" that Russia was outspending the United States by more than $10 billion a year. Barry M. Blechman of the Brookings Institution, writing in the fall of 1975, said that U.S. defense expenditures exceeded those of the Soviet Union by almost 20 per cent in 1964 but "are now only 70 per cent of the Soviet total."[13]

---

[12] Interview published in *U.S. News & World Report*, Nov. 30, 1975, p. 22.

[13] Barry M. Blechman, "Handicapping the Arms Race," *The New Republic*, Oct. 11, 1975.

James R. Schlesinger, the former Defense Secretary, said in Washington on Dec. 4, "the Soviets are producing 70 per cent more tactical aircraft" and "today have twice as many men under arms as we have." He said further that in recent years they had produced four times as many submarines and surface combat ships as the United States did. The International Institute for Strategic Studies reported that the Soviet Union has 40,000 tanks and the U.S. Army 10,000. While the United States has been reducing its armed forces at the rate of about 40,000 a year, the Soviet Union has been increasing its forces by about the same number.

The United States has asked Russia in the continuing Vienna Conference on Mutual Force Reductions to remove part of its tank forces in central Europe in return for the West's removal of some of its tactical nuclear weapons. At the NATO meeting in Brussels in December 1975, Kissinger proposed that 1,000 U.S. tactical nuclear weapons and 29,000 U.S. troops be removed from Europe in return for the pullback of 1,600 Soviet tanks and 68,000 soldiers. The Soviets first agreed to study the proposals intended to break the two-year deadlock in negotiations, but then turned them down in January. Moscow wants equal cuts on both sides to preserve its manpower superiority.

## Ineffectiveness of Helsinki Pact on Human Rights

The Helsinki agreement which 33 European nations, the United States and Canada signed Aug. 1, 1975, was regarded by Moscow as a necessary substitute for a peace treaty formally ending World War II and securing Russia's western borders. The agreement, the final document of the Conference on Security and Cooperation in Europe, expressed principles for (1) securing a permanent peace in Europe, (2) cooperation between nations and (3) establishment of inviolable boundaries on the continent. The document was non-binding and had no legal status as a treaty.

The agreement's provisions on human rights have become scornfully regarded in much of the West as a collection of platitudes and empty promises. *The Economist* of London commented that Brezhnev "gave a tongue-in-cheek promise to do something about human rights in eastern Europe."[14] But his assurances were not followed up by domestic reforms. Milan Kubic has reported in *Newsweek* that many East Europeans regarded the agreement as a sell-out.[15] He said that since the Communist nations signed pledges to respect "human rights and fundamental freedom," liberties have in fact been reduced.

[14] "And a bumpy new year," *The Economist*, Jan. 3, 1976, p. 7. See also "Helsinki's Poor Harvest" in the magazine's Jan. 31 issue, p. 13.
[15] Alfred Friendly Jr., "Running to Stay in Place," *Newsweek* international edition, Jan. 5, 1976, p. 16.

# Soviet Foreign Policy's Unclear Aims

S OVIET foreign policy offers a confusing and, often, an adventurist image to the West. To some analysts it would seem either illogical or perfidious for the Soviet Union to pursue détente on the one hand and to preach revolution on the other; to advocate "peaceful coexistence" with the United States but to pursue confrontation in Angola; to denounce the "opportunists" and "contemporary compromisers" in France and Italy who want to achieve power by peaceful means and also to denounce the "Trotskyists" and "modern revisionists" who want to achieve power by violent means. Inevitably, these contradictions reflect the differing viewpoints of ill-defined factions in the Kremlin.

Edward Crankshaw has observed that the Kremlin "still cannot resist the old traditional, stupid urge to make trouble for the NATO powers simply for the sake of making trouble when the opportunity occurs."[16] But larger ambitions are also evident. *The Economist* recently viewed Soviet tactics in Portugal, Angola and the Middle East as part of a persistent Soviet attempt to change the social and political balance of forces in the world. Kissinger warned the Russians of the consequences of such a policy in a statement in Washington on Jan. 14. He said, "It must be clear that when one great power attempts to obtain a special position of influence based on military intervention... the other power will sooner or later act to upset this advantage."

There is a debate among western scholars of Soviet affairs as to whether the Kremlin regards détente as merely a holding action while waiting for an advantage or as a relatively permanent relationship with the West. In a *Foreign Affairs* article[17] in 1973 that drew much attention, Marshall D. Shulman, a professor of international relations at Columbia University, wrote: "Undoubtedly, the present course offers tactical advantages to the Soviet Union, but there is reason to believe that something more fundamental may be involved." He went on to say that the Soviet leadership might be responding to a situation "which requires a long-term commitment to a policy of low tension abroad and consolidation in the Soviet sphere."

A different appraisal was offered the following year in *Survey*, a journal of East-West studies published in London. Eleven scholars representing several countries signed an essay in which they argued that Moscow regarded détente as "essentially a transitory—although possibly prolonged—phase in relations between the Soviet Union and the non-Communist

---

[16] Edward Crankshaw, "Consensus in Russia," *The New York Times Magazine*, Nov. 30, 1975, p. 15.

[17] "Toward a Western Philosophy of Coexistence," October 1973.

states pending the final triumph of communism.' "[18] Professor Richard Pipes of Harvard, one of the 11 authors, elaborated on the thought in the same magazine a year later: "Détente has been deployed...whenever the Soviet Union was militarily or economically weak and needed peace and western assistance."[19]

An internal debate apparently developed in the Kremlin in 1975 over whether the rapidly maturing "revolutionary situation" in the West, brought on by the economic weakening of the capitalist nations and a lessening of western resolve following Vietnam, did not call for a change in tactics. Certain analysts in the Kremlin wrote that the opportunity for seizure of power by a number of national Communist parties was ripe, and thus Moscow needed to take a more revolutionary stance.

Despite such invocations of Marxist-Leninist doctrine, Moscow tends to be viewed from Washington as playing a superpower role in which ideology takes a back seat. Daniel Seligman, writing in *Fortune* on "Communist Ideology and Soviet Power,"[20] makes this point. He said that "the emphasis on most State Department formulations is not on Communist ideology but on Soviet power." Citing remarks from department officials, such as "Soviet Russia is only just beginning its truly 'imperial' phase,"[21] Seligman commented: "[It] sounds as though the State Department is anticipating a lot of trouble from the Russians. Actually, it is hopeful that they will stick to détente. The hope rests on a number of trends.... One, of course, is the ongoing fragmentation of the Communist world."

## Continuing Verbal Warfare With Maoist China

Many of the Kremlin's foreign-policy impulses seem to proceed from its concern over China and the independent assertion of communism in western Europe. Each in its own way challenges Russian notions of primacy in world communism and, by extension, has had a constraining influence on Moscow's exercise of its foreign policy options. The conflict with China is enduring and it is extremely vexing to the Soviet leadership.

Both Russia and China maintain the bulk of their ground forces along their lengthy borders. The Russians accuse the Chinese of trying to instigate war between the Soviet Union and the West, of opposing détente and peace, and of inciting the "Third World" of developing nations against Moscow, most

---

[18] "Détente: An Evaluation," *Survey*, spring-summer 1974. The essay was signed by Robert Conquest, Brian Crozier, John Erickson, Joseph Godson, Gregory Grossman, Leopold Labedz, Bernard Lewis, Richard Pipes, Leonard Schapiro, Edward Shils, P. J. Vatikiotis.

[19] Richard Pipes, "The Preconditions of Détente," *Survey*, spring 1975, p. 45.

[20] Title of his article, the first of a three-part series, January 1976. The second part, "Communism's Crisis of Authority," appeared in the February issue.

[21] Remark in a speech by Helmut Sonnefeldt, State Department Counselor, to the Naval War College in 1975.

recently over the issue of Angola. Domestically, the Russians accuse the Chinese of governing through the Army, of suppressing workers and of running a "military-bureaucratic regime" which would perpetuate Maoism after Mao Tse-tung dies.[22]

The ideological attacks against China continue unabated. The theoretical Soviet journal *Kommunist* published a lengthy editorial in the summer of 1975 calling for action to "smash Maoism theoretically and politically." On Jan. 16, 1976, *Pravda* issued a warning to the leaders in Peking that one day the Chinese people would rise against them. The article was signed I. Alexandrov, which is widely believed to be a pseudonym used to indicate that an article had high-level Kremlin approval. It described Chairman Mao and his colleagues as "renegades who have usurped power."

Peking replies in kind. In December, Teng Hsiao-ping, who was then deputy premier of China, predicted in his opening toast to the visiting President Ford[23] that war with Russia was inevitable. Teng had expressed similar thoughts on other occasions, notably while on an official visit to France the previous May. Despite the war of words, western observers do not discount the possibility that both sides may well attempt to reach an accommodation after Mao passes from the scene. Until there is a reconciliation, if indeed there ever is, China will remain a worrisome problem to Russia.

## Moscow's Testing of Western Resolve in Angola

Angola has been regarded in some quarters as a testing ground for Soviet expansionism in Africa. When Portugal announced its firm intention to carry out its deadline for granting Angola independence on Nov. 11, 1975, the Russians decided to step up their hitherto small-scale support for the Movement for the Popular Liberation of Angola. Some observers have suggested that Moscow may simply have wanted to frustrate Peking, which backed a rival faction in Angola.

Ford and Kissinger obviously take another view. They have been outspoken in their belief that Soviet intervention in Angola is a testing of western resolve. The Secretary of State has argued repeatedly, before Congress and elsewhere, that American credibility as a world power is at stake and that a victory by the Soviet-backed Movement for the Popular Liberation would be a sign to the world that Moscow had freedom of action to transform events elsewhere too.

---

[22] See "China After Mao," *E.R.R.*, 1974 Vol. I, pp. 101-120.

[23] Ford visited China, Dec. 1-5, 1975. Teng, expected to succeed to the premiership upon chou En-lai's death, Jan. 8, 1976, was instead passed over and apparently relegated to political oblivion. Hau Kuo-feng, who as public security minister had been a relatively obscure figure to China specialists in the West, became Acting Premier.

At a news conference in Washington on Feb. 12, he voiced angry frustration over the apparent victory of the pro-Soviet faction in Angola and the refusal by Congress to support the administration's efforts to aid pro-western factions in the Angolan civil war: "It cannot be in the interest of the United States to create the impression that, in times of crisis, either threats or promises of the United States may not mean anything because our divisions may paralyze us."

In a major policy speech in San Francisco on Feb. 3, Kissinger had said: "Angola represents the first time that the Soviets have moved militarily at long distances to impose a regime of their choice. It is the first time the United States has failed to respond to Soviet military moves outside the immediate Soviet orbit. And it is the first time that Congress has halted national action in the middle of a crisis." The speech gained wide attention for Kissinger's use of the phrase "contain and isolate," though in the context of the American response to Soviet expansionism after World War II. "These policies served us well," Kissinger said. "Soviet expansion was checked."

Victor Zorza, writing in *The Washington Post* on Feb. 5, said that the mere mention of containment—a policy presumably replaced by détente—"ought to start the alarm bells ringing in the Kremlin." George F. Kennan, the former diplomat who authored the containment policy,[24] wrote in the same newspaper on Feb. 16, "there are some nuances and reservations that could usefully be added to what Dr. Kissinger had to say." Among Kennan's points was that "not all places and regions are of equal importance" to American interests.

Zorza quoted Helmut Sonnenfeldt, who accompanied Kissinger to Moscow, as saying in regard to the discussions held with Brezhnev on Angola: "We made it clear to the Soviets that...when such—perhaps marginal—shifts occur in the power relationship, the other superpower is going to look for and find compensation. And if we proceed upon that route, we become prisoners of the iron law...that sooner or later there will be a conflict."

In the meantime, on Jan. 29, the official Soviet newspaper *Izvestia*[25] published a statement implying the possibility of a political solution in Angola, perhaps in response to the congressional decision[26] to cut off additional funds for American aid

---

[24] The origin is traced to the famous unsigned article he wrote in *Foreign Affairs* in 1947. Kennan later disavowed the militaristic turn that the policy took.

[25] It is published by the Presidium of the Supreme Soviet and considered authoritative, especially on foreign affairs.

[26] The House on Jan. 27 voted 323 to 99 to approve the cutoff amendment (to the fiscal 1976 defense appropriations bill) which the Senate had adopted on Dec. 19 by a vote of 54 to 22.

in that country. Arthur Schlesinger Jr., the author-historian, wrote in *The Wall Street Journal* on Feb. 9 generally in support of this congressional action and advised the Ford administration to "reexamine its policy of selling Russia the wheat and computers it so desperately needs" if Russia does not remove Cuban troops from Angola in the near future.

## Effect of U.S. Election on Russia's Options

Domestic election-year politics may be a consideration in Washington's reluctance to threaten to stop or reduce grain sales to Russia. In a speech to the American Farm Bureau Federation in St. Louis on Jan. 5, President Ford spoke of a temporary withholding of grain exports which had occurred in the past for other reasons. It was done, "I can assure you, with extreme reluctance," Ford added. Wheat and corn sales to Russia have been extremely popular in the Midwest where higher farm prices mean greater local prosperity.

The Russians are aware that they can influence the American electoral process. Nikita Khrushchev boasted that he had helped John F. Kennedy in the 1960 election, and the Russians openly admitted in the strategic arms limitation talks in Helsinki in 1972 that the agreements would be signed before the presidential nominating conventions were held in order to help Richard M. Nixon. However, Brezhnev has never accepted the American doctrine that détente obliges him to cease maneuvering for advantage. Brezhnev has it in his power to offer just enough signs of compromise on arms control, Angola and other issues to prevent the breakdown of détente and a return to the confrontation of the Cold War.

The Russians also realize the extent to which President Ford's negotiating positions are limited by domestic political realities. Republican contender Ronald Reagan has demanded that Ford "order his negotiators to get a real equality in every area of agreement." Sen. Jackson on the Democratic side charges that Ford's pursuit of détente "continues to rest on a series of unequal bargains and unilateral American concessions."

While Moscow assuredly would like to seek maximum advantage from a President whose political survival is being challenged at home, the Kremlin is undoubtedly also aware that it cannot expect a President who is seeking election to make an international accommodation that will have to be defended strongly before the electorate. Any basic agreement now would presumably have to be ratified by the American voters in November.

# Selected Bibliography
## Books

Brezhnev, L., *On the Policy of the Soviet Union and the International Situation*, Doubleday (through the Novotski Press Agency Publishing House, Moscow), 1973.

Brown, Archie and Michael Kaser, *The Soviet Union Since the Fall of Khrushchev*, Macmillan (London), 1975.

Dornberg, John, *Brezhnev: The Masks of Power*, Andre Deutsch (London), 1974.

——*The New Tsars*, Doubleday, 1972.

Ulam, Adam B., *Expansion and Coexistence: Soviet Foreign Policy 1917-1973*, Praeger, 1974 (2nd ed.).

## Articles

Coffey, J. I., "Détente, Arms Control and European Security," *International Affairs*, January 1976.

Connor, Walter D., "Generations and Politics in the U.S.S.R.," *Problems of Communism*, October 1975.

Crankshaw, Edward, "Consensus in Russia," *The New York Times Magazine*, Nov. 30, 1975.

"Détente: An Evaluation," *Survey*, spring-summer 1974.

"Disputes Over New Weapons Imperil Arms Pact," *Congressional Quarterly*, Nov. 29, 1975.

Devlin, Kevin, "The Interplay Drama," *Problems of Communism*, August 1975.

Goldman, Marshall I, "The Soviet Economy is Not Immune," *Foreign Policy*, winter 1975-76.

Gurney, Ramsdell Jr., "Arms and the Men," *The Bulletin of the Atomic Scientists*, December 1975.

Legum, Colin, "How Angola's Agony Trapped the World," *The Observer*, Dec. 21, 1975.

Murarka, Dev, "Brezhnev's Bitter Harvest," *New Statesman*, Dec. 12, 1975.

Nitze, Paul, "Assuring Strategic Stability in the Era of Détente," *Foreign Affairs*, January 1976.

Pipes, Richard, "The Preconditions of Détente," *Survey*, spring 1975.

Seligman, Daniel, "Communist Ideology and Soviet Power," *Fortune*, January 1976.

——"Communism's Crisis of Authority," *Fortune*, February 1976.

Shattan, Joseph, "How the Soviets See Détente," *The New Leader*, Feb. 2, 1976.

Shulman, Marshall D., "Toward a Western Philosophy of Coexistence," *Foreign Affairs*, October 1973.

## Studies and Reports

Editorial Research Reports, "American Global Strategy," 1976 Vol. I, p. 87; "Russia's Diplomatic Offensive," 1972 Vol. I; "Kremlin Succession," 1969 Vol. II, p. 897.

The International Institute for Strategic Studies, "The Military Balance, 1975-76," 1975.

# PANAMA AND LATIN POLICY

by

## Richard C. Schroeder

**1 9 7 5**
**Oct. 24**

# PANAMA AND LATIN POLICY

**F**OR YEARS Latin America has been a soporific to the American body politic. Candidates searching for viable issues in U.S. relations with the nations to the south have come up perennially empty-handed. Not since the early 1960s, when the Bay of Pigs invasion and the Cuban missile crisis stirred wide concern, has there been any substantial interest within the United States in Latin American affairs. "Americans," James Reston of *The New York Times* once remarked, "will do anything for Latin America, except read about it."

That situation may change as the United States moves into the 1976 presidential campaign. The Ford administration is faced with a number of potentially explosive problems in Latin America, any one of which could be seized upon by opposition politicians as a campaign issue. Included among them are Cuba's bid to end the U.S. trade embargo, charges of Central Intelligence Agency (CIA) subversion of Latin American governments, control of the international drug traffic, illegal immigration into this country, treatment of multinational corporations, trade, energy and Latin America's new-found solidarity with the Third World of developing nations in Asia and Africa.

Far overshadowing any of these, however, are the delicate and volatile negotiations on the future status of the Panama Canal. Panamanians view the U.S. presence in the Canal Zone as an anachronism and an insult to their national dignity. Latin American governments are virtually unanimous in their support of the Panamanian position. In the United States, however, a substantial portion of the population and influential members of Congress are adamant in their opposition to any American withdrawal from control of the strategic waterway.

Negotiations have been carried on sporadically between the United States and Panama since 1964. Three draft treaties have already been rejected by both sides. Violence has erupted in Panama on more than one occasion, most recently in the stoning of the U.S. embassy in Panama City on Sept. 23. The embassy attack drew a strong protest from the U.S. government and an apology from Panama. At the State Department, officials report "considerable progress" in the current round of talks between U.S. negotiators, headed by Ellsworth Bunker, the 81-year-old veteran diplomat, and a Panamanian team under Foreign Minister Juan Tack. But, in view of the intransigence on both sides, observers doubt that any satisfactory solution is in the offing, at least not until after the 1976 elections. Meanwhile, the dispute remains an open sore in U.S.-Latin American relations and a point of contention between the Ford administration and Congress.

## Issues at Stake in the Negotiations With Panama

At the center of the controversy are proposed changes in a 72-year-old treaty giving the United States perpetual control over a 10-mile-wide strip of land that bisects the Republic of Panama. Running through the middle of the strip for a distance of 50 miles between the Atlantic and Pacific Oceans is the Panama Canal, built by the United States more than 60 years ago at a cost of some $387 million. The Canal is one of the more heavily traveled waterways of the world. Each year, more than 14,000 ships, carrying over 125 million tons of cargo, pass through its locks, avoiding an 8,000-mile journey around the South American continent.

Some 70 per cent of the tonnage carried through the Canal either originates in the United States or is destined for U.S. ports. Sixteen per cent of all U.S. imports and exports pass through the Canal.[1] On a relative basis, however, the Canal is far more important to the oceanic trade of 10 other countries.[2]

For its rights in the Zone, the United States pays Panama an annuity of $2.3 million a year.[3] The economic value of the Canal to Panama goes far beyond the direct official payment, however. More than 40 per cent of Panama's foreign exchange earnings and nearly one-third of its gross national product are directly or indirectly attributable to the Canal—from purchases made by the Panama Canal Company, its employees and the U.S. military establishment, sales made to ships and crews passing through, and wages.[4]

---

[1] Department of State, *Background and Status of the Panama Canal Treaty Negotiations*, Jan. 25, 1974.

[2] The countries and trade percentages, as of 1971, were: Costa Rica (30.9), Guatemala (30.9), Chile (39.6), Peru (39.0), Ecuador (72.4), Colombia (22.2), Panama (31.5), El Salvador (68.1), Nicaragua (55.1), and New Zealand (17.6). The figures were cited by Ambassador John C. Mundt, Special Representative of the United States for Panama Treaty Negotiations, in testimony to the Subcommittee on the Panama Canal of the House Committee on Merchant Marine and Fisheries, Nov. 29, 1971.

[3] Robert S. Strother, writing in Sept. 12, 1975 issue of *National Review*, contends that the annuity is actually compensation for the trans-isthmian Panama Railroad, which predates the Canal by more than half a century. The State Department denies this, citing Article 14 of the Hay-Bunau-Varilla Treaty of 1903, which authorizes an annuity as part compensation for all U.S. rights in the Canal Zone, including the building and maintenance of the Canal.

[4] Department of State news release, "U.S., Panama Agree on Principles for Canal Negotiations," Feb. 7, 1974.

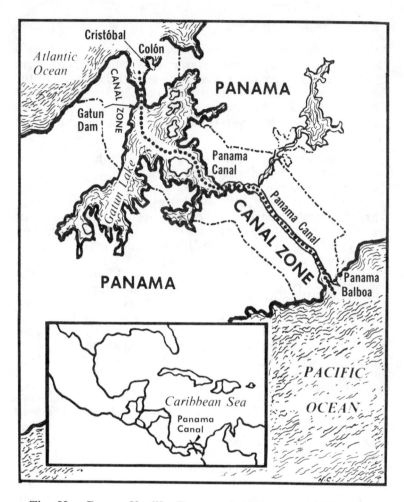

The Hay-Bunau-Varilla Treaty of 1903 granted the United States—"in perpetuity"—the use of 648 square miles of Panamanian territory for the "construction, maintenance, operation and protection" of a canal which the U.S. proposed to build. Within that area—the Canal Zone—the United States was given "rights, powers and authority...which the United States would possess...if it were the sovereign of the territory." Over the years, the United States has built up a self-contained ministate within the Zone. The Canal is operated by the U.S.-owned Panama Canal Company and the Zone is governed by a U.S. agency, the Canal Zone Government, both headed by a single U.S. presidential appointee.

Approximately 40,000 Americans live within the Zone—5,000 civilian employees, 10,000 military personnel and their dependents. The Zone is under U.S. law; the Zonian government maintains a police force, courts and jails to enforce U.S. laws on

American citizens and Panamanians alike. It has a virtual monopoly on all commercial enterprises within the Zone, from movie theaters to commissaries. It also controls nearly all the deep-water port facilities which serve Panama. In the words of Ellsworth Bunker, the United States "operates, on Panama's territory, a full-fledged government—a government which has no reference to the government of Panama, its host."[5]

The omnipresence of the Zone government dates from the earliest years of American activity in Panama. Even while the Canal was under construction, Zone administrators set up government-owned department stores, bakeries, ice cream plants, printing shops, cleaners and social clubs, and even organized leisure-time activities for wives of construction employees.[6] One element of the U.S. operation in the Zone, the military establishment, has changed over the years, however. The 1903 treaty authorized the presence of U.S. troops for the defense of the Canal. In the intervening years, the military has expanded its Canal Zone operations into what has been called a "miniature Pentagon," with such diverse responsibilities as training of U.S. personnel and officers of friendly Latin American nations, military assistance programs, disaster relief, mapping of remote areas of the hemisphere, supervision of U.S. military missions in Latin American countries, communications and intelligence.

The heart of the U.S. military presence in the Canal Zone is the Army's Southern Command (SOUTHCOM), with its headquarters on a steep hill overlooking Panama City, the capital. Among the facilities are a chain of golf courses, which have helped give the installation the nickname "Southern Comfort." More important, however, are facilities such as Albrook Air Force Base; Howard Air Force Base; Ft. Gulick, site of the U.S. Army School of the Americas; Ft. Clayton, site of a cartographic school; and the Army Jungle Warfare School.

The Zone is also the locale for periodic maneuvers involving U.S. troops and friendly foreign military personnel, and is the headquarters for Mobile Training Teams which fan out to countries throughout the hemisphere.[7] Since World War II, SOUTHCOM has trained more than 30,000 Latin American officers and enlisted men, many of whom occupy high positions in their governments and armies. Among them is Brig. Gen. Omar Torrijos, Panama's Chief of Govern-

---

[5] Ellsworth Bunker, "Panama and the United States: Toward a New Relationship," address to the Rainier Club, Seattle, Wash., May 22, 1975.

[6] Arthur Bullard, *Panama: The Canal, The Country and The People* (1911), pp. 557-578.

[7] For more detail on Zone military operations, see Gary MacEoin's *Revolution Next Door* (1971), pp. 132-157. See also Nathan Haverstock's and Richard C. Schroeder's *Dateline Latin America* (1971), pp. 80-88.

ment and the principal opponent of the U.S. military presence in the Zone. In addition, the CIA operates a technical support base at Ft. Amador in the Zone for supplying equipment and specialized personnel to CIA stations throughout Latin America.[8]

## Panamanian Demands and American Responses

Panamanians have felt aggrieved by the 1903 treaty almost from the start. The clauses on "perpetuity" and "sovereignty" have particularly angered them. From the beginning, as well, the United States has felt a sense of uneasiness over how much the Panamanians conceded. John Hay, Secretary of State at the time the treaty was signed, told the Senate when it was considering ratification: "We shall have a Treaty very satisfactory, vastly advantageous to the United States, and we must confess, not so advantageous to Panama." An official State Department assessment half a century later takes note of the Panamanian position:

> Panama has been dissatisfied with the treaty for many years. Part of this dissatisfaction has derived from Panama's views of two aspects of the negotiation of the Treaty of 1903: (1) that Panama's dependence upon the United States to protect its new-found independence from Colombia placed it in a position in which it felt that it had to accede to U.S. desires respecting the content of the treaty; and (2) that Panama's principal negotiator was a Frenchman who stood to benefit considerably if the United States purchased the private French concession to build a trans-isthmian canal.[9]

In 1905, the United States recognized Panama's titular sovereignty over the Canal Zone. It revised the Treaty in 1936, and again in 1955, increasing Panama's revenues *(see box, p. 774)* and removing some particularly troublesome provisions, such as the right to interfere in Panama's internal affairs. Panamanian resentment continued to smolder, however, and culminated in violence in January 1964. The United States had conceded the right of Panamanians to fly their flag in the Zone. When Panamanian students attempted to do so, American students resisted. In the ensuing riots that spread to the general population, 20 Panamanians and four Americans were killed.[10]

The riots brought the Canal issue to the attention of the United Nations, the Organization of American States (OAS) and other international bodies. Under prodding from these agencies, the United States and Panama opened negotiations on a new treaty. During the negotiations, the United States agreed, for

---

[8] Philip Agee, *Inside the Company: CIA Diary* (1975), pp. 184, 190.

[9] State Department news release, Feb. 7, 1974. The treaty was ratified by the Senate, Feb. 23, 1904.

[10] See "Panama Settlement," *E.R.R.,* 1964 Vol. I, pp. 143-160.

the first time, that American control and operation of the Canal should cease after a definite period of time. The United States, in effect, gave up the "perpetuity" clause of the 1903 treaty. By 1967, the negotiations had produced three draft treaties, providing (1) for joint operation of the present Canal, (2) construction and operation of a new sea-level Canal under joint authority, and (3) U.S. defense of both canals during the duration of the treaties. In the United States, congressional opposition to the treaties was so strong that they were never submitted for ratification.[11] In Panama, a military coup headed by Col. (now Brig. Gen.) Omar Torrijos in 1968 ousted the civilian government that had carried on negotiations.

Negotiations were opened again in 1971. At that time the United States submitted a draft treaty of its own, which was quickly turned down by Panama. A new start at writing a treaty was made in late 1972; that initiative was derailed when the U.N. Security Council—at Panamanian initiative—met in Panama City in March 1973. The Council passed a resolution supporting Panama's insistence on recapturing its sovereignty in the Zone. The United States vetoed the resolution.

The latest phase of the 11-year marathon began with the appointment in September 1973 of Ellsworth Bunker as chief U.S. negotiator. Bunker, a former ambassador to the OAS and principal mediator during the 1965 crisis in the Dominican Republic, had also been this country's envoy to South Vietnam during the later war years. Preliminary conversations led to the signing, in February 1974, of an eight-point "Agreement in Principle" to govern future negotiations. Signing for the United States was Secretary of State Henry Kissinger and for Panama, Foreign Minister Juan Tack.

Major points of the agreement looked toward a new treaty with a fixed termination date that would return to Panama the territory in which the Canal is located, grant the country a "just and equitable" share of the benefits from the Canal, and provide a role for Panama in administering the Canal during the life of the new treaty. Moreover, the agreement envisioned joint protection and defense of the Canal by the two countries, operation and maintenance of the Canal by the United States, and provisions for enlargement and modernization of the waterway.

Despite the "Agreement in Principle," subsequent negotiations have been hung up on a number of specifics. Panama insists on a maximum treaty life of 25 years; Gen. Torrijos has said the United States must be out of Panama by the end of the century. "The year 2000 is a sacred number," he is

---

[11] For background, see "Global Waterways: Access and Control," *E.R.R.*, 1967 Vol. II, pp. 837-842.

reported to have declared.[12] The United States wants, at the minimum, a provision for U.S. defense of the Canal over a 50-year period. Another negotiating obstacle is compensation; the United States has proposed raising the annual payment to $25 million a year. Panama reportedly wants more, but how much more is not clear. There is also disagreement on how much of the Canal Zone is to be turned over to Panama immediately when the proposed treaty enters into force.

Two of the stickiest issues involve the phase-out of the U.S. military establishment and the phase-in of Panamanian civil jurisdiction. As long ago as 1972, General Torrijos called for the removal of SOUTHCOM, claiming that its presence, and particularly its counter-insurgency training activities, compromise Panama's sovereignty and foreign policy. Panamanian negotiators want the U.S. military establishment reduced to the minimum necessary for Canal defense, with all other operations moved out. They also want the Zone rapidly integrated into Panama's national territory, placing it under Panamanian legal and law-enforcement jurisdiction.

The 1974 "Agreement in Principle" took some of the heat out of the negotiations, but as time has passed without further visible progress, the atmosphere has begun to grow more tense. In September 1975, at a meeting of southern U.S. governors, Secretary of State Kissinger remarked that the United States must maintain the right to defend the Panama Canal "unilaterally" and for "an indefinite future." Kissinger subsequently amended the remark, using the term "long future," but in the meantime the Panamanian government issued an angry denunciation. It further said that the United States and Panama were still far apart on details of a new treaty. A week after Kissinger's remark, a mob of 600 to 800 rock-throwing demonstrators attacked the U.S. embassy in Panama City.

## Political Difficulties Facing Both Governments

Negotiations are made exceedingly difficult by political pressures on both governments. For Panamanians, sovereignty in the Zone is akin to motherhood and God. Any appearance of backing down before the United States could quickly topple the Torrijos government. In an interview with *New York Times* correspondent David Binder last summer, Torrijos expressed fears of massive violence and his own death if negotiations stalled. "I am the man in the middle, caught between the students who want action and the oligarchs who would like to get rid of me," he was quoted as saying. "For almost seven years, I have been careful to promote peaceful relations all around the Canal Zone. That the students haven't broken anything over there yet is

---

[12] Quoted in *Newsweek*, Sept. 29, 1975, p. 55.

## Panama Canal at a Glance

Completed—1914
Total length—50.4 miles
Size of locks—1,000 feet long, 110 feet wide (accommodating tankers up to 90,000 tons)
Annual ship passages—14,000 plus
Annual tonnage—125 million
Annual toll revenue—$143 million (1974-75)
Construction cost—$387 million
Payments to Panama—$10 million initial payment and $250,000 a year until 1936; $430,000 a year until 1955; $1,930,000 a year until 1974; $2,300,000 a year since 1974.
U.S. population in Zone—40,000 (5,000 civilian workers; 10,000 military; 25,000 dependents)
Population of Panama—1.7 million

possible only because they have faith in the people leading the negotiations. I haven't lost hope, but I just cannot live on hope."[13]

The Ford administration, likewise, must contend with hostile public opinion and an intransigent Congress. A national poll conducted in June[14] indicated that Americans by a majority of 5 to 1 favor the continued U.S. ownership of the Canal. The prevailing view is that the Canal Zone is, indeed, American property. Nearly $7 billion has gone into the construction and maintenance of the Canal and U.S. facilities in the Zone since America assumed control 72 years ago.[15] This opinion is shared almost to a fault by the 40,000 "Zonians," American residents of the Canal Zone, many of whom are second and third generation descendants of the original American construction and operation crews. From the outset, the transplanted Americans considered the Zone their native soil, and they proceeded to build a model of American suburban life there. Visitors to Panama are immediately struck by the contrast between the slums of Panama City and the neat, ordered, small-town atmosphere of the Zone.

The Zonians and others who favor continued American control of the Canal have powerful allies in Congress, which makes the negotiators' task a delicate one. In 1974, 34 senators—

---

[13] *The New York Times*, July 27, 1975.
[14] By the Opinion Research Corporation, Princeton, N.J., for the American Council for World Freedom, Washington, D.C. Of the 1,021 adults polled, 66 per cent favored U.S. ownership and 12 per cent favored Panamanian ownership. Twenty-two per cent offered no opinion.
[15] Figure cited by Sen. Harry F. Byrd Jr. (Ind. Va.) in a bylined article which appeared, among other places, in the *Los Angeles Times*, May 18, 1975, and *The Denver Post*, May 25, 1975.

enough to block ratification of any new treaty—supported a resolution introduced by Sen. Strom Thurmond (R S.C.) insisting on "undiluted sovereignty" over the Canal. In 1975, a similar resolution drew 37 supporters. In the House, a majority of members voted twice this year, on June 26 and Sept. 24, to block funds "to negotiate the surrender" of the U.S. rights in the Zone.

Under heavy pressure from the Ford administration, the House softened its stand on Oct. 7, approving language saying that U.S. interests in the Canal should be protected under any new treaty or agreement. The House action, in effect, cleared the way for continuing negotiations, but served notice on the administration that any new treaty will face intense scrutiny—and probably strong opposition—when it is presented. Significantly, although the Senate has sole power to ratify treaties, the House must also vote on an agreement with Panama if it involves the transfer of any American property.

The administration's negotiating position has also been weakened by an internal division in the executive department between the Departments of Defense and State. For months, Defense held out for much harder terms in the proposed treaty than State was willing to press for. At one time, a projected negotiating trip by Ambassador Bunker was held up while the infighting raged over retention of bases and the duration of American rights to defend the Canal. In August, President Ford decided in favor of the State Department position, thus unifying the executive branch approach. But it is not at all certain that even he can hold the line if, or when, a new treaty comes up for national debate.[16]

# Origins of Panama Canal Controversy

T HE REPUBLIC of Panama owes its existence to a geographical curiosity. The entire western hemispheric land mass narrows to a 50-mile-wide neck of land within its borders.[17] In 1513, Balboa became the first European to cross the Panamian jungles to the Pacific.[18] He claimed the ocean for the

---

[16] For a detailed treatment of the Defense-State disagreement, see Stephen S. Rosenfeld's "The Panama Negotiations—A Close-Run Thing," *Foreign Policy*, October 1975, pp. 10-12.

[17] For geographic background, see Preston E. James, *Latin America* (1959, third edition).

[18] An event later attributed—erroneously—to Cortez, by John Keats, in his sonnet "On First Looking into Chapman's Homer:"

"Or like stout Cortez when with eagle eyes
He star'd at the Pacific—and all his men
Look'd at each other with a wild surmise—
Silent, upon a peak in Darien."

rulers of Spain. In 1519, a Spanish expedition founded Panama City on the Pacific shore. With the conquest of Peru, the isthmian crossing became the principal trans-shipment point for gold and other commodities from the western coast of South America to Spain. The vulnerability of the Spanish mule trains on their way through the jungles and across the isthmian mountains made them easy prey for English pirates, such as Drake and Morgan, both of whom raided Panama during the 16th century, waylaying treasure caravans and sacking port cities on both coasts.

Panama temporarily lost its importance when the Spanish Empire collapsed in the early 19th century. It joined the Federation of Gran Colombia, along with present-day Venezuela, Colombia and Ecuador in 1821. When the federation fell apart in 1830, Panama remained a province of Colombia. In 1848, the U.S.-Mexican War fully opened up the American West to U.S. settlers; in 1849, the discovery of gold in California sent thousands from the East Coast to the new western territory. Many found it more convenient to go by sea to Panama, make the jungle crossing, and then sail on to California.

In 1850, Colombia granted a concession for a trans-isthmian railroad to an American group headed by John L. Stephens. In one of the most remarkable railroad construction projects of all time, the Stephens group built the Panama Railroad mile by mile, carrying passengers from the city of Colón on the Atlantic Coast to the farthest point of completion, and then by mule and river boat to the Pacific Coast. The railroad did not reach Panama City on the Pacific until 1855, but by that time its revenues had nearly equaled the construction cost.

### Early U.S. Interest; Panamanian Independence

A French group, headed by Ferdinand de Lesseps, builder of the Suez Canal, bought the Panama Railroad in 1880, intending to build a sea-level canal along its route. Malaria and yellow fever decimated the crews of the French company, and financial scandals led to its ultimate collapse in 1889. The interests of the company—consisting principally of the railroad, by then hopelessly rundown, and the right to build a canal—were taken over by a group headed by Philippe Bunau-Varilla, a French engineer. By 1890, the United States had become interested in constructing a canal somewhere in Central America. An abortive effort was made to dig a sea-level canal through Nicaragua, but it was abandoned after three months of work.

The Spanish-American War of 1898 underscored America's strategic need for a canal, however; it took the battleship *Oregon* 90 days to make the passage from its Pacific station around South America to Cuba. Negotiations were then begun, with the French company for its Panama property and with the Colombian government for new canal-building rights. In December 1902, a treaty was signed between Secretary of State John Hay and Colombian Chargé Tomás Herran, permitting the United States to buy out the French company and build a canal in return for $10 million and an annual rental. The treaty was quickly ratified by the U.S. Senate, but in August 1903 it was rejected by the Colombian Senate, which was holding out for higher stakes.

The following November, Panama rebelled against Colombia, with the encouragement of the United States and the discreet assistance of a handful of U.S. troops sent to the isthmus to "protect" the Panama Railroad. Independence was declared on Nov. 4, and the United States recognized the new country on Nov. 6. Bunau-Varilla was appointed Minister Plenipotentiary to negotiate a canal treaty with the United States. With $40 million at stake—the amount the United States proposed to pay for the company's rights—Bunau-Varilla offered the United States terms so favorable that Secretary of State Hay wrote to Sen. John C. Spooner (R Wis.): "You and I know very well how many points are in the Treaty to which many patriotic Panamanians would object."[19] Soon after the Panamanian revolt, President Theodore Roosevelt remarked, "I took the Canal Zone and let Congress debate." A later observer has remarked that Roosevelt "did *not* steal the Panama Canal. What he stole was Panama."[20]

## Construction of Canal as an American Milestone

The political work involved in obtaining the Zone and the right to build the Canal was minor in comparison to the actual construction of the waterway. The enormous effort and ingenuity that the United States put into the Canal has always been a source of national pride. Understanding this is essential to comprehending American attitudes toward the Canal even today. There is a pervasive feeling in this country that "nobody else could have done it," and since we did it, the Canal is by right "ours."

Work on the Canal started in 1904. The first task was to rid the Zone and surrounding areas of the mosquito-borne diseases that had taken thousands of lives in the construction of the Panama Railroad and the ill-fated French attempt at canal-building. American sanitary teams under Col. William C. Gorgas swarmed all over the Zone, spraying stagnant streams, laying sewer lines, cleaning up fetid slums, paving roads,

---

[19] Quoted by Ellsworth Bunker in his Seattle speech (*see footnote 5*).

[20] Will Sparks, writing in *The Washington Post*, June 25, 1975. Sparks was Assistant Secretary of Defense in 1964-1965 and an assistant to President Johnson in 1965-1968.

building hospitals and administering to the sick. Disease research went on simultaneously, and even today, much of what is known about insect-borne diseases stems from the Panama experience.

Construction was a more difficult task. The first three years of the American effort were characterized by bickering over the relative merits of a sea-level canal versus a lock canal.[21] Absentee administrators tried to supervise work from Washington. Finally, in 1907, the job was handed over to the Army. Col. George W. Goethals turned the Zone into a virtual "company town," with strict discipline and careful attention to detail, ranging from procurement of supplies and machinery to planned social and recreational activities. He personally acted as judge in everything from family disputes to work rules and punishment for crime.

The work was prodigious. It is estimated that 175 million cubic yards of earth were shoveled out to create the "big ditch." A huge earthen dam—then the world's largest—was constructed to impound the waters of the Chagres River and create a lake 85 feet above sea level. It supplies most of the water to operate the system of parallel locks that raise and lower ocean-going ships. Canal builders used more dynamite and more concrete than on any other construction job in history. At the end, the Canal was called "the greatest liberty man has ever taken with nature." The first ship passed through the Canal on Aug. 9, 1914, although final construction was not completed until six years later.

### Strategic and Commercial Importance of the Canal

When the Canal was being built, its locks—1,000 feet long, 110 feet wide and 41 feet deep—were more than sufficient to hold the largest ship afloat. That is no longer true. The Canal can handle ships of up to 90,000 tons, which excludes a substantial portion of the vessels now in world trade, especially the supertankers of 250,000 tons or more. In similar manner, the Navy's biggest warships passed easily through the Canal in 1914; most of the fleet can still negotiate the Canal, but large aircraft carriers, a key to strategic warfare, cannot.

Thus, in the midst of the debate over keeping or giving up control of the Canal, it is apparent that the Canal itself, to some degree, is outmoded. It is pointed out that the multi-ocean Navy possessed by the U.S. today obviates the need for a dramatic round-the-Horn dash like that made by the *Oregon* in 1898. Aircraft carriers are on station, not only in the Atlantic and Pacific, but also in the Indian Ocean. Commercially, although

---

[21] See Hubert Herring's *A History of Latin America* (1967), p. 503.

## Panama Canal Chronology

**1903.** U.S. buys canal rights from French company, proposes treaty for canal-building to Colombia, which rejects it. Panama revolts against Colombia, with U.S. aid, and declares independence. U.S. granted rights in Canal Zone "in perpetuity" and "as if sovereign."

**1905.** U.S. recognizes Panamanian "titular sovereignty" over Zone.

**1907-1914.** U.S. builds lock canal from Atlantic to Pacific.

**1936, 1955.** Minor revisions in Hay-Bunau-Varilla Treaty of 1903.

**1964.** Riots in Canal Zone kill 20 Panamanians, 4 Americans. Negotiations begin on new Canal treaty.

**1967.** Three treaties proposed for joint operation of Canal and construction of new canal.

**1968.** Military coup in Panama. Three treaties rejected.

**1971.** New treaty proposed by United States turned down by Panama.

**1973.** U.N. Security Council session in Panama urges Panamanian sovereignty in Zone. United States vetoes resolution, names new negotiating team headed by Ellsworth Bunker.

**1974.** U.S. and Panama sign eight-point agreement to guide future negotiations. U.S. abandons claim to perpetual control of Zone.

**1975.** Negotiations stall. Mob attacks U.S. Embassy in Panama City.

the Canal carries one-sixth of the sea-borne trade of a dozen nations, its annual tonnage amounts to only about 1 per cent of all world trade. Critics of a hard-line U.S. position say this country would suffer little if it gave up control. If, in fact, a Central American waterway is vitally needed, they say, the United States should concentrate on negotiations to build a new, bigger, sea-level canal in the region.

A bonus from a sea-level canal would be to reduce the vulnerability of the present waterway. Various U.S. officials have pointed out the dangers of sabotage if current negotiations fail. Secretary of State Kissinger warned in July 1975 of a "nationalistic, guerrilla-type of operation that we have not seen before in the western hemisphere." Ambassador Bunker has spoken of the Canal's "growing vulnerability to hostile attack." Sen. Gale W. McGee (D Wyo.), a supporter of negotiations for a new Canal treaty, has said that "in these times of briefcase bombs, it's almost indefensible in a hostile situation." Noting that damage to the big dam at Gatun could put the Canal out of business for up to two years, McGee added, "The littlest guy in the world can bust that dam."

Opponents of a new treaty concede the possibility of sabotage but discount the chances of out-and-out guerrilla warfare.

Panama, they say, has too much to gain from continued operation of the Canal to consider such a step. As for sabotage, Sen. Harry F. Byrd Jr. (Ind. Va.) declares that "if the U.S. cannot defend its property in a country the size of Panama, our country is, indeed, in grave condition."[22] Set against that view is the contention of Gen. George Brown, chairman of the U.S. Joint Chiefs of Staff, that the Canal can be better protected with, than without, the consent of the Panamanians.[23]

Anti-treaty forces also challenge the assertion that the Canal has lost much of its strategic and commercial value. Rep. Daniel J. Flood (D Pa.) calls the Canal Zone the "jugular vein of hemispheric defense."[24] Senator Byrd cites figures drawn up by the U.S. Maritime Commission indicating that if the Canal were closed, there would be:

—A 17 per cent increase in average annual fuel consumption by carriers of U.S. foreign trade.
—A 31-day increase in average shipping time.
—A $932 million increase in the yearly total delivered price of all exports.
—A $583 million increase in the yearly total delivered price of all imports.

What the anti-treaty forces worry most about is stability in Panama. If the United States were to turn the Canal over to the Panamanians, they ask, what guarantees would there be that tolls would remain at reasonable levels and that the Canal would not be used as an instrument of international politics, as was the Suez Canal when the Egyptians closed it to Israeli shipping? No guarantee at all, answers Sen. Paul J. Fannin (R Ariz.). Only a "powerful and stable government like the United States" can guarantee an open Canal, he asserts.

There are strong arguments on both sides relating to the Canal's utility and vulnerability. In the end, however, the decision to approve or kill a new treaty is likely to depend on other factors. Is a determined insistence on U.S. sovereignty and a long-term U.S. military presence in the Zone the best way to accomplish our basic aim, which is to keep the Canal open and functioning, while an alternative waterway is being developed? And if it is the best way, is the inevitable damage to U.S.-Latin American relations a price that the United States can afford to pay?

---

[22] Senators Byrd and McGee offered their opposing views in *U.S. News & World Report*, Oct. 6, 1975, pp. 37-38.
[23] Cited by Rosenfeld in *Foreign Policy*, p. 11.
[24] Quoted in *Congressional Quarterly*, July 1, 1975, p. 1444.

# Implications of Policy Toward Panama

IN THE ASSESSMENT of the State Department, the Panama Canal issue is not likely to be an important factor in the 1976 presidential campaign. William D. Rogers, Assistant Secretary of State for Inter-American Affairs, said in a recent interview[25] that he did not expect any foreign relations questions to figure heavily in the coming campaign, "at least not to the extent that they have in every campaign since 1960. There is much less domestic preoccupation today with foreign affairs."

There are signs, however, that the Canal issue may prove to be much more divisive than the administration thinks. The sides are clearly drawn between supporters and opponents of a new treaty. There are deep-seated emotional factors, running far beyond the Canal itself. Having suffered the debacle of an American withdrawal in Southeast Asia, can this country afford to back away from confrontation with a ministate such as Panama? On the other hand, is the public ready to risk another guerrilla-type operation in defense of a claim to sovereignty over another nation's territory? The elements are present for a major political clash, if that is what both sides want.

The administration may, in fact, have misjudged the depth of feelings on the issue. A few months ago, Rep. W. Henson Moore (R La.) told Secretary of State Kissinger: "No matter how rational you are about the treaty, you will be bitterly opposed in Baton Rouge, and Ford will lose Louisiana."[26] At the same time, administration officials sense that if U.S. intransigence leads to new violence and confrontation in Panama, the Democrats can become the "peace" party, much as the Republicans were in 1968.

For those reasons, there is a suspicion that the United States is not pushing hard for a rapid draft of a new treaty. The most propitious time for submission of a treaty draft to Congress would be after the November 1976 elections. Administration officials deny any purposeful foot-dragging, but Secretary Rogers said: "There is no arbitrary time limit on submitting a treaty to the Senate. We are neither rushing nor stalling. Torrijos has been good on this. He has said the question is not when, but how."

The word from Panama is less reassuring than that from Washington. Torrijos, according to observers, is willing to bide

---

[25] With Editorial Research Reports, Oct. 10, 1975.
[26] Quoted by Rosenfeld in *Foreign Policy*, p. 9.

his time, but only if the United States shows a genuine intent to accede to Panama's demands. "Panama considers that 18 or 24 months of delay is nothing in the struggle of a people for its liberation, when there exists an intent on the other side to leave," he recently told *Newsweek* magazine. "But 18 to 24 months is a long time if they intend to stay."[27] Foreign Minister Juan Tack is more adamant. "We are not talking about minor changes in fees or geography," he told the U.N. Security Council. "We want effective sovereignty immediately." Speaking in Mexico in July, Tack declared, "The patience of the people of Panama has reached its limit in the struggle to recover the Canal Zone."

Panama is bolstered in its urgency by the near-unanimous support of the other Latin American nations. The Canal Zone is regarded in Latin America as a particularly objectionable vestige of U.S. colonialism. The "big stick" diplomacy that created the Republic of Panama still angers Latin Americans. "All Latin America favors a quick solution to this problem, so that Panama will regain its sovereignty over the Canal Zone," Luis Echeverria, president of Mexico, said recently.

Latin solidarity on the Panama issue is reflected in recent conversations with two hemispheric leaders. Shortly before he left office, Galo Plaza, the retiring Secretary-General of the Organization of American States, said:

> Panama is an issue that brings Latin Americans together. Whoever thinks that this is an issue between Panama and the United States is highly mistaken. It's a Latin American issue.[28]

Alejandro Orfila, Plaza's successor at the OAS, recently called the Canal negotiations "definitely the most important issue between the United States and Latin America right now." Said Orfila: "The outcome of the negotiations will make or break U.S.-Latin American relations."[29]

### Latin American Issues Beyond Canal Question

Ellsworth Bunker has said, "The Latin American nations have made our handling of the Panama negotiation a test of our intentions in the hemisphere." Two years ago, Bunker noted, the Latin American foreign ministers, meeting in Bogotá, Colombia, voted to put the Canal question on the agenda of the "New Dialogue" proposed by Secretary of State Kissinger. If, in fact, the current negotiations are a testing ground, the issues in Panama go beyond the Canal itself, and the retention or relinquishing of sovereignty in the Zone. The agenda of the "New

---

[27] "Panama's Magic Number," *Newsweek*, Sept. 29, 1975.
[28] Editorial Research Reports interview with Galo Plaza, May 7, 1975.
[29] Editorial Research Reports interview with Alejandro Orfila, Oct. 10, 1975.

Dialogue," if it still exists, is exceptionally crowded. The failure to reach a satisfactory agreement with Panama could seriously erode American influence and interests throughout the hemisphere. It could, for example, disrupt efforts to "normalize" relations between the United States and Cuba.

High on the U.S. side of the "dialogue" agenda are two issues which Latin Americans consider of relative unimportance: the flow of illicit drugs—cocaine, heroin and marijuana—from Latin America to this country, and the mounting problem of illegal immigrants in the United States from Latin America, principally Mexico and the Caribbean islands. For the moment, at least, the United States prefers to deal with the two problems on a bilateral basis, rather than raising the issues in multilateral forums such as the OAS.[30] For Latin America, economic issues are far more important.

In the long run, the trend that will be watched most closely—in this country and in Latin America, as well—is Latin America's increasing identification with the Third World, the bloc of underdeveloped, non-aligned nations. Strictly speaking, Latin America represents a panorama of underdeveloped, semi-developed and relatively well-developed countries. The economic interests of such countries as Brazil, Mexico and Argentina cannot be said to coincide with the world's least-developed countries. Nor can oil-producing Venezuela, Ecuador and Trinidad and Tobago be readily identified with the world's poorest nations. Nonetheless, in recent international forums, including the U.N. General Assembly, Latin America has politically aligned itself with the Third World bloc in its confrontation with the industrialized countries.

The drift toward the Third World may reflect a Latin consensus that its economic and political interests no longer coincide—as they were once seen to—with those of the United States. Or they may reflect Latin American frustration and disenchantment with U.S. policies in Panama, Cuba and elsewhere. It is quite probable that they are a reaction to U.S. indifference to Latin America.

American officials caution against overstating the degree to which Latin America is moving out of the U.S. orbit. Assistant Secretary Rogers acknowledges some "fundamental ideological differences," particularly in economic matters. But, he adds, such disagreements have not damaged America's good bilateral relations in the hemisphere. Still, in the light of the dispute over the Panama Canal it may be well to ponder the words of Galo Plaza: "Latin America is more important to the United States than Vietnam ever was."

---

[30] For a discussion of the illicit drug trade, see Richard C. Schroeder's *The Politics of Drugs: From Mainlining to Marijuana* (1975), published by Congressional Quarterly Inc.

# Selected Bibliography

## Books

Abbot, Willis J., *Panama and the Canal*, Syndicate Publishing Co., 1913.

Agee, Philip, *Inside the Company: CIA Diary*, Stonehill Publishing Co., 1975.

Bullard, Arthur (Albert Edwards), *Panama: The Canal, the Country and the People*, The Macmillan Co., 1914.

Busey, James L., *Latin American Political Guide*, Juniper Editions, 1975.

Clark, Gerald, *The Coming Explosion in Latin America*, David McKay Co., 1963.

Haverstock, Nathan A. and Richard C. Schroeder, *Dateline Latin America*, The Latin American Service, 1971.

Herring, Hubert, *A History of Latin America*, Alfred A. Knopf, 1969.

James, Preston E., *Latin America*, The Odyssey Press, 1959.

MacEoin, Gary, *Revolution Next Door*, Holt, Rinehart and Winston, 1971.

Schroeder, Richard C., *The Politics of Drugs*, Congressional Quarterly, 1975.

## Articles

"Kissinger Sets Canal Conditions," *The Vision Letter*, Sept. 30, 1975, pp. 1-2.

McGee, Gale and Harry F. Byrd Jr., "Should U.S. Give up the Panama Canal? Two Sides of the Issue," *U.S. News & World Report*, Oct. 6, 1975, pp. 37-38.

Rosenfeld, Stephen S., "The Panama Negotiations—A Close-run Thing," *Foreign Policy*, October 1975, pp. 1-13.

Strother, Robert S., "The Panama Question: An Alternative to U.S. Defeatism," *National Review*, Sept. 12, 1975, pp. 986-989.

Young, C. W. Bill, "The Canal Belongs to the U.S.," *Eastern Europe*, July 7, 1975, pp. 18-20.

## Studies and Reports

Bunker, Ellsworth, "Panama and the United States: Toward a New Relationship," Address to the Rainier Club, Seattle, Wash., May 22, 1975.

Department of State, "Background and Status of Panama Canal Treaty Negotiations," Jan. 25, 1974.

—"U.S. Policy Toward Latin America: Recognition and Nonrecognition of Governments and Interruptions in Diplomatic Relations, 1933-1974," Historical Studies, Interamerican Series, June 1975.

—"U.S., Panama Agree on Principles for Canal Negotiations," State Department news release, Feb. 7, 1974.

Editorial Research Reports, "Panama Settlement," 1964 Vol. I, p. 141; "International Waterways: Access and Control," 1967 Vol. I, p. 837.

Rogers, William D., "Statement to the Subcommittee on International Trade and Commerce and the Subcommittee on International Organizations of the House Committee on International Relations," Sept. 23, 1975.

# PHILIPPINE INSTABILITY

by

## John Hamer

**1 9 7 5**
**Apr. 25**

# PHILIPPINE INSTABILITY

A S SOUTH VIETNAM AND CAMBODIA fall, both believers and skeptics of the so-called "domino theory" look with trepidation toward such longtime U.S. allies as Thailand and the Philippines. Thailand's government already has demanded the prompt departure of all American forces from that country. And the Philippine government in mid-April announced that it would reassess its security ties with the United States because of America's "apparent new perception" of its commitments in Southeast Asia.

Philippine President Ferdinand E. Marcos, in an address April 15 at the National Defense College in Manila, said that "Prudence requires any political leader in the area today to look into these matters in view of the debacle in the Indochina areas." And the next day, in a lengthy policy statement, Marcos said: "There is no certainty that in case of external aggression the United States would come to the rescue of the Philippines.... The future of our relationship, which is perhaps the oldest in Asia, must be discussed as early as possible on the basis of complete reciprocity of interest."

Lying some 600 miles across the South China Sea from Vietnam and China, with Taiwan to the north and Malaysia and Indonesia to the south, the Philippine archipelago occupies a strategic position in Asia and the Pacific. American military bases in the Philippines include Clark Air Force Base north of Manila, the largest U.S. overseas air facility, and Subic Bay Naval Base, the largest U.S. naval base in the western Pacific. Both had heavy use during the Vietnam War and are being used today in the removal of remaining Americans from Indochina. Rent-free lease agreements for the bases run until 1991 but are now being reconsidered by the Marcos government. It fears that the bases may be more of a liability than an asset, even though they employ large numbers of Filipinos and provide a payroll of at least $150 million annually. It is estimated that U.S. military spending and employment account for nearly 10 per cent of the Philippines' gross national product.

Nonetheless, Marcos has strongly suggested that the Philippines might either take over the bases or begin charging substantial rent payments. On April 18, in his strongest statement since the sudden deterioration in Indochina, Marcos said: "If it is to the national interest to discard the mutual defense pact and to take over the bases, we will do so. Let no man, friend or foe, think in terms other than the national interest." Marcos called a meeting of the Philippines' Foreign Policy Council for April 25 to consider various security options.

America and the Philippines have a long history of close military and economic ties, and the U.S. government clearly would like to maintain the relationship. Their mutual defense treaty of 1951 provides that an attack on the Philippines will be considered an attack on the United States.[1] Presidents Eisenhower and Johnson are believed to have promised immediate assistance in case of attack. But the U.S. War Powers Act of 1973 set a 60-day limit on any presidential commitment of American forces abroad without specific approval by Congress, a limit to which Marcos alluded.

Although President Ford did not mention the Philippines in his State of the World address, he said at a news conference on April 3: "I believe there is a great deal of credibility to the domino theory.... I hope that other countries in Southeast Asia, Thailand, the Philippines, don't misread the will of the American people and the leadership of this country to believing that we're going to abandon our position in Southeast Asia. We are not." However, President Marcos later said that recent events in Indochina may have undermined the U.S. position.

### Mixed Results of 'New Society' Under Marcos

Once known as the "showcase of democracy" in Asia, the Philippines today is under a state of martial law declared by President Marcos in September 1972. Marcos calls the prevailing system "constitutional authoritarianism," and he has undertaken an ambitious reform program labeled the "New Society." But results have been mixed, at best. On the surface, most of the nation is more peaceful and orderly than before the Marcos decree. The crime rate in Manila—one of the most dangerous cities in Asia only a few years ago—dropped dramatically after the government clamped on a midnight to 4 a.m. curfew, banned the ownership of firearms and confiscated thousands of guns.

Marcos also imposed censorship on the press, which traditionally had been uninhibited and often irresponsible. Direct censorship has now been lifted, but the press continues

---

[1] The Philippines and the United States are members of the Southeast Asia Treaty Organization, organized expressly in 1954 at the urging of Secretary of State John Foster Dulles to provide for collective action against the spread of communism in Southeast Asia. However, the United States received little help in Vietnam from its SEATO allies—Australia, France, New Zealand, Pakistan, Thailand and the Philippines—and the organization today is considered ineffective.

to practice self-censorship. Open criticism of the government is rare. In the early days of martial law, there were widespread arrests of Marcos' political opponents and others who might undermine his authority. The exact number of initial arrests is unknown, but some estimates exceed 10,000, and at least 5,000 prisoners are still being held.[2] Marcos has the strong support of the armed forces, which numbered only about 55,000 a few years

---

[2] President Marcos on Dec. 11, 1974, said in a public statement that 5,234 prisoners were still in detention, including 1,165 "political detainees" charged under anti-subversion laws or with crimes against the security of the state. A few days later, Marcos said that the number released thus far was 1,076. However, Marcos also said that 2,727 cases were "pending trial" and 2,948 cases were "pending preliminary investigation," which together add up to 441 more than the number he said were still under arrest. (Figures supplied by U.S. State Department.)

ago but has nearly doubled to reach a goal of 110,000 men. This includes about 25,000 members of the Philippine Constabulary, a national military police force. The Army and the Constabulary traditionally have been small and weak, but their build-up under the Marcos government has led to charges of increased military arrogance and corruption. With the Philippine Congress and judiciary ineffectual under martial law, the military has been given administrative and governmental functions nationwide. But it is often unresponsive to local needs, and generally inexperienced in implementing new programs.

Economically, the Philippines has fared reasonably well under martial law. Foreign investments are up, due largely to improvements in law and order and reductions in governmental red tape. Preliminary figures showed a 6 per cent growth in gross national product in 1974, although per capita GNP is only about $265 per year. The country's balance of trade was favorable in 1973, but it fell to a deficit in 1974 because of high petroleum prices and is likely to show a deficit for the next few years. Government measures imposed under martial law have had beneficial effects on general price stability, but inflation has caused a decline in average real wages and unemployment is around 7 per cent.

A recent detailed analysis by the *Far Eastern Economic Review* concluded that: "Overall, Marcos has been exceedingly fortunate since martial law.... Now, while much of the world economy is looking hopefully towards recovery later this year and through 1976, the nature of the Philippine economy suggests that a time-lag with the industrialized world will make the next 18 months particularly difficult. Marcos will be under the gun of the most unfavorable economic circumstances since martial law...."[3]

Most Filipinos adopted a wait-and-see attitude when Marcos declared martial law. Despite press censorship, political arrests and the general suspension of civil rights, the majority of Filipinos appear to be going along with the Marcos policy for the time being. About 70 per cent of the population of 44 million are tenant farmers and peasants who have lived under feudal land barons for many years, so martial law has not greatly changed their lives. Indeed, a highly publicized land reform program has given them some hope of eventual land ownership and a better way of life (see p. 98).

Among the wealthy and educated elite, there is some dissatisfaction with martial law, especially on the part of Marcos' political opponents who have been deprived of their civil rights.

---

[3] Phillip Bowring, "Test of Strength in the Philippines," *Far Eastern Economic Review,* April 4, 1975, p. 51.

Some have accused Marcos of appropriating their land holdings or other economic interests while they were in detention. However, the nation's most important pressure group consists of the impoverished peasants in the countryside. They are traditionally patient, but if they continue to see the gap between rich and poor widen and find that glowing government promises go unfulfilled, Marcos' rule might be threatened.

## Rising Church Opposition to Political Arrests

The Philippines is the only Christian nation in Asia, with more baptized persons than all other Asian nations combined. More than 80 per cent of all Filipinos are Roman Catholic, and the church is the only nationwide organization aside from the government and the military. While the church leadership traditionally has been conservative and politically inactive, there is evidence of growing opposition to some of the abuses which have occurred under martial law.

The Catholic archbishop of Manila, the Most Rev. Jaime L. Sin, in November 1974 made the most severe public criticism of the government since Marcos imposed martial law. "Martial law and all it connotes...is for emergencies only, and not for the normal state of things," Sin told a group of reporters. "We cannot jail a man indefinitely and still call ourselves Christian."[4] Last September, Catholic bishops of the Philippines submitted a petition asking Marcos to lift martial law and restore civil liberties. A call for freedom and justice, couched in pastoral language, was read at masses and lay meetings throughout the country.

In January 1975, the Philippine Supreme Court rejected a document signed by five Catholic bishops challenging the legality of a national referendum which Marcos had scheduled on the continuance of martial law. The bishops then urged the people to boycott the referendum despite the risk of criminal penalties for not voting. The government announced after the referendum on Feb. 27 that 90 per cent of the voters approved the continuance of martial law. Critics said the voting was meaningless because the people had little choice.[5]

The top hierarchy of the church is divided on the issue of martial law, but some young activist priests have become increasingly outspoken, especially in their concern for political prisoners. Archbishop Sin last November objected to holding people for vague "security reasons" and called for a "clear-cut definition of what subversion is." The prelate also charged that some prisoners had suffered "diabolical torture" while in captivity. But disunity among the church leadership probably will preclude a direct confrontation with Marcos. "And even if the

---

[4] Quoted by Harvey Stockwin, *The Washington Post*, Nov. 23, 1974.

[5] Marcos held two previous referenda, in January and July 1973, with similar results.

church openly challenged Marcos on libertarian issues," wrote Peter R. Kann, Asia correspondent for *The Wall Street Journal,* "it is far from certain that the pulpit would prove as powerful as the throne."[6]

## Struggle of Muslims for Independence in South

The Marcos government is facing an open revolution in the southern Philippine islands where Muslim guerrillas have been fighting government troops for several years. The war has heated up since Marcos declared martial law. Muslim rebels refused to turn over their firearms and began coordinated attacks on government outposts in Mindanao and the islands of the Sulu Archipelago. There are only about three million Muslims in the Philippines—less than 5 per cent of the total population—but they are proud and independent people who resisted the Spanish colonialists for centuries. The Muslims are divided into about six primary groups, each with its own language, but leadership has been assumed by the Moro National Liberation Front (MNLF), led by Nur Misuari, a former political science professor at the University of the Philippines.

The Muslim rebellion is more a cultural and economic problem than a political or military issue, however. Until the end of World War II, Muslims were a majority in most of the southern Philippines. They had very different traditions from the Catholic north, including the communal ownership of land without formal titles. In the 1950s, Christians started moving southward into the relatively underpopulated areas and began staking land claims where they outnumbered the Muslims. Even so, Muslims and Christians coexisted in relative, if polarized, peace until Marcos declared martial law and the Muslims saw their hopes for more local power shut off.

In the past two years there have been increasingly fierce and bloody battles between the Muslim guerrillas, who total perhaps 20,000, and government troops, who have been reinforced steadily and now number more than 35,000. In February 1974, most of the city of Jolo—including the Muslim mosque and the Catholic cathedral—was destroyed in a battle between rebels and government forces. Several hundred persons were killed and thousands of refugees were forced to flee Jolo island. The Marcos government refuses to release casualty figures, but observers estimate that perhaps as many as 3,000 rebels, civilians and soldiers have been killed in more than two years of fighting.

The conflict has thus far resisted either a military solution or a negotiated settlement. The MNLF has demanded political autonomy for all the southern islands, including Mindanao,

⁶ Peter R. Kann, "The Philippines Without Democracy," *Foreign Affairs*, April 1974, p. 629.

Palawan and the Sulu Archipelago. But the Marcos government
has rejected this demand on the basis that much of Palawan and
Mindanao are Christian-majority areas. Marcos is attempting to
win over the Muslim populace with a broad program of social
and economic aid, while at the same time inviting rebel leaders
to observe a ceasefire and hold peace talks *(see p. 323)*. However,
as a recent analysis by *Far Eastern Economic Review* concluded:
"Amid the scattered violence, talk of 'cease-fires' is meaningless.
The calmer atmosphere in which peace talks could be minimally
productive simply does not exist. To the contrary, the continued
deterioration of the situation on both the talking and fighting
fronts suggests that a grim situation will tend to become
grimmer."[7]

## Scattered Resistance From Communist Guerrillas

The Marcos government must also deal with scattered
guerrilla actions by the New People's Army (NPA), technically
the military arm of the Communist Party of the Philippines.
Although the Philippines has had a Communist problem for
many years *(see p. 196)*, the NPA is a new generation of Maoist-
oriented rebels. They number perhaps 2,000 armed men, backed
by several thousand propagandists, and enjoy considerable support among some segments of the rural populace. Although the
NPA has operated primarily in remote provinces of Luzon, it has
recently begun showing up on other islands. "A map of the
Philippines marked with NPA appearances looks like measles,"
wrote Henry S. Bradsher in the *Washington Star-News*, Dec. 2,
1974.

NPA rebels, some of them sons of middle- and upper-class
families who are concerned about rural poverty and land
reform, try to convince peasants that a Communist revolution
offers their best hope for breaking out of poverty. Bradsher
quoted the mayor of a town in Sorsogon Province, a rugged jungle region on the extreme southeastern tip of Luzon, as saying
that the masses support the NPA. "They don't cooperate with the
government, never tell us anything," he wrote. "People are
afraid. But the NPA has won their sympathy, too. They're very
good at that."

The NPA figured prominently in Marcos' declaration of martial law in September 1972. After his re-election to the
presidency in 1969, leftist groups seemed to be winning many
converts. Manila was rocked by student riots in 1970, and the
1971 congressional elections were marked by violence, including
a bombing incident at a rally held by the opposition Liberal Party. There was no evidence that the NPA was responsible and, in
fact, some blamed the bombing on the Marcos administration,
which is of the Nationalist Party. Nevertheless, the government

[7] "A Crucial Time in the South," *Far Eastern Economic Review*, April 4, 1975, p. 30.

## U.S. Interests in the Philippines

American business holdings in the Philippines are extensive. The actual value of American investments in the islands is open to debate, but it is at least $1 billion and may be as high as $3 billion. A detailed study by the Corporate Information Center of the National Council of Churches in November 1973, entitled "The Philippines: American Corporations, Martial Law, and Underdevelopment," stated:

"U.S. investment in the Philippines represents the first or second largest amount of U.S. investment in Southeast Asia. While that investment may only be 1 per cent of the total book value of U.S. investment worldwide, it also represents 80 per cent of the foreign investment in the Philippines."

Americans own about one-third of the total equity capital of the 900 largest corporations in the Philippines, the study found, with 47 U.S. companies ranking among the top 200 corporations there. Furthermore, American businesses in the Philippines have historically been highly profitable. Studies of selected U.S. companies found that their profits were up to 300 per cent greater than capital investments.

The climate for U.S. businesses in the Philippines has been favorable since 1913, when Congress established free trade between the two lands. After World War II, the Philippine Trade Act of 1946 called for an eight-year continuation of free trade on one condition—Americans were to be given "parity," or equal rights with Filipinos in the development of all natural resources and the operation of public utilities.

The Philippines' new constitution contained a provision prohibiting parity, but the nation was forced to amend its constitution by plebiscite. In the Laurel-Langley Act of 1955, the U.S. Congress specified that parity would end on July 3, 1974. Perhaps the most difficult post-parity issue concerns the right of Americans to own land. But Marcos extended until May 27, 1975, the deadline for U.S. firms to turn over their land holdings to Filipinos, and most companies are leasing the land back with little change in operations. Marcos extended other privileges to American firms until the spring of 1976.

used the bombing as its justification for further crackdowns on leftist radicals.

Then in the late summer of 1972, a fishing trawler seized by government troops in Luzon's northern Palanan Province was reported to contain several thousand M-14 rifles and other military supplies supposedly intended for the NPA. The government made a major issue of the incident and warned of the growing seriousness of the "Communist menace." Critics contended that the incident had been staged by the Marcos government. In early September of that year there was a series of mysterious bombings in Manila for which Marcos blamed the Communists and his critics blamed him. Finally, on Sept. 22, there was an alleged assassination attempt against Defense Secretary Juan Ponce Enrile, whose government car was sprayed with bullets by gunmen. Enrile, it turned out, was riding in a following vehicle. That night Marcos declared martial law, although it was later discovered that he had signed the proclamation the day before, on Sept. 21.

The United States government has never commented official-ly on the declaration of martial law in the Philippines, although silence is seen by many observers as an expression of support. U.S. Ambassador Henry A. Byroade reportedly met with Mar-cos for two hours shortly after he issued the declaration. Reporter Keyes Beech of the *San Francisco Examiner* wrote (Sept. 28, 1972) of the meeting: "President Ferdinand Marcos promised to protect a $1 billion American economic stake in the Philippines in return for tacit U.S. approval of martial law." The charge has never been confirmed or denied.

However, one immediate response to martial law was the following telegram to President Marcos: "The American Chamber of Commerce of the Philippines wishes you every success in your endeavors to restore peace and order, business confidence, economic growth, and the well-being of the Filipino people and nation. We assure you of our confidence and coopera-tion in achieving these objectives." And a U.S. oilman in the Philippines was quoted in *Business Week* magazine (Nov. 4, 1972) as saying: "Marcos says, 'We'll pass the laws you need—just tell us what you want.'" The response of U.S. business to martial law generally has been favorable.

## Origins of U.S.-Philippine Links

THE PHILIPPINES has been called "America's first Vietnam." Although the analogy is imprecise, there are disturbing similarities. The Philippines was the site of the first U.S. land war in Asia, a savage conflict in which American troops battled Filipino guerrillas for more than three years. Little remembered in America today, that war involved 74,000 U.S. soldiers—of whom 4,165 died—and cost the United States $170 million. Some 16,000 Filipino guerrillas were killed and as many as 200,000 civilians died as a result of the war, according to some sources.[8] It was an all-out war, with villages burned, civilians massacred, prisoners tortured and hostages killed by both sides.

---

[8] George Farwell, *Mask of Asia: The Philippines* (1966), p. 52.

The origins of the war—which is usually called the "Philippine Insurrection" in the United States and the "Second War for Philippine Independence" by Filipinos—lay in nearly four centuries of Spanish colonial rule of the Philippines. The islands came under Spanish control in 1565, when Miguel de Legaspi claimed them in the name of Prince Philip (later King Philip II) of Spain. Ferdinand Magellan had "discovered" the islands in 1521 during his voyage to prove the world was round—and was killed there by a Malay chieftan. The Spanish succeeded in converting the majority of Filipinos to Catholicism but did little to develop the Philippine economy. Spanish neglect and exploitation led to smoldering discontent among Filipinos, who organized more than 100 revolts against Spanish authority.

The final revolt against the Spaniards began in 1896, under the leadership of the Filipino patriot Andrés Bonifacio. It gained strength after the execution of José Rizal, a popular novelist who had attacked the greed of the Spanish clergy and the arrogance of Spanish officials. The revolution's leadership was taken over by the young Gen. Emilio Aguinaldo, but Spain reinforced its troops and put down the uprising, forcing Aguinaldo and 34 other rebel leaders into exile in Hong Kong. Nonetheless, the desire for independence remained strong among Filipinos.

## U.S. Intervention After Spanish-American War

Meanwhile, events were taking shape which would draw the United States into the Philippines. The Spanish-American War had broken out in Cuba in April 1898 following the sinking of the *U.S.S. Maine* in Havana harbor. The U.S. Asiatic Squadron, led by Commodore George Dewey, was ordered to Manila to engage the Spanish fleet. The battle of Manila Bay, May 1, 1898, began with Dewey's memorable command, "You may fire when you are ready, Gridley," and the Spanish fleet was largely destroyed.

Aguinaldo and his staff returned from exile aboard an American vessel and immediately met with Dewey, who promised them freedom for the Philippines in return for their cooperation in helping U.S. forces defeat Spain—a promise Dewey later did not recall making.[9] Aguinaldo mustered some 12,000 men and encircled the Spanish forces in Manila, awaiting the arrival of American troops. On June 12, 1898, the Filipino rebels proclaimed independence for their country—making the Philippines the first democratic republic in Asia—and began drafting a constitution. But the euphoria of independence was short-lived.

After U.S. troops arrived in Manila and the Spanish surrendered on Aug. 13, the Stars and Stripes were raised over the city—not the new Philippine flag of independence. The

---

[9] Beth Day, *The Philippines: Shattered Showcase of Democracy in Asia* (1974), p. 76.

# GOVERNMENT

The Philippines is now under martial law declared by President Ferdinand E. Marcos in September 1972. A new constitution was ratified in January 1973 establishing a parliamentary republic, but Marcos continues to rule under "transitory provisions" and has not convened a national assembly to elect a new president and prime minister. The Supreme Court is also under Marcos' control. The Philippines is a member of the United Nations, SEATO, ASEAN, the Asia and Pacific Council, and the Asian Development Bank.

# LAND

There are 7,107 islands in the Philippine archipelago comprising 115,707 square miles, with most of the land mass in the 11 largest islands. The climate is tropical, with abundant rainfall. About 35 per cent of the land is under cultivation. Rice and corn are the main cash crops; sugar, copra, coconut oil and hemp are the main export crops. Hardwood forests cover 42 per cent of the land, with logging a growing industry. The islands contain rich copper, nickel, chromite, silver, gold, and iron deposits.

# PEOPLE

There are now about 44.4 million Filipinos; the annual population growth rate of 3.3 per cent is one of the world's highest. Most Filipinos are descended from the Indonesians and Malays who migrated to the islands centuries ago, but many now have Chinese, Spanish or English blood. The official language is Pilipino, which is based on Tagalog, but English is widely spoken. The literacy rate is 83 per cent. The dominant religion is Roman Catholic (83 per cent), followed by Protestant (9 per cent), Muslim (5 per cent) and animist (3 per cent).

Americans warned Aguinaldo not to enter Manila while officials of the United States and Spain met in Paris to discuss peace terms. "Too late the Filipino general found that he had been tricked, and that his 'liberators' were actually 'imperialists,'" wrote Beth Day. "The Filipino army withdrew from Manila and set up a rebel government in Malolos, about 50 miles north."

The rebels soon adopted a constitution remarkable for its sweeping bill of rights and its overtones of social reform, but this document, the Malolos constitution, was never put into effect because fighting broke out between U.S. and Filipino troops on Feb. 4, 1899. The fighting influenced the U.S. Senate, after a month of bitter debate, to approve the Treaty of Paris on Feb. 6, 1899, ceding the Philippines from Spain to the United

States for an indemnity of $20 million. When the fighting finally ended in April 1902, it had cost the United States eight and a half times the indemnity paid to Spain and more than one-half as much as the Spanish-American War itself had cost.

## Development of Philippines Under U.S. Tutelage

American public opinion was deeply divided over the wisdom of involvement in the Philippines, and U.S.-Philippine relations have always been laced with ambiguity. This was so from the beginning, when President William McKinley made the initial decision to take over the islands. Official policy at the time was inclined toward isolationism, and McKinley had spoken out against the "greed of conquest" and "criminal aggression." But enthusiastic expansionists such as Senator Henry Cabot Lodge (R Mass., Senate 1893-1924) and Assistant Secretary of the Navy Theodore Roosevelt, aided by newspaper magnate William Randolph Hearst, had fanned the flames of imperialist sentiment.

In a long night of prayer and soul-searching in the White House, McKinley had decided that "there was nothing left for us to do but to take them all and to educate the Filipinos and uplift them and civilize and Christianize them and by God's grace do the very best we could by them...." That the Filipinos had a Christian religion which antedated Jamestown was a fact that apparently eluded McKinley and much of the American public. There were other reasons for U.S. interest in the Philippines, such as the search by American businessmen for new markets, the desire of militarists for bases in the Pacific, and the lust of expansionists to pursue America's "manifest destiny." But the idea that a great and rich nation like the United States had an obligation to guide a backward and unfortunate country like the Philippines played a central role. This notion was captured in the ironic tone of a poem Rudyard Kipling addressed to Americans, "The White Man's Burden," which first appeared in *McClure's* magazine, February 1899:

> Take up the white man's burden—
> Send forth the best ye breed—
> Go, bind your sons to exile
> To serve your captives' need;
> To wait, in heavy harness,
> On fluttered folk and wild—
> Your new-caught sullen peoples,
> Half devil and half child....

But the poem did not have its intended effect—the title became a proud catchword for imperialists. Nonetheless, the period of American control over the Philippines was generally benign and enlightened. Even the most nationalistic Filipinos were amazed at how American soldiers laid down their rifles and began helping the natives rebuild their schools and villages after the war. Sanitary and medical conditions in rural areas were vastly improved. The Philippine Commission, initially headed by William Howard Taft—who popularized the term, "little brown brother" to describe the Philippine people—included Filipinos in its membership, and in 1907 began to share legislative powers with an elected Philippine Assembly. An American Governor-General continued to exercise executive authority, but most of the various department secretaries were Filipinos. In 1916, Congress enacted the Jones Law confirming the American intention to grant the Philippines independence when conditions were right.

The final step toward self-government was taken in 1934 when Congress passed the Philippine Independence Act (also known as the Tydings-McDuffie Act) after considerable lobbying by Filipinos in Washington. It provided for creation of a commonwealth and a 10-year transition period leading to complete independence. During that time the islands were to be self-governing except for matters of defense, foreign relations, currency and tariffs. Meeting for six months in 1934-35, elected Filipino delegates hammered out a new constitution, and President Franklin D. Roosevelt in March 1935 certified that it was acceptable to the United States. The Philippine Commonwealth's first President, Manuel L. Quezon, was sworn in on Nov. 15, 1935. The islands were scheduled to become independent on July 4, 1946.

## Devastation by Japanese During World War II

Tokyo, however, had a different timetable. The Japanese bombed Clark Field eight hours after the surprise attack on Pearl Harbor on Dec. 7, 1941, and landed in the islands two weeks later. They overran Manila on Jan. 2, 1942, trapping the meager American and Filipino forces on Bataan Peninsula and finally on the island fortress of Corregidor. Quezon and other Filipino leaders escaped from Corregidor by submarine and established a government in exile, but the island fell in May. The long march of mistreated prisoners back along the Bataan Peninsula to Manila is infamous as one of the most brutal events in the war in the Pacific.

Gen. Douglas MacArthur, the American commander in the Far East, had left the Philippines in 1941 with the promise, "I shall return." On Oct. 20, 1944, return he did as American forces landed on the island of Leyte. Quezon had died of tuberculosis in the United States, but the commonwealth's new president, Sergio Osmena, waded ashore at MacArthur's side. The liberating troops faced fierce Japanese resistance, as they fought from island to island toward Manila. The Japanese soldiers went into a suicidal frenzy as American forces approached the capital, murdering some 60,000 civilians and devastating much of the city as they withdrew into an ever-tightening defensive circle. When the Japanese finally were cleared from Manila, the historic city was largely rubble.[10]

Food, clothing and other relief supplies were furnished initially by the U.S. Army, the Red Cross and Philippine War Relief, Inc. But restoration of the Philippine economy was slowed by a long and violent controversy over wartime collaboration. This centered on the record of Manuel Roxas, a Filipino senator and former member of General MacArthur's staff who had accepted a post in the puppet government under the Japanese. Roxas was portrayed as having exerted a restraining influence on the Japanese and was nominated to run for president against Osmena. In what has been called a blatantly corrupt election, Roxas defeated Osmena and was inaugurated as president, to preside when the Philippines became independent, as scheduled, on July 4, 1946.

## Internal Problems After Independence in 1946

Roxas had a short and troubled term in office. He managed to get the national government staffed and functioning, and to clean up most of the war's debris. But in the struggle for survival, the nation had no time to tackle long-term problems. Moreover, the Americans working to aid the Philippines in self-government made the mistake of selecting only highly educated and socially elite Filipinos for training. The new ruling class thus was drawn largely from the wealthy, landowning aristocracy, while the poor remained dependent on the rich for patronage jobs or political favors. This led to widespread corruption and helped perpetuate the feudal order which had characterized four centuries of Spanish rule. Roxas died of a heart attack in April 1948 and was replaced by Elpidio Quirino, who made some headway against favoritism and inefficiency in government. But the fundamental problems, especially the deepening misery of small farmers, remained unchecked.

Economic distress and internal dissent led to a resurgence of the Hukbalahap guerrilla movement.[11] The Huks, as they were called, had been founded with Communist help as a peasant revolutionary movement. During the war they fought in the hills against Japanese and Filipino landlords alike, and for a while had almost complete control over north-central Luzon, even electing local commanders and mayors by popular vote. They seized big estates, killed the owners and gave land to farmers who cooperated with them. They emerged as an open opposition group after the war, and Roxas outlawed the movement in 1948. But the Huks, with many sympathizers among the

---

[10] See "Rehabilitation of the Philippines," *E.R.R.*, 1945 Vol. I, pp. 261-279, and "Philippines in Transition," *E.R.R.*, 1950 Vol. I, pp. 355-374.

exploited peasantry, fought on and by 1950 they numbered about 20,000 and were on the verge of overthrowing the Quirino government.

At this point the U.S. government became concerned and urged Quirino to appoint Ramon Magsaysay as Secretary of Defense. A popular ex-guerrilla with a reputation as a "man of the people," Magsaysay regained the farmers' support with a large-scale public works and economic aid program, while at the same time offering the Huks amnesty and land in Mindanao if they surrendered. His greatest coup was infiltrating the Huk leadership in Manila and arresting the leaders just as the Huk army had surrounded the city. With no leaders, the peasant soldiers fell back into the hills, where by 1953 they had been reduced to a hard core of only a few hundred. Magsaysay was elected president as a result of his success in putting down the Huk rebellion, to the delight of his American advisers, but he was killed in a plane crash in 1957.

The late 1950s and early 1960s were marked by bitter in-fighting and widespread corruption in the Philippines as first Carlos P. Garcia, a Nationalist, and then Diosdado Macapagal, a Liberal, held the presidency. Garcia permitted Magsaysay's liberal programs to continue, but saw no need for further changes. Macapagal, on the other hand, was an idealist who never learned to handle Congress. His land reform program was riddled with loopholes. Smuggling also became common practice. Marcos, another Nationalist, was elected president in 1965, and to an unprecedented second term in 1969.

---

# Crucial Issues Facing Marcos

---

THE MOST VOLATILE problem facing the Marcos government today is the Muslim rebellion. A major step toward defusing the conflict may have been taken April 21 when Marcos agreed to in-tegrate insurgents into the Philippine military command. Meeting in Manila with 142 leaders of 27 rebel groups, Marcos directed the formation of a new engineering battalion to be com-posed of Muslims. He commissioned 12 rebel leaders as second lieutenants in the Philippine armed forces and gave them the oath of office. Marcos also announced the creation of two regional offices in the Mindanao-Sulu area under Muslim direc-tors with Cabinet-level powers.

However, the dominant MNLF boycotted the Manila talks. The MNLF has said it will negotiate only if the government first acknowledges its demand for complete autonomy as a basis for peace talks. Marcos refuses to do this, saying that he will not compromise the "territorial integrity" of the Philippines. "The way to peace does not lie in dismembering the republic," Marcos said April 16 in a conciliatory appeal to the Muslims to stop fighting and start talking. But at talks held last January in Jeddah, Saudi Arabia, Philippine government negotiators withdrew after the MNLF refused to modify its demand for autonomous status for the southern islands.[12]

The Muslim rebellion is a delicate problem for Marcos. If he cracks down too hard he risks alienating rulers of the Middle Eastern countries that supply most of the Philippines' oil. Another complication is that Libya's unpredictable leader, Muammar Qaddafi, has begun supplying the MNLF with arms through the Malaysian state of Sabah, on the island of Borneo. The rebellion has caused divisions in the five member[13] Association of Southeast Asian Nations (ASEAN). Malaysia has been accused of aiding the rebels, while Indonesia has tried to be a mediator. Since the war resists a military or political solution, Marcos has attempted to win over the Muslims with social and economic programs. Marcos on April 21 announced creation of a Southern Philippines Development Administration and released $7 million for development projects in Mindanao. There are plans to build more roads, schools, hospitals and irrigation systems in Muslim-dominated provinces.

### Slow Progress of Vaunted Land Reform Plan

The land reform program is supposedly the cornerstone of Marcos' "New Society." In October 1973, Marcos said: "The land reform program is the only gauge for the success or failure of the New Society. If land reform fails, there is no New Society." The original program required all landowners holding more than seven hectares[14] to begin turning over ownership to tenants through certificates of land transfer. However, the government found that most rice and corn land was not owned by large landowners, but rather by middle-class teachers, lawyers, small businessmen and military men who had invested their life savings to have a small stake or a place to retire. Four of every five landowners—far more than the government initially estimated—were found to own less than 10 hectares.

So the government raised the figure to 24 hectares, and then found that roughly 800,000 of the estimated one million tenants who plant rice or corn would be excluded from the program.

---

[12] The talks were held under the auspices of the World Islamic League, which has tried to negotiate a political solution to the dispute. In June 1974, foreign ministers of Islamic countries, meeting in Kuala Lumpur, Malaysia, called on Marcos to "desist from all measures which resulted in the killing of Muslims."

[13] The Philippines, Malaysia, Indonesia, Thailand and Singapore.

[14] A hectare is 2.47 acres.

When the 800,000 are added to the 280,000 tenants who planted crops other than rice or corn, this meant that 1,080,000 of the Philippines' approximately 1,280,000 tenants would be excluded.[15] Critics of Marcos question whether he really wants to accomplish meaningful land reform, pointing out that the government has imprisoned many of the strongest advocates of land redistribution, has outlawed peasant organizations or demonstrations, and has banned strikes.

The Marcos government must also deal with unemployment. The jobless rate is currently at least 7 per cent nationally and approaches 12 per cent in some urban areas. In addition, perhaps 20 per cent of the Filipinos are underemployed; the efficient educational system turns out more teachers and other professionals than there are jobs. Meanwhile, prices of basic foodstuffs and manufactured goods have been rising much faster than wages. Yet the gross national product is expected to maintain a continued growth of about 7 per cent after inflation through 1975.[16]

Filipinos—rich and poor—are also becoming more numerous at an alarming rate. The 3.3 per cent annual population growth rate, one of the world's highest, threatens to double the nation's population to almost 90 million by the year 2000. "All our resources will not be enough to feed, clothe, and house 89 million people," warns Dr. Conrado Lorenzo, the Harvard-trained obstetrician who heads the government's population commission. The government population program aims to cut the growth rate to 2.5 per cent in 1980.

**Diplomatic Initiatives With Communist Nations**

In the face of changing political realities in Southeast Asia and the rest of the world, Marcos has begun to re-examine and in some cases to readjust traditional Philippine foreign policy. The Philippines until the early 1970s had always followed the United States' lead in shunning diplomatic relations with Communist countries. In March 1973, the Philippines established diplomatic ties with Yugoslavia and Romania, and later that year with East Germany, Poland, Hungary, Czechoslovakia and Outer Mongolia. A trade mission visited Communist China the same year, and Mrs. Imelda Marcos, the president's attractive and ambitious wife, later went to China and met with Mao Tse-Tung. Marcos himself plans to visit China in 1975 and formal diplomatic relations may be established soon afterward. The Philippines also has substantial trade and diplomatic relations with the Soviet Union, and formal relations are being con-

---

[15] "Benedict J. Kerkvliet, "Land Reform in the Philippines Since the Marcos Coup," *Pacific Affairs*, fall 1974, p. 295.

[16] "Philippines Aim to Steady Growth and Restrain Inflation," *Commerce Today*, (U.S. Department of Commerce publication) Jan. 20, 1975, p. 42.

sidered. Marcos is also discussing the possibility of preliminary talks with the leaders of North Korea. After the fall of Phnom Penh, the Philippines announced recognition of the Khmer Rouge insurgent government in Cambodia. And Marcos said April 21 that developments in Indochina have made it "urgent" for the Philippines to establish direct communication lines with North Vietnam.

The Philippines today is moving toward new relationships with its traditional ally, the United States, with its Asian neighbors and with the rest of the world. At the same time, the Philippines is threatened internally by rebellions and tensions that will challenge the capacity of Marcos' authoritarian regime to govern. Marcos has said that martial law is not a permanent condition, but has given no indication of when it will be lifted. The "New Society" has had some successes, but more unkept promises could strain the patience of Filipinos. In the Philippines, instability may be endemic for the foreseeable future.

## Selected Bibliography

### Books

Day, Beth, *The Philippines: Shattered Showcase of Democracy in Asia*, M. Evans and Company, 1974.

Farwell, George, *Mask of Asia: The Philippines*, Frederick A. Praeger, 1966.

Kuhn, Delia and Ferdinand, *The Philippines: Yesterday and Today*, Holt, Rinehart and Winston, 1966.

Lightfoot, Keith, *The Philippines*, Praeger Publishers, 1973.

### Articles

Anderson, Gerald H., "Our Man Marcos—U.S. Investment in the Philippines," *The New Republic*, Dec. 1, 1973.

*Far Eastern Economic Review*, selected issues.

Kann, Peter R., "The Philippines Without Democracy," *Foreign Affairs*, April 1974.

Kerkvliet, Benedict J., "Land Reform in the Philippines—All Show, No Go," *The Nation*, May 11, 1974.

Schirmer, Daniel B., "Marcos—Sophisticated Dictator," *Commonweal*, April 11, 1975.

Shaplen, Robert, "Letter From Manila," *The New Yorker*, April 14, 1973.

Suhrke, Astri, "U.S.-Philippines: The End of a Special Relationship," *The World Today*, February 1975.

### Studies and Reports

Center for Strategic and International Studies, Georgetown University, "U.S.-Philippines Economic Relations," 1971.

Corporate Information Center, National Council of Churches of Christ in the U.S.A., "The Philippines: American Corporations, Martial Law, and Underdevelopment," November 1973.

Editorial Research Reports, "The Philippines: Time of Frictions," 1967 Vol. I, p. 361; "Philippines in Transition," 1950 Vol. I, p. 355; "Rehabilitation of the Philippines," 1954 Vol. I, p. 261.

# UNITED NATIONS AT THIRTY

by

## Helen B. Shaffer

1 9 7 5
Vol. II

# UNITED NATIONS AT THIRTY

T HE UNITED NATIONS is approaching its 30th birthday, on Oct. 24,[1] at a critical juncture in its short, stormy life. The road it will choose at the forthcoming session of the General Assembly, which convenes on Sept. 16, could determine whether the U.N. can become a more effective instrument of global cooperation than in the past or whether it will repeat the dismal fate of its predecessor, the League of Nations (see p. 109).

"The future of the United Nations is clouded," Secretary of State Henry A. Kissinger said in an address to the Institute of World Affairs in Milwaukee on July 14. "...Troubling trends have appeared in the General Assembly and some of its specialized agencies. Ideological confrontation, bloc voting and new attempts to manipulate the charter to achieve unilateral ends threaten to turn the United Nations into a weapon of political warfare rather than a healer of political conflict and a promoter of human welfare."

## Special Session on New Economic Relationship

The United Nations is changing, and no wonder. Circumstances in the world that gave birth to the United Nations in 1945 are vastly different today. The configurations of political and economic power have shifted. The cartel of oil-producing nations has introduced a new factor in the relationships between members of the United Nations. New issues are being raised and new voices are being heard.

The new voices come mainly from the once-silent "Third World" of poor, underdeveloped nations, some of which only recently have attained independence. These nations have found common cause with the Arab bloc, sometimes joined by the U.N.'s 13 Communist members, to form a large majority in the General Assembly. They are often in opposition to the United States and other western powers that long have been the main support of the United Nations.

---

[1] The United Nations held a special ceremony on June 26 to commemorate the 30th anniversary of the signing of the U.N. charter, but Oct. 24 is its official birthday, marking the anniversary of the date when the charter had been ratified by all of the "big five" nations (United States, U.S.S.R., United Kingdom, France, China) and a majority of other signers.

The strength of this new majority is clear from the increasing attention given by the General Assembly and other U.N. agencies to the demands of Third World countries for fundamental changes in the prevailing system of economic relationships between the poorer and the richer nations of the world. The underdeveloped countries are making stronger and stronger demands for a bigger share of the world's pie. It was in the face of such pressure that the 29th (1974) session of the General Assembly called for a special session, to be held Sept. 1-12, 1975, just before the convening of the 30th regular General Assembly session.

Special sessions are called only to deal with matters of particular urgency. In the entire history of the United Nations, there have been only six special sessions. The first five dealt with peace-keeping matters, the area of primary concern under the U.N. charter.[2] The sixth, held in 1974, was the first to reflect Third World demands for major economic change. It was concerned with raw materials and development, and produced a "Declaration and a Program of Action on the Establishment of a New Economic Order." The 1975 special session has been called to discuss "major themes of the development process."

The agenda includes a critique of the United Nations' basic structure and its suitability for undertaking needed economic and social tasks. An important item on the agenda is a report by a group of representatives from 25 nations, appointed by Secretary-General Kurt Waldheim in accordance with a General Assembly resolution last year, to propose changes in the U.N. structure to help overhaul the existing system of international economic relations. The report, entitled "A New United Nations Structure for Global Economic Cooperation," has been described as "a complex and radical document."[3] On first receiving a copy on May 20, 1975, Waldheim said it was "a historic moment in the life of the United Nations."

### Threat of Israel's Expulsion by General Assembly

The United States, while still powerful, no longer holds the same degree of control over the procedures and policy of the United Nations that it exercised in the organization's early years. How the United States responds to this and other changes may well be the key to the U.N.'s future. Disillusionment with the United Nations is spreading in the United States, even among those who once were its strong advocates. The prospect of a U.S. withdrawal is not so startling as it was a few years ago.

---

[2] Special sessions were called to consider the Palestine problem (1947 and 1948), the future of Tunisia (1961), the Congo (1963), and South West Africa, now called Namibia (1967).

[3] Paxton T. Dunn, "Restructuring world relations: The U.N.'s last chance?" *the inter dependent* (monthly newspaper of the United Nations Association), June 1975, p. 6.

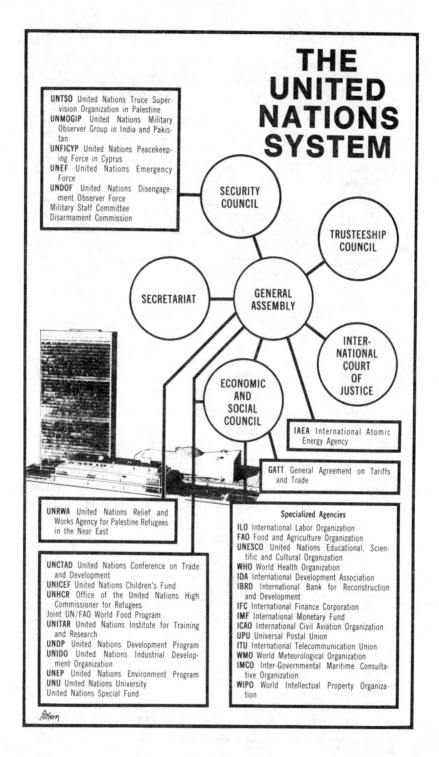

# THE UNITED NATIONS SYSTEM

**SECURITY COUNCIL**

**UNTSO** United Nations Truce Supervision Organization in Palestine
**UNMOGIP** United Nations Military Observer Group in India and Pakistan
**UNFICYP** United Nations Peacekeeping Force in Cyprus
**UNEF** United Nations Emergency Force
**UNDOF** United Nations Disengagement Observer Force
Military Staff Committee
Disarmament Commission

**TRUSTEESHIP COUNCIL**

**SECRETARIAT**

**GENERAL ASSEMBLY**

**INTER-NATIONAL COURT OF JUSTICE**

**ECONOMIC AND SOCIAL COUNCIL**

**IAEA** International Atomic Energy Agency

**GATT** General Agreement on Tariffs and Trade

**UNRWA** United Nations Relief and Works Agency for Palestine Refugees in the Near East

**UNCTAD** United Nations Conference on Trade and Development
**UNICEF** United Nations Children's Fund
**UNHCR** Office of the United Nations High Commissioner for Refugees
Joint UN/FAO World Food Program
**UNITAR** United Nations Institute for Training and Research
**UNDP** United Nations Development Program
**UNIDO** United Nations Industrial Development Organization
**UNEP** United Nations Environment Program
**UNU** United Nations University
United Nations Special Fund

**Specialized Agencies**

**ILO** International Labor Organization
**FAO** Food and Agriculture Organization
**UNESCO** United Nations Educational, Scientific and Cultural Organization
**WHO** World Health Organization
**IDA** International Development Association
**IBRD** International Bank for Reconstruction and Development
**IFC** International Finance Corporation
**IMF** International Monetary Fund
**ICAO** International Civil Aviation Organization
**UPU** Universal Postal Union
**ITU** International Telecommunication Union
**WMO** World Meteorological Organization
**IMCO** Inter-Governmental Maritime Consultative Organization
**WIPO** World Intellectual Property Organization

If current truce negotiations between Israel and Egypt,[4] with the United States as mediator, fail to reach agreement before the General Assembly convenes, the likelihood of an Assembly vote to expel Israel will be increased. Should the General Assembly expel Israel, as it has previously threatened to do, some form of U.S. reprisal against the United Nations could be expected. The consequences for the United Nations would be considerable. Its very survival would be at stake. The loss of U.S. funding alone would be nearly fatal *(see p. 119)*.

*(see p. 119)*

Current tensions in the United Nations are, in part, a result of its success in attracting new members. Nationalism may be the dominant political mode of the day, but application for admission to the United Nations inevitably follows the acquisition of nationhood.[5] Thus the organization's membership has grown from 51 at its founding to 138 today. Several more applicants will be considered in the next Assembly session. Of the 138 members, approximately 100 "can be identified as Third World countries, developing countries or non-aligned countries," according to former U.S. Ambassador John Scali, while the remainder includes states "more or less aligned with the Atlantic community or with the Socialist bloc."[6] Changes wrought by this growth are most apparent in the General Assembly, where the one-nation, one-vote rule prevails.

## U.N. Actions Opposed by the United States

The United States took exception to a number of actions taken by the General Assembly during the 29th session that reflected the domination of that 100-member Third World bloc. Abdelaziz Bouteflika of Algeria served as Assembly president during 1974. A special State Department report cited major actions that were carried with large majorities over strenuous U.S. objections:[7]

1. The General Assembly, following the special session's "Declaration," adopted on Dec. 12, 1974, a "Charter of Economic Rights and Duties" by a vote of 120-6 with 10 abstentions. This lengthy document was designed, according to its preamble, to further "acceleration of the economic growth of developing countries with a view to bridging the economic gap between developing and developed countries." The United States opposed the charter because it encouraged formation of raw material cartels similar to the oil cartel.

---

[4] On July 24, Egypt announced that it would extend permission for a U.N. peace-keeping force to continue patrolling a buffer zone in the Sinai Peninsula for another three months. The force was placed in the Sinai in January 1974 following a cease-fire agreement that terminated hostilities during the "Yom Kippur War" between Israel and neighboring Arab countries in October 1973.

[5] North Korea is an exception, never having sought U.N. membership.

[6] Testimony before the House Foreign Affairs Subcommittee on International Organizations, Feb. 4, 1975.

[7] The Department of State, "Special Report: U.S. Positions at 29th U.N. General Assembly," 1975.

2. The Assembly on Nov. 12, 1974, supported a ruling of Assembly President Bouteflika suspending South Africa (a charter member of the United Nations) from participating in the Assembly by a vote of 91-22, 19 abstaining. This action was taken because of South Africa's policy of apartheid. The U.S. position has been that while it opposes apartheid, it believes the United Nations cannot properly function if it expels accredited members because of their domestic policies.

3. The Assembly voted on Oct. 14, 1974, 105-4 with 20 abstentions, to invite the Palestine Liberation Organization (PLO) to participate in the Assembly's debate on the Palestine issue. Additional resolutions, with large majorities, granted the PLO observer status in all U.N.-sponsored meetings and propounded a position favoring the Palestinian cause. The United States objected that it was unprecedented and contrary to U.N. rules for a non-government entity to be given participation privileges and that the Assembly's action could be interpreted as prejudging a conflict in process of being negotiated. The United States also was embarrassed by the invitation extended to PLO leader Yasir Arafat to address the Assembly, which he did on Nov. 13, 1974.

4. The United States also is concerned by the reluctance of the United Nations to unite against terrorism, a subject that will come up again in the forthcoming session. U.S. Ambassador Scali deplored the fact that during the debate on the Middle East, certain speakers "sought to equate terror with revolution [and] profess to see no difference between the slaughter of the innocents and a struggle for national liberation."

Even before he succeeded Scali as U.S. ambassador to the United Nations, last June,[8] Daniel P. Moynihan became known as an advocate of a tougher U.S. line, especially with regard to the emerging Third World force. He feels the United States has been too accommodating to unrealistic demands and the anti-American rhetoric of the new majority. "It is time for the United States to go into the United Nations and every other international forum and start raising hell," he said in an interview last February.[9] When it became known that he was the administration's choice for the U.N. post, considerable attention centered on an article Moynihan wrote amplifying his views in the March issue of *Commentary*.[10]

## Congressional Concern Over Trends in World Body

Meanwhile, Congress showed exceptional interest in 1975 in United Nations developments and trends. The House Foreign Affairs Subcommittee on International Organizations held hearings in February to review activities of the General Assembly and the U.S. role in the United Nations. The Senate

[8] Moynihan's appointment was confirmed by the Senate on June 9, 1975, and he was sworn in on June 20.
[9] *The New York Times*, Feb. 26, 1975.
[10] Daniel P. Moynihan, "The United States in Opposition," *Commentary*, March 1975, pp. 31-44.

Foreign Relations Committee in May called a number of specialists on international relations to testify during six days of seminars on "The United States and the United Nations." Some of the topics covered by the Senate panels indicate the areas of current concern in Congress: "The U.S. Role in the U.N.: the Vision and the Reality," "The United Nations as a Weapon in International Politics," "The Impact of Détente," "The Impact of the Third World," and "Is the U.N. Working?"

The Senate on July 18 adopted a resolution that said it "looks with disfavor...over persistent attempts by some nations among the so-called non-aligned nations of the Third World to expel Israel from membership in the United Nations." If this should occur, the resolution said, "the Senate will review all present U.S. commitments to the Third World nations involved in the expulsion and will consider seriously the implication of continued membership in the United Nations under such circumstances."

Minority Leader Hugh Scott (R Pa.), chief sponsor of the resolution, said that while the United Nations had "served the world well in many respects" and could continue to do so, it ran "a very grave danger of becoming too politicized, too susceptible to the arrogant militancy of some of its members." The trend was "counterproductive," Scott said, insofar as any long-term peace settlement in the Middle East was concerned. If a group of small nations could expel Israel from the General Assembly, Scott said, there was nothing to prevent it from doing the same thing to the United States.

Several of Scott's co-sponsors took even stronger positions in rebuking the United Nations. "We pay a good bit of the expenses, we provide a location, we are usually outvoted," said Assistant Majority Leader Robert Byrd (D W.Va.), "and, so far as I am personally concerned, we can just withdraw now."

Two bills were introduced in the Senate on Aug. 1 reflecting the deepening concern over trends in the United Nations and looking to a revision of U.S. policy toward that body. Sen. Lloyd Bentsen (D Texas), with Scott as a co-sponsor, introduced a bill that would authorize the President to suspend participation in and withhold payments "with respect to any organ, commission or other body of the United Nations...which the President determines discriminates [against] another member" or "if the President determines that a member is expelled or suspended for reasons contrary to the spirit of the U.N. charter." On the same day, Sen. J. Glenn Beall (R Md.) introduced a bill to establish a 15-member Commission on United States Participation in the United Nations to conduct a complete review of all aspects of U.S. membership and to report on its findings within a year.

# Goals and Structure of United Nations

T HE IDEA of a United Nations was born in the midst of the most destructive, widest-ranging war in history, World War II. The primary objective of its founders was to create an organization that could prevent the repetition of such a devastating calamity. The United Nations constituted a second try at global peace-keeping. The League of Nations, founded at the end of World War I,[11] had proved incapable of coping with the aggressions of militarist dictatorships. It could not stop Japan's invasion of Manchuria in 1929, fascist Italy's attack on Ethiopia in 1935, or Nazi Germany's remilitarization of the Rhine in 1936 and its subsequent invasions of Austria (1938) and Czechoslovakia (1939). The outbreak of World War II, following Germany's invasion of Poland in September 1939, put the final seal on its failure.

The League began with a major handicap: despite the fact that President Woodrow Wilson was a founding father of the League, the United States chose—by a negative vote in the Senate—not to join. Later, when it suited their purposes, other major powers fell away. At one time or another, 63 nations were members of the League, including nearly all (23) nations of Europe and the 41 charter members that had been signers of the Versailles Treaty of 1919, the most important of the treaties which ended World War I. But over the years 17 nations withdrew, four were forcibly annexed by other League members or ex-members[12] and one, the Soviet Union, was expelled five years after its tardy admission in 1935.

Among the withdrawals were those of the three major aggressors: Germany, admitted in 1926, withdrew in 1933 when Adolf Hitler became dictator; Japan and Italy, both charter members, withdrew in 1933 and 1937, respectively. The Soviet Union was ousted in 1939 as a rebuke for having invaded Finland, a League action that has been described as its "last dying, feverish gesture."[13] The crippled League nevertheless lived on, performing various services throughout World War II. It was not formally disbanded until April 18, 1946, when the new United Nations took over its residual assets and functions.

## U.N. Origin as Result of World War II Concerns

The suggestion that a new union of nations be formed was first put forward by British Prime Minister Winston Churchill

[11] The League of Nations came into existence on Jan. 10, 1920, at Geneva, Switzerland.

[12] Among League members that lost their independence by aggression before World War II were: Ethiopia, conquered by Italy in 1936; Austria, annexed by Germany in 1938; Czechoslovakia, dismembered and placed under German control after the invasion of March 1939; and Albania, annexed by Italy in 1939.

[13] Leland Goodrich, *The United Nations in a Changing World* (1974), p. 7.

at his Atlantic rendezvous with President Roosevelt in 1941. The name "United Nations" was first formally used in a "Declaration by United Nations," a statement issued on Jan. 1, 1942, in which representatives of 26 countries pledged a continuing fight against the Axis powers (Germany, Italy, Japan).

The four major Allied powers—the United States, the United Kingdom, China and the U.S.S.R.—agreed at a meeting in Moscow in 1943 to seek some form of international organization that would continue to serve against militarist aggression after victory had been won over the Axis powers. Representatives of these four nations met the following year at Dumbarton Oaks in Washington, D.C., where they drafted proposals for forming such an organization.

Their proposals were taken up at a United Nations Conference on International Organization in April-June 1945 in San Francisco, to which representatives of 50 nations then lined up against the Axis were invited.[14] The charter for the United Nations was drawn up and approved at the San Francisco Conference. It came into effect on Oct. 24, 1945.

The primary function of the United Nations, as stated in the words of the preamble to its charter, was "to save succeeding generations from the scourge of war, which twice in our lifetime has brought untold sorrow to mankind." A second stated goal was a product of the prevailing belief that the war was being fought not only to put down military. aggression but to protect mankind against the oppressive character of fascism: it was "to reaffirm faith in fundamental rights, in the dignity and worth of the human person, in the equal rights of men and women and of nations large and small."

A third goal showed recognition of the need for acceptance of some form of world law if peace was to be sustained. Signers of the charter would strive "to establish conditions under which justice and respect for the obligations arising from treaties and other sources of international law can be maintained." The fourth stated goal derived from the lessons of the 1930s, which suggested a link between economic distress and warfare. It pledged U.N. members "to promote social progress and better standards of life."

Membership in the United Nations was opened to "all...peace-loving states [that] accept the obligations contained in the...charter and, in the judgment of the Organization, are able and willing to carry out these obligations...." Admission of a new state would be by decision of the General Assembly "upon the

---

[14] Although Poland was not represented at the San Francisco Conference, it signed the charter later and became one of the original 51 members of the United Nations.

# Member States of the United Nations
*(by years of admission)*

1945 - (Charter members) Argentina, Australia, Belgium, Bolivia, Brazil, Byelorussian Soviet Socialist Republic, Canada, Chile, China,[1] Colombia, Costa Rica, Cuba, Czechoslovakia, Denmark, Dominican Republic, Ecuador, Egypt,[2] El Salvador, Ethiopia, France, Greece, Guatemala, Haiti, Honduras, India, Iran, Iraq, Lebanon, Liberia, Luxembourg, Mexico, Netherlands, New Zealand, Nicaragua, Norway, Panama, Paraguay, Peru, Philippines, Poland, Saudi Arabia, South Africa, Syrian Arab Republic,[2] Turkey, Ukrainian Soviet Socialist Republic, Union of Soviet Socialist Republics, United Kingdom of Great Britain and Northern Ireland, United States, Uruguay, Venezuela, Yugoslavia

1946 - Afghanistan, Iceland, Sweden, Thailand

1947 - Pakistan, Yemen

1948 - Burma

1949 - Israel

1950 - Indonesia[3]

1955 - Albania, Austria, Bulgaria, Finland, Hungary, Ireland, Italy, Jordan, Khmer Republic, Laos, Libyan Arab Republic, Nepal, Portugal, Romania, Spain, Sri Lanka

1956 - Japan, Morocco, Sudan, Tunisia

1957 - Ghana, Malaysia[4]

1958 - Guinea

1960 - Cameroon, Central African Republic, Chad, Congo, Cyprus, Dahomey, Gabon, Ivory Coast, Madagascar, Mali, Niger, Nigeria, Senegal, Somalia, Togo, Upper Volta, Zaire

1961 - Mauritania, Mongolia, Sierra Leone, United Republic of Tanzania[5]

1962 - Algeria, Burundi, Jamaica, Rwanda, Trinidad and Tobago, Uganda

1963 - Kenya, Kuwait

1964 - Malawi, Malta, Zambia

1965 - Gambia, Maldives, Singapore

1966 - Barbados, Botswana, Guyana, Lesotho

1967 - Democratic Yemen

1968 - Equatorial Guinea, Mauritius, Swaziland

1970 - Fiji

1971 - Bahrain, Bhutan, Oman, Qatar, United Arab Emirates

1973 - Bahamas, German Democratic Republic, Federal Republic of Germany

1974 - Bangladesh, Grenada, Guinea-Bissau

[1] Nationalist China was replaced in 1971 by the People's Republic of China.

[2] Egypt and Syria in 1955 united to form the United Arab Republic, but in 1961 Syria resumed its status as an independent state and its U.N. membership and in 1971 the United Arab Republic changed its name to the Arab Republic of Egypt.

[3] Indonesia in 1965 announced a decision to withdraw but decided in 1966 to resume membership in the United Nations.

[4] Originally entered the U.N. as the Federation of Malaysia but changed its name in 1963 to simply Malaysia after Singapore, Sabah (North Borneo) and Sarawak were admitted to the federation. Singapore later became an independent state.

[5] A union of Tanganyika and Zanzibar, the union dating from 1964; Tanganyika had been admitted in 1961, Zanzibar in 1963.

recommendation of the Security Council." The final article of
the charter provided that the document itself, in five equally
authentic texts (Chinese, French, Russian, English and
Spanish), would be deposited in the archives of the U.S. government in Washington, D.C., and certified copies transmitted by
the United States to the governments of other member states.
The five languages of the original charter have become, with the
addition of Arabic, official languages of the United Nations.

## Power Focus in Security Council's 'Big Five'

Perhaps the most important lesson learned from the League
experience and applied to the United Nations was that no
significant action could be taken by the international body unless it suited the interests of all of the major powers or at least
did not offend seriously the interests of any one of them. This
explains the structure of the Security Council and the fact that
it alone among all U.N. agencies was given authority to make
decisions that would be binding on members to carry out. This
applies with particular force to peace-keeping actions.

The charter established that the Security Council was to be
made up of 11 members, five of which would be Nationalist
China, France, the U.S.S.R., the United Kingdom and the
United States. These five would hold their seats permanently;
the other six would be elected for two-year terms by the General
Assembly, which was to give consideration to their contributions to the U.N. and their geographical distribution. Security Council decisions were to require a majority of seven, but the
majority would have to include all five permanent members.
Any one of these five could exercise a veto over a majority
decision. An amendment that went into force in 1965 increased
the membership of the Security Council to 15 and set the required majority at nine, but the veto power of the five same permanent members has remained in force for all substantive (non-
procedural) matters.

This power was given to the five because these nations were
then considered major bulwarks against militarist and expansionist activity by Germany and Japan. The late U.S. Secretary
of State Edward R. Stettinius, Jr., in presenting the United
Nations Charter to the Senate Foreign Relations Committee in
1945, explained that giving the five Great Powers permanent
seats and the veto in the Security Council was simply recogniz-
ing the facts of life. The United Nations, he said, would depend
for its success upon the unanimity of these five. Others referred
to them as "the world's policemen."[15]

The Security Council was given authority to investigate
tinderbox situations, to mediate disputes between nations, to

---

[15] Clark M. Eichelberger, *The United Nations: The First Twenty-Five Years* (1970), p. 4.

determine when a threat to peace existed, to call on members to apply economic sanctions or other measures to prevent or stop aggression and—most significant of all—to take military action. Article 42 states that, should other measures prove inadequate, "it [the Security Council] may take such action by air, sea, or land forces as may be necessary to maintain or restore international peace and security."

## Functions and Limitations of Other U.N. Organs

Four other central units of the United Nations were established by the charter: the General Assembly, in which all U.N. members would be represented and where the rule of one-nation, one-vote would prevail; the Economic and Social Council (ECOSOC), originally 18 members elected by the General Assembly with the number later increased to 27 and most recently to 54; the Trusteeship Council, made up of representatives of the "Big Five," the trust-administering countries, and an equal number of non-administering countries; the International Court of Justice, consisting of 15 judges elected by the General Assembly and the Security Council; and the Secretariat, which consists of an independent international staff under the Secretary-General.

The General Assembly was conceived as a kind of open forum, often referred to as "the town hall of the world." Its functions are to discuss, to study, to recommend and to call world attention to problems and recommended solutions. It was given no powers for committing U.N. members to direct action, however. The influence of the General Assembly was expanded in 1950 by its adoption of the "Uniting for Peace" resolution. This provided that in the event the Security Council was stopped by a veto from taking action when there appeared to be a threat to peace, the Assembly was to take up the matter immediately and recommend that members take collective measures, including the use of armed force if necessary.

The General Assembly goes into session every year on the third Tuesday of September and continues to meet for about three months. Its various committees, however, function throughout the year and the Assembly can be called into special or emergency session by the Security Council or by a majority of U.N. members. Decisions in the Assembly require a two-thirds majority for important matters and a simple majority for other matters.

ECOSOC is responsible for much of the U.N.'s actual service functions, aside from peace-keeping. From it have sprouted numerous commissions and other bodies that deal with a wide range of subjects requiring international cooperation—health, trade, food, women's rights, narcotics control and many others.

The Trusteeship Council supervises the administration of trust territories by members given this responsibility under the U.N. aegis. The functions of this Council are more or less self-liquidating as dependent territories attain independence either alone or in union with neighboring territories. Of the original 11 trust territories only two remain: Papua in New Guinea, administered by Australia, and Pacific Islands, administered by the United States.

The Court hears disputes brought before it and offers advisory opinions at the request of other U.N. agencies. Its powers are limited. Nations may, if they wish, agree in advance to abide by its decisions on particular disputes. The Court does not have the power to hand down binding interpretations of provisions in the charter, in the manner of the U.S. Supreme Court dealing with constitutional issues. Since many of the charter's provisions were written in general terms—the inevitable consequence of compromise—there are a number of areas of dispute as to the legality of certain actions taken by U.N. agencies or its members under the charter.[16]

The Secretariat carries out the various tasks assigned to it by other U.N. agencies. Staff members, who come from more than 100 countries, take an oath, in accordance with Article 100 of the charter, that they will "not seek or receive instructions from any government or from any other authority external to the Organization." U.N. members similarly promise "not to seek to influence [the Secretary-General and other members of the Secretariat] in the discharge of their responsibilities."

In addition to the constituent bodies within the United Nations, there are a number of so-called "specialized agencies" that have separate autonomous identities but maintain a special relationship with the organization. Most of these work through the Economic and Social Council. Some of the specialized agencies were inherited from the League of Nations, while some long predated even the League.[17]

The U.N. charter by no means sets up a world government. Article 2 emphasizes "the sovereign equality of all its members" and provides that nothing in the document "shall authorize the United Nations to intervene in matters which are essentially within the domestic jurisdiction of any state." The charter recognizes and encourages reliance on other multi-national organizations sympathetic to U.N. goals.

---

[16] The right of the General Assembly to expel members is one of these questions. The charter states that members may be suspended or expelled by the Assembly "on the recommendation of the Security Council" or "if they persistently violate the principles of the charter."

[17] United Nations, "Basic Facts About the United Nations" 1975.

# Prospect of a More Effective U.N.

Looking back over 30 years, those who can recall the hopes that attended the birth of the United Nations have reason to register both satisfaction and disappointment. The United Nations has not abolished war, but it has managed to confine some outbreaks to limited areas and it has helped to maintain uneasy truces in a number of hot spots around the globe. The United Nations has not restrained certain of its members from offending the ban on "use of force against the territorial integrity or political independence of any state"[18] and there are a number of states whose practices hardly conform with the charter's requirement of respect for "human rights."

Some say too much was expected of the U.N., that sovereign states were bound to put national interests ahead of those of the international community. The general feeling, however, is that the United Nations, for good or ill, has become a necessity. Too many problems and situations confronting the world's nations require multinational if not global handling. Also, too many nations have come to depend on the numerous services and technical expertise of the United Nations. The very fact that a world without an organization of its kind is no longer conceivable is testament to the durability of the United Nations.

## Limited Success of U.N. Peace-Keeping Efforts

It is considered a good sign that the U.N. has become virtually a universal society, despite the problems this development has brought. The two Germanys were admitted only in 1973. Switzerland is alone among the advanced nations of the West in preferring to remain outside the organization. Still to be admitted are the two Vietnams and the two Koreas.[19] It is probable that the General Assembly will grant observer status to the two Vietnams at the coming session.

Certain expectations of the founders failed to materialize. There is no U.N. army as such. The only time a U.N. fighting force was mobilized to fight a war was in 1950-53 to repel North Korea's invasion of South Korea. Despite its status as a U.N. operation, however, the Korean conflict has been regarded as primarily a U.S. undertaking. The United States pressed for the action and contributed most of the men, materiel and financing.[20]

[18] Article 2, No. 4.

[19] The United States on Aug. 11 vetoed a Security Council proposal to admit the two Vietnams, in retaliation for the Soviet veto of the application for admission of South Korea. North Korea has not applied for admission.

[20] Fifteen countries apart from the United States and South Korea contributed a total of 45,000 combat troops to the U.N. command for the Korean operation. See "United Nations Peacekeeping," *E.R.R.*, 1964 Vol. II, pp. 611-612.

U.N. peace-keeping activities have consisted of mediation efforts and the dispatching of neutral patrols, made up of volunteered contingents of troops from nations not involved in the disputes, to keep watch over cease-fires or buffer zones between adversaries. These efforts have not prevented sporadic bursts of commando-like violence and several outbreaks of warfare in the Middle East and on Cyprus. There are three such U.N. forces now deployed in these two areas: the United Nations Peace-Keeping Force on Cyprus (UNFICYP), the United Nations Emergency Force (UNEF) on the Egyptian-Israeli border, and the United Nations Disengagement Observer Force (UNDOF) on the Israeli-Syrian border.

U.N. peace-keeping action in the Middle East dates back to 1948, shortly after the General Assembly in November 1947 adopted the Palestine partition plan, which led to the founding of Israel the following May. UNEF was first established in 1956 after the U.N. intervened in the Suez crisis, and has served intermittently, with time out for brief wars, ever since. UNFICYP dates from March 1964 when it was stationed in Cyprus to prevent recurrent fighting between Greek and Turkish Cypriots. The mandate for these forces is usually extended every six months.

Another disappointment has been the United Nations' failure to do much about checking the proliferation of armaments. Sen. Stuart Symington (D Mo.), who served as a member of the U.S. delegations to the United Nations in 1968 and again in 1974, has criticized what he considers excessive caution in the U.S. approach to the arms control issue in the United Nations. [21] Most U.N. members, he said, appear to want to bring the arms race—especially the nuclear arms race—under control. He has urged the United States to take the initiative in pressing for wider-based agreements, via the United Nations, rather than taking the limited bilateral or multilateral approaches now favored.

## Possible Modification of Use of Veto Powers

Among the great unknowns about the future of the United Nations is the effect of détente between the United States and the Soviet Union on procedures in the Security Council. The early years of the United Nations were marked by the onset of the Cold War and also by the dawn of the atomic age. The fre-

---

[21] As evidence of this caution, Symington cited U.S. abstention from a request to the U.N. Conference Committee on Disarmament (CCD) to give highest priority to conclusion of a Comprehensive Test Ban Treaty; U.S. abstention from a resolution urging it and the Soviet Union to broaden the scope and accelerate the pace of the SALT discussions, and U.S. abstention from a resolution urging continuing efforts toward agreement on rules restricting use of napalm or other weapons causing extreme suffering. See "The United Nations, the United States, and Arms Control," Report to the Senate Committee on Foreign Relations, May 1975, pp. 2-6.

# Secretaries-General of the United Nations

Trygve Lie (Norway) 1945-1953

Dag Hammarskjöld (Sweden) 1953-1961

U Thant (Burma) 1961-1971

Kurt Waldheim (Austria) 1971-

quent use of the veto by the Soviet Union was often criticized in the first decade as a restraint on the effectiveness of U.N. procedures, but in retrospect the availability of the veto may be seen as having helped to preserve the universality of the organization. Any split-off from the United Nations on ideological grounds would only heighten dangerous confrontations, and the principle of unanimity of the great powers for the preservation of relative peace in the world would go by the boards.

A question which may come up in future sessions is whether to continue the veto power as it now stands. A less drastic practice—refraining from voting in the Security Council—has come into occasional use. A non-vote does not count as a negative vote or a veto. China has resorted to this at times. So far, China's role in the United Nations has been fairly quiet; what it might be in the future is another question. The practice of not voting in both the Security Council and the General Assembly has suggested to some U.N.-watchers that a helpful practice might be to take positions by "consensus" without open voting. "Consensus," it is felt, might permit a nation not vitally concerned over a particular issue to go along without the possible embarrassment of having to take a positive public stand on the issue.

The United Nations in the immediate future will unquestionably have to deal with Third World demands for more parity in distribution of the wealth of the world. And related to this prospect is the likelihood that the new majority in the General Assembly will press for charter revision to give it the power to push for the international economic reforms the Third World seeks. Amendments to the charter require a vote of two-thirds of the members of the General Assembly, ratified by two-thirds of the members of the United Nations, including all permanent members of the Security Council. An amendment adopted in December 1965 provides that a general conference of member states for reviewing the charter may be held at a date and place to be fixed by a two-thirds vote of members of the General Assembly and by any nine members of the Security Council.

The United States has taken the position that the charter should not be substantively revised, because it has proved to be a flexible instrument, readily adaptable to new situations "by the normal process of interpretation and evolution." Significant modifications in U.N. procedures are said to have come about gradually "as new members with new views have joined" and as older members gain experience. "Such an evolution is...an invaluable way in which the charter is maintained as a living, current document—an avenue of change vastly preferable to sudden, radical shifts which, by virtue of the extreme diversity among the member states, almost inevitably would result in loss of fundamental consensus which is the foundation of the charter."[22]

## Hope for Consensus on Closing Economic Gaps

Some American critics of the United Nations take the position that the United States should take the initiative in pressing for reforms that would restore some of the power and influence the United States exercised in the international body in its early years. At least, it is felt, U.S. influence should be a bit more commensurate with its contribution. Since its founding, the United States has contributed more than $1.5 billion to the

---

[22] U.S. Department of State, "Special Report: U.S. Positions at 29th U.N. General Assembly," 1975, p. 20.

United Nations and its specialized agencies, exclusive of contributions for peace-keeping forces and numerous voluntary programs under U.N. aegis, such as various funds for humanitarian assistance, development aid, drug abuse control and the like.

The United Nations assesses member-nations according to their ability to pay. From the beginning, the United States has paid the lion's share of costs. In 1972 Congress put a lid of 25 per cent of the basic U.N. budget on the amount the United States could contribute. This reduced the percentage from about 31.5 per cent, cutting out some $13.2 million from the 1974 U.S. contribution.

---

*"We are at a watershed...a period which...is either going to be seen as a period of extraordinary creativity or a period when...the international order came apart, politically, economically and morally."*

Henry A. Kissinger,
Secretary of State

---

Members of Congress complain from time to time about the disparity between the large contributions by the United States and the minuscule amounts of money and expertise provided by smaller nations that take pleasure in abusing their rich benefactor on the floor of the General Assembly. "More than half of the U.N. membership are assessed at the minimum rate of 0.02 per cent of the budget or $56,030 for 1975 [compared with 25 per cent or $81.3 million for the United States]," Rep. Lester L. Wolff (D N.Y.) told the House International Organizations Subcommittee on Feb. 4. The oil-producing countries, he added, pay "a combined total of 1.28 per cent of the total budget."

Few would object to the cost, however, if the United Nations could serve effectively as an instrument of worldwide cooperation for peace, security and human well-being, as proclaimed by its charter. With economic issues coming to the fore, the best hope for the future of the organization would seem to be the development of some kind of détente between the have and the have-not countries that would bring a consensus on terms of mutual benefit. Moves in that direction, with an end to name-calling, have already been taken on both sides of the economic gap. The two sessions ahead will show which way the wind is blowing.

# Selected Bibliography

## Books

Eichelberger, Clark M., *The United Nations: The First 25 Years*, Harper & Row, 1970.

Fabian, Larry L., *Soldiers Without Enemies: Preparing the United Nations for Peacekeeping*, Brookings Institution, 1971.

Goodrich, Leland M., *The United Nations in a Changing World*, Columbia University Press, 1974.

Russell, Ruth B., *The United Nations and United States Security Policy*, Brookings Institution, 1968.

## Articles

Cleveland, Harland, "The U.S. vs. the U.N.?", *The New York Times Magazine*, May 4, 1975.

Dunn, Paxton T., "Restructuring World Relations: The UN's Last Chance?" *the inter dependent* (monthly newspaper of the United Nations Association), June 1975.

Hottelet, Richard C., "Crisis at the U.N.," *Commonweal*, Feb. 28, 1975.

Moynihan, Daniel P., "The United States in Opposition," *Commentary*, March 1975.

"The Question of Reducing the U.S. Financial Role in the United Nations," *Congressional Digest*, March 1975.

Tuckerman, Anne, "The United Nations at 30: More Than an Echo Chamber," *The Nation*, Nov. 2, 1974.

*UN Chronicle*, selected issues.

Yost, Charles, "How to Save the United Nations," *Saturday Review/World*, Dec. 14, 1974.

## Studies and Reports

*Congressional Record*, statements of witnesses before Senate Committee on Foreign Relations, May 15, 1975, pp. 8363-8382, and May 22, 1975, pp. S 9002-9008.

Department of State, "Special Report: U.S. Positions at 29th UN General Assembly" 1975.

Editorial Research Reports, "United Nations: 1945-1960," 1960 Vol. I, pp. 439-462, and "United Nations Peacekeeping," 1964 Vol. II, pp. 601-620.

House Committee on Foreign Affairs, Subcommittee on International Organizations, report on "The United Nations: Expendable or Indispensable?" March 1974, and hearings, "Review of the 1974 General Assembly and the United States Position in the United Nations," Feb. 3-5, 1975.

Senate Committee on Foreign Relations, "The United Nations," report by Sen. Charles H. Percy (R Ill.).

—"The United Nations, the United States, and Arms Control," report by Sen. Stuart Symington (D Mo.).

The Stanley Foundation, "Decision-Making Processes of the United Nations," 19th Conference on The United Nations of the Next Decade, at Vail, Colo., June 9-16, 1974.

United Nations Office of Public Information, "Basic Facts About the United Nations," 1975, and other selected documents and publications.

# BRITAIN IN CRISIS

by

## Yorick Blumenfeld

# BRITAIN IN CRISIS

B RITAIN has experienced such a succession of shocks since the end of World War II that it is difficult even for Anglophiles to grasp the full measure of the current crisis. Britain's long-established democratic and parliamentary institutions may ultimately be undermined if economic problems grow more critical and further erode public confidence in the ability of the political system to deal with them. The people are being subjected to the worst inflation in their history, to record postwar unemployment levels, and to falling production and declining business investment.

Britons see this combination of problems coming to a head early next year. The Chancellor of the Exchequer, Denis Healy, has said 1976 will be the country's most critical year since 1940, when Britain stood virtually alone against the might of Nazi Germany. The growth of political extremism has added to, and perhaps fed upon, the pervasive discontent. The killing in Northern Ireland has spilled over into England in the form of terrorist bombings, even in central London *(see p. 138)*. Parliament, returning from its summer recess on Oct. 13, will engage in the coming session in a prolonged debate over how far to go toward meeting nationalist demands in Scotland and Wales for self-rule *(see p. 137)*. Lord Robens, chairman of the Vickers industrial complex and a former government minister, has gone so far as to say: "We are almost at the stage of the Weimar Republic before Hitler. The political consequences of that are a dictatorship of the right or left. I wouldn't care to say which."

The British face the challenge ahead with a lack of confidence that results from a long and nagging national failure. For a generation both the Labor and Tory governments have prescribed a succession of remedies for the nation's chronic ills and none of them has worked. The consequence is that in 25 years Britain has slipped from being the second-richest nation in Europe, behind Sweden, to being one of the poorest. Britain's plight has become the subject of an almost endless stream of assessments both at home and abroad, especially in America *(see box, p. 127)*. Among the recent commentaries columnist Vermont Royster wrote in *The Wall Street Journal:* "Britain's undoing is its own doing. It has been brought to this by the calculated policies of its government and by their resigned acceptance by the people."[1]

The postwar socialist momentum in Britain has been such that most governments have been concerned more with the distribution of wealth than with its creation. Rather than stimulate new plant investment, as was done in France and West Germany, Britain's Labor governments concentrated on the nationalization of industry and on the establishment of a welfare state. Industrial production lagged behind that of Britain's foreign trade rivals. The welfare system, it is argued, was greater than the nation could support.

### Dangers Perceived in Nation's Worst Inflation

Whatever the underlying causes may be, the economic problem of gravest concern today is inflation. The retail price index, as recorded in late August, had risen 26.2 per cent in the previous 12 months despite some slowdown during the summer. This rise followed a 16.2 per cent inflationary jump between August 1973 and August 1974. In the past year, basic hourly wage rates have shot up as much as 30 per cent. So steep has been the postwar inflation, especially in recent years, that the purchasing power of the pound sterling has fallen from a level of 100 in 1946 to less than 19 this autumn. Roy Jenkins, the Home Secretary, said on July 2 that an inflation at these levels "discourages individuals from holding on to a proper sense of perspective and generates a feeling of uncertainty about the future which touches all aspects of public affairs." A government phamphlet,[2] delivered to 21 million homes in Britain during the first week of September, warned that "Inflation, if not brought under control, means industrial collapse and national bankruptcy."

The causes of the current runaway inflation are multiple. Monetarists believe that the government's mistake has been to increase the money supply too quickly. It has more than tripled since 1964. Others point out that an unprecedented rise in government expenditures from £19.9 billion ($42 billion) in 1973 to £26.8 billion ($56 billion) in 1974, was primarily responsible. Last year the government had to borrow $15.7 billion and this year the figure is expected to exceed $21 billion because of record pay increases in the public sector.

The Chancellor of the Exchequer acknowledged in the House of Commons on July 20 that "for the past 18 months we have been living above what we were earning." He explained: "We have been able to do this because foreigners have been prepared

---

[1] *The Wall Street Journal*, Aug. 20, 1975.
[2] Titled "Attack on Inflation: A Policy for Survival."

to back us with their money." However, with the Treasury spending $100 for every $80 it was gathering in revenue, many bankers were worried about how long Britain's creditworthiness was likely to last. One measure of the fall in international confidence in Britain's management of the economy was the decline of the pound in international trade. In relation to the American dollar, it fell in value from about $2.35 in January to below $2.10 in September.

The deficit in Britain's international balance of payments is likely to be well over $2.5 billion this year, and an anticipated increase in fuel prices this autumn could add considerably to that figure. Tory M.P. Enoch Powell has warned that if the foreign lending should happen to stop, "the government could find itself forced to manufacture billions of pounds of new money, which would drive inflation sky-high." To keep foreign reserves in Britain, the government has been forced to pay interest rates of over 12 per cent to depositors. The high cost of borrowing domestically has stoked the inflationary fire.

### Rise of Unemployment to Record Postwar Level

In a grim warning over television, Prime Minister Harold Wilson said on Aug. 20 that "for hundreds of thousands of British homes this autumn the shadow—for so many of them the reality—of unemployment is threatening standards each family has taken for granted for years past." Unemployment passed the million mark in July and the following month rose to a million and a quarter, over 5 per cent of the working population. While the figure includes large numbers who recently left school and is not especially high by current American standards, it is significant in a country whose Labor government has long attempted to banish unemployment.

The prospects for this winter are particularly bleak. Industry is anticipating the need to reduce employment in the coming months at a rate that has not been witnessed in Britain since the depression of the the the 1930s. The number of workers in manufacturing now working a short week is believed to have reached 250,000. Three-quarters of British industry has plant and equipment standing idle and, *The Economist* reported recently,[3] below-capacity work is more widespread than it was in early 1974 when the combination of coal miner strikes and an Arab oil embargo forced the nation on a three-day work week.

Although Labor has always been, above all else, the party of full employment, the Labor government's present policy apparently is aimed at bringing inflation under control even at the

---

[3] *The Economist,* Aug. 9, 1975, p. 55.

expense of creating more unemployment. *The Economist* commented on July 26, "The country has discovered that it cannot, without intolerable inflation, operate at full employment while still enjoying the old system of free collective bargaining backed by irresistible strikes." Labor M.P. Ian Mikardo said in the House of Commons that his party's commitment to full employment had been abandoned by the prime minister and that a Labor government was doing the unthinkable, "introducing measures deliberately to create unemployment." The Secretary for Energy, Tony Benn, said Sept. 8 that Britain's traditional economic and industrial system had failed to meet the challenge of mounting unemployment.

### Declining Production and Investment in U.K.

"All of us, government and industry included, share the responsibility for industry's failure over the past 20 years to invest in new plant, machinery, factory buildings, industrial modernization," Wilson said in his broadcast on Aug. 20. Production has fallen by 8 per cent over the past year and productivity by 10 per cent in the past three months. A survey of industrial trends by the Confederation of British Industry[4] reads like a catalogue of gloomy superlatives. Companies cite a lack of orders and sales as major factors in limiting their output. A high proportion of the companies report a greater decline in new export orders than for the last quarter of any previous year surveyed.

The chronic lack of investment in British industry is due partly to the fact that the trade union movement continues to lean heavily on its traditional belief that profits are a form of antisocial exploitation. This attitude has resulted in levels of taxation that have caused a mounting number of bankruptcies. Although many economists point to last year's halving of real profits as the major cause of the investment slump, the government has put into effect a statutory order forbidding dividends of companies to rise by more than 10 per cent a year. Return on investment has become so low that many companies, including American-owned companies in Britain, see no point in making further investment at this time.

Because of chronic over-manning, industrial unrest, government interference, low investment and high taxation, Britain is now at the bottom of European production figures in almost every industry. James Ensor, business editor of the *Financial Times*, has calculated that key British industries get less production in cash terms from each worker than their rivals on the European continent.

---

[4] A central body representing British industry nationally.

## Britons' View of Americans Viewing Them

"...Britain remains the foreign country (with the possible, rather mixed exception of Canada) that Americans by and large feel to be closest to themselves. British examples still abound in American writings about history, politics, economics, literature, medicine and the law.

"There is much in British society and British culture that Americans remain disposed to like and respect. Some even admit to a sneaking admiration for the determination with which, as they see it, the British collectively subordinate considerations of solvency to the joys of doing their thing—a sign, if one were needed, that the microorganisms of the British sickness are in the American bloodstream too.

"That is what troubles [American commentators].... The bad example Britain might set for America is recognized even (or, perhaps, particularly) by the highly intelligent conservative economists at the Federal Reserve Board, one of whom [Chairman Arthur F. Burns] mused the other day that the United States was manifestly on the British track, but how far behind? Once it used to be perhaps 50 years, he thought. Now the interval seems to have shortened, maybe to as short as 15 years...."

*—The Economist,* Sept. 13, 1975

British workers take longer to produce goods than those in other industrial countries partly because of antiquated machinery. The British motor industry, which employs one British worker in 20, is a case in point. While every British Leyland worker is turning out a meager six cars a year, a worker at Datsun in Japan is rolling off 377. The result is that British Leyland's inefficiency forced it to go into bankruptcy and it was nationalized by the government. *The Observer* wrote editorially, Aug. 17, 1975: "We British must soon make up our minds whether we intend to take our leisure in working hours behind the factory gates or to earn more time off by improving our working methods."

Nearly half of Britain's work force is employed by the government in the public sector, which is insulated from the discipline of market forces. Large parts of the nationalized industries are now bankrupt and under normal commercial conditions would have closed long ago. Because of their monopoly position, they tend to cover deficits by raising prices. Prime Minister Wilson, speaking at the annual conference of the National Union of Miners on July 8, said the government has made it clear that "every public industry must now pay its way within what it earns." But inevitably, this will fuel the inflationary process.

The government's contribution to the railways, a total of $827 million last year, is expected to exceed $930 million this year—excluding pensions. The number of passengers carried over the past decade has fallen by 12 per cent and the freight volume has declined by 20 per cent. The steel industry is likely to be the hardest hit during the coming months. Sir Montague Finniston, chairman of the British Steel Corporation, said the mills had been operating at half of capacity during the past summer. Huge loans, totaling as much as $1.5 billion, are being sought by the corporation which is now reported to be losing $10.5 million a week and lacks cash to meet its payroll.

There is general agreement that steel, like most of the nationalized industries, is vastly overmanned. Despite the fact that demand for steel fell last year, the corporation wound up with an additional 8,000 employees. *The Economist* has noted that the Japanese would manage to produce the same amount of steel with about one-third of the British work force. British Steel finds itself boxed in by a world recession which prevents it from raising steel prices, by the government's unwillingness to close antiquated plants, by unions that refuse to accept cuts in manpower, and by the inability of the government to invest in modern plants.

# Historic Parallels to the Present

B RITAIN has evolved through many changes over the centuries. From a feudal society it developed into an absolute monarchy, and then from an aristocracy into a 19th century middle-class democracy. Much of the strength and continuity of Britain have been based on the fact that its constitution is unwritten and highly flexible. While the adaptability of this constitution has been proved, it has also exposed the country to certain weaknesses in times of emergency. There are no statutes, for example, spelling out the selection and functioning of either a prime minister or his cabinet.

Within a generation, the United Kingdom has experienced a transformation from being the leading imperial power in the world and the seat of the Commonwealth to a secondary European power.[5] The effect of this transformation upon the institutional and social stability of the country has been enormous. But there has been a continuing adherence to con-

---

[5] See "Britain in the 1960's: Descent From Power," *E.R.R.*, 1967 Vol. II, p. 697.

stitutional forms, and this has made the preservation of democracy in Britain a matter of importance to the entire western world.

Those who worry in the mid-Seventies about the concerted threats of organized labor and the possible effects of a depression on the continuation of democratic rule always look back to the General Strike of 1926 and the economic crises of the 1930s in search of parallels. Indeed the similarities seem startling. Britain in the beginning of 1925 did not offer the Conservative government of Stanley Baldwin a very hopeful prospect. There was an uneasy feeling in the country that labor and capital were splitting into opposite and conflicting camps. The immediate danger was from the coal miners.

---

*"The coal industry was almost inevitably the field of conflict. It was by far the largest single industry [in 1925-26].... It had always been the symbol of class struggle."*

A. J. P. Taylor, *English History 1914-1945*

---

The coal industry after World War I had suffered a severe slump and profitability was declining. Because of increasing losses, Baldwin decided to end government subsidies to the coal industry. This was greeted with hostility by the miners because only the subsidies had enabled the owners to maintain the prevailing wage levels. The coal operators announced in June 1925 that they would either be forced to cut wages or increase working hours for the same pay. The miners attributed the trouble to wastefulness of private ownership and demanded nationalization of the mines. The miners wanted to place the returns of the profitable mines in a common pool with the others and thus enable the poorer mines to keep up the wage levels.

Baldwin appointed a Royal Commission to look into the problems of the mines. Pending its investigation, the subsidy was to continue. Meanwhile, the Trades Union Congress (TUC), angry over high unemployment and the Tory government's policies, made preparations for a national strike to bring the government to its knees. As a countermeasure, the government announced a national plan to provide essential services in time of emergency. Commissioners, with the necessary volunteer staff, were placed in charge of 10 districts into which the country was divided. Each of these districts would maintain such essential services as food supply, law and order, and public transportation.

When the Royal Commission recommended in March 1926 that the government stop the subsidy, a confrontation was inevitable. The subsidy ended on May 1, 1926, and the mine owners posted a reduced scale of wages. At the same time the government proclaimed a state of emergency. Because of the suspension of most of the newspapers, no one was sure how near the country might be to civil war. When the general strike came on May 3, volunteers managed to maintain essential services. That broke the back of the strike and by May 11 most of the three million strikers returned to work. Only the miners continued their walkout.

This strike aroused the antipathy of the middle class toward the unions and made Baldwin a hero. It was a humiliating lesson the TUC has not yet forgotten. The British historian A.J.P. Taylor sees still another legacy from that struggle. "In the end, the owners were destroyed by their victory," he writes. "The class war continued in the coal districts when it was fading elsewhere, and the miners insisted on nationalization as soon as power passed to their hands."[6]

### Formation of Coalition Cabinet in Depression

Britain withstood the worst effects of the world depression longer than most industrial countries. However, its economy began to deteriorate as world trade began to fall off sharply after 1931. By 1933 nearly three million workers, or a quarter of the entire work force, were on the dole. Because the Labor government of the day was hopelessly divided on the question of reducing public expenditures and increasing taxes, Prime Minister Ramsay MacDonald resigned on Aug. 24, 1931, and summoned the leaders of all three parties—Tory, Labor and Liberal—to serve in a coalition (Nationalist) government.

The reaction of the TUC and the labor movement was to repudiate MacDonald's decision to cooperate with Liberals and Conservatives. The Labor M.P.'s joined to form a Parliamentary Labor Party which expelled MacDonald and his supporters from its ranks. However, when MacDonald called for a general election in October 1932, his coalition Nationalists won an overwhelming 502 seats in the House of Commons, in contrast to only 52 for the Labor Party. The electorate had given MacDonald a mandate to take whatever steps were necessary to try to heal the sick economy.

The first measure of the new government had been to go off the gold standard—in effect, to devalue sterling. Enormous

---

[6] A.J.P. Taylor, *English History 1914-1945* (1965), p. 248.

pressures built up to protect domestic industries by instituting tariffs. First the "Abnormal Importations Act" enabled the Board of Trade to impose duties of up to 50 per cent on articles which were allegedly "dumped"—brought into Britain at low prices in unusually large quantities. In addition, the government passed an ad valorem duty of 10 per cent on all imports. The policy of protecting industry against outside competition had now been clearly established.

While most of the country welcomed the experience of coalition government, the Parliamentary Labor Party in its isolated position rejected the coalition as a denial of its responsibilities toward the working class. Its views were largely undercut by an economic recovery that began in 1933 and carried employment and production to a prewar peak in 1937. By then the coming of World War II was diverting the nation's attention from domestic concerns. Class divisions were submerged during the war years to the common goal of first withstanding and then defeating the Axis powers. Soon after V-E Day, the Labor Party regained power at the polls and set in motion the welfare state.

---

# The Arena of Political Struggle

---

O VER the past century the British people have managed to keep almost all of their principal struggles within the parliamentary arena. The national belief was that the parliamentary system enabled governments to represent the will of the people and that the Commons would provide a high quality of leadership in any crisis. For a complex set of reasons this situation began to change in the 1960s. Lord Shawcross, who was a member of the first postwar Labor government, writes that there is open defiance of Parliament and government because of "a general realization by the mass of the people that Parliament no longer represents the mass of the people."[7]

Shawcross points to the election of the Wilson government in October 1974 with 39.3 per cent of the votes cast *(see box, p. 717)* and speaks of a minority forcing "upon an unwilling people policies of which the mass of them disapprove." Indeed, neither of the two major parties has won decisively at the polls since the Labor victory in 1966. An unusually large vote for the third-party Liberals in October 1974—18.3 per cent of the 29,188,637 votes cast—was widely interpreted as a "no" vote for both Labor and Conservatives.

---

[7] Lord Shawcross, "Who are the Masters Now?" *Encounter,* September 1975, p. 95.

Each new government in Britain regards itself as duty bound to its extremist wing to repeal the economic, industrial and social programs of its predecessor. Wilson, like Edward Heath before him, continues to make U-turns on economic policy, first renouncing any form of incomes policy and then adopting one. Enoch Powell, who has sometimes been called "Britain's George Wallace," told the House of Commons earlier this year that the nation expects to be deceived by its politicians. Liberal M.P. Jo Grimond, the former leader of his party, has said that it is "all too clear that the democratic system has been frustrated." He said that a new type of political organization is needed because "Parliament has played singularly little part in dealing with the disastrous economic events of the past three years."

There have been national campaigns for a more equitable form of popular representation. It is pointed out that although 5.4 million people voted Liberal in the last election, they are represented by only 13 Members of Parliament whereas proportional representation would have given them 116 M.P.'s. There have also been suggestions that if Parliament is going to meet the coming challenges, it will have to overhaul its own procedures. When Parliament reconvenes Oct. 13 it will need an entire month to clear up old business from the last session.

## Growing Domination by Trade Union Movement

The big unions have gotten bigger and more militant during the past decade. Until the early Sixties the Transport and General Workers Union and the Amalgamated Union of Engineering Workers were dominated by strong but moderate leaders. Since 1968 they have been run by men—Jack Jones and Hugh Scanlon, respectively—who have been eager to battle both management and government for higher wages, shorter hours, and a highly sectarian economic policy.

The power of the trade unions to raise their own members' wages beyond any increase that could be justified by productivity ultimately brought down the Heath government in the winter of 1974. The unions had opposed the enactment of the Industrial Relations Act[8] by the Tories and caused major industrial unrest in trying to repeal it. When in December 1973 Heath refused to budge from the government's offer of a 16½ per cent pay increase to striking miners who were demanding more than 30 per cent, the economy almost ground to a halt. The lack of coal and energy forced the introduction of a three-day work week. Heath called a general election and lost. In the past 10 years the only major national strike to fail was that of the postmen who held out for seven weeks in 1971.

---

[8] For background, see "Industrial Strife in Western Europe," *E.R.R.*, 1971 Vol. I, pp. 418-419, 422-425.

## Labor Governments Since 1945

In the election of July 1945, the first in Britain in a decade, Labor was voted in with an absolute majority in the House of Commons. Under Clement Attlee the party governed from Aug. 1, 1945, to Feb. 5, 1950. The Labor Party was returned again in 1950, with a majority of 17 over the Conservative opposition, but of only six overall.

On October 25, 1951, the voters turned to the Conservatives under Winston Churchill, giving them an all-party majority of 17. Labor did not win another election until 1964. Then, on Oct. 15, under the leadership of Harold Wilson, the Labor Party was returned with an all-party majority of four. With this slim edge Wilson governed until March 31, 1966, when the country again voted him in—this time with a substantial overall majority of 96.

The tide swung back to the Conservatives on June 18, 1970, but since then the number of votes cast for each of the two major parties has been extremely close. In 1970 there was a difference of 3.4 per cent; in February 1974 this dropped to a mere one per cent (with the Conservatives polling the larger figure although Labor gained more seats and formed the government); on Oct. 10 the difference was only 3.6 per cent.

### OCT. 10, 1974, ELECTION

| Parties | At Dissolution | Oct. 10 Results |
|---|---|---|
| Labor | 298 | 319 |
| Conservative | 296 | 276 |
| Liberal | 15 | 13 |
| Scottish Nationalists | 7 | 11 |
| Welsh Nationalists | 2 | 3 |
| Ulster Unionists (NI) | 11 | 10 |
| Other | 6 | 3 |
| Number of Seats | 635 | 635 |

SOURCE: British Information Services

*The Guardian* wrote editorially on Sept. 1, 1975: "In the last 18 months, the government has deferred to the TUC in an unprecedented degree. Government by consent has come to mean specifically government with the consent of the TUC." An example of union consent being sought, and obtained, was witnessed two days later at the annual conference in Blackpool when representatives of the 10.3 million members[9] of the Trades Union

---

[9] The TUC is composed of 110 unions. The other 385 British unions represent only about 10 per cent of the country's 11.5 million organized workers.

Congress endorsed the motion of Jack Jones, by a majority of more than 2 to 1, to support a key element of the government's anti-inflation program—a ceiling on wage increases *(see p. 719)*.

The press tended to see the vote in terms of the unions' recognition that inflation had to be brought under control before unemployment could be attacked. "Yesterday afternoon was the moment when fear curbed greed," the independent *Daily Mail* commented editorially on Sept. 4, the day after the voting. The pro-Labor *Daily Mirror* said, "The TUC...showed Britain how to face reality." On the opposite side of the Atlantic, *The New York Times* proclaimed that the news from Blackpool "will hearten Britain's friends everywhere." *Time* magazine, in a long article on Britain's industrial distress, cautioned that "the optimism is probably premature." "The social conflicts that underlie Britain's labor problems are nowhere being resolved...."[10]

### Left-Wing Challenge Within Labor Party Ranks

The Labor Party, like the Tory Party, is a coalition of political factions whose points of view cover a broad range of the ideological spectrum. While in opposition between 1970 and 1974, the Labor Party organization fell increasingly under the control of left-wing activists who wanted to create a classless, egalitarian society. This left wing, most of whose militant representatives in Parliament belong to the "Tribune Group," captured both the party conference and the national executive of the party.

**Harold Wilson**

The Labor left flexed its muscle in July when a moderate in the cabinet, Reginald Prentice, the Minister for Overseas Development, was rejected by the constituency management committee of his district and invited to retire as M.P. for Newham. The radicals who had captured the local committee were incensed that Prentice had not voted in Parliament according to their instructions. It was the first time a sitting cabinet minister had been dropped as a candidate for the next general election.

---

[10] "Upstairs/Downstairs at the Factory," *Time*, Sept. 15, 1975, p. 58.

Prime Minister Wilson was unsuccessful in trying to intervene in Prentice's behalf but he has adroitly managed to split the Tribune Group and the trade union movement. His policy has been to divide those who genuinely disagree with the prevailing doctrine about wages and inflation from the fundamentalists who believe that only the breakdown and ultimate transformation of the present economic and social system can solve the country's problems.

# Efforts to Stave Off Disaster

IT WILL be "a hell of a slog for the next couple of years," said Wilson the morning after his last election. The going has been rough and, by common consent, it is going to get a lot rougher if, as expected, production continues to fall and unemployment climbs toward the two million mark. The squeeze on incomes, while prices continue to rise, will lead to a further decline in living standards. Trouble stares the government in the face no matter which course it may take. At the time of his election last October, Wilson said that only in wartime would he contemplate the use of statutory powers to hold back incomes and prices. At first he tried to hew to a policy of voluntary wage restraints. As wages soared, this political exercise made both the union leaders and the public aware that a firmer policy was needed. The *Times* of London has remarked editorially that every government since 1959 has come to power opposed to an official incomes policy and that every government has adopted one.

### Labor's Hopes for Its Anti-Inflation Program

Wilson outlined to Parliament on July 11 his plan to contain inflation, saying in these words: "This is a plan to save our country. If we do not over the next 12 months achieve a drastic reduction in the present disastrous rate of inflation by the measures outlined...the British people will be engulfed in a general economic catastrophe of incalculable proportions." A key element of the plan, that of limiting pay raises to £6 ($12.60) a week, went into effect Aug. 1. The intent is to bring the rate of domestic inflation down to 10 per cent by the third quarter (July-October) of 1976.

Another part of the plan would provide increases for all workers earning less than £8,500 ($18,700) a year. This part originated with Jack Jones and received the overwhelming support of the TUC. However, there were notable differences from the start. Len Murray, the General Secretary of the TUC, made it clear that all workers would be entitled to a full £6 raise and that the TUC would regard strikes in support of claims of £6 as legitimate. But £6 a week, if given to all the 25 million workers in Britain, would add up to £7.8 billion ($16.4 billion) a year. This would be a high cost for industry to absorb in a year during which real production is expected to fall.

The Tories criticized the plan for not controlling public expenditure. Margaret Thatcher, the party leader, said that by April 1976, government spending would have increased in two years by nearly $900 for every man, woman and child in the United Kingdom. In response, the Secretary for the Environment, Anthony Crosland, announced in Parliament on Aug. 5 that there would be a "standstill" in local government expenditures.

### Critical Issue of Unions' Stand on Wage Limits

Although the specter of an early election and the return of a Conservative-led coalition under Margaret Thatcher was used by the TUC leaders to convince delegates at Blackpool to abide by the wage limits set by the government, there are doubts as to how long such support can last. Kenneth Gill, general secretary of the Amalgamated Union of Engineering Workers, said the £6-a-week limit was interference with the process of free collective bargaining. "Wage control is as voluntary as rape," he said. For its part, the government has made clear that if a union attempts to break the voluntary agreement, it would enact the necessary legal sanctions to make the policy statutory.

**Margaret Thatcher**

Until the new year no major union is likely to launch a policy-breaking strike. The big labor contracts in the public sector for the railwaymen, miners, gasmen and power workers will not come until after Christmas. If at that time prices continue to rise along with unemployment and there is no sign of an economic upturn, a massive squeeze on the government will begin. The best paid workers, who tend to be the ones with the most bargaining strength, will be the ones affected most seriously.

# Breaking up the United Kingdom?

The United Kingdom of England, Scotland, Wales and Northern Ireland is beset by separatist sentiment in Scotland and Wales. Welsh nationalism is of cultural origin and centers on concern for the perpetuity of the ancient Celtic language. Scottish nationalism, on the other hand, is largely an economic matter. The impetus is North Sea oil.

The first oil from huge undersea deposits off the coast of Scotland was brought ashore June 18, 1975, an event marked by ceremonies at which the Secretary of State for Energy, Tony Benn, proclaimed that "in time we shall be one of the top 10 oil producers in the world."

A lot of Scotsmen are now saying that "we" should refer only to the five million Scots, not the entire 55 million Britons. *The Economist* writes of "an avaricious nationalism" being "on the march in Scotland," threatening Britain's hope for an economic miracle founded on immense oil revenues it expects within a decade. "The country is kept afloat by massive foreign borrowing using North Sea oil as collateral," the magazine added.*

Although Scotland's quarrel with England goes far into history—the two were separate and warring kingdoms until 1603—the contemporary resurgence of Scottish nationalism is only about a decade old. The Scottish Nationalist Party won a mere 2 per cent of the popular vote in 1964 but 30 per cent in October 1974, second only to the Labor Party in Scotland.

It is not clear, however, how much of SNP's electoral growth represented merely a protest vote against Labor and Conservatives. Public opinion polls taken in May 1975 indicated that 22 per cent of the Scots endorsed independence and 29 per cent a federal form of government such as now exists. Only 18 per cent favored the present British government's devolution proposals.**

All of the political parties in Britain are committed to changing Scotland's status within the United Kingdom. A government White Paper issued in December 1974 on "Democracy and Devolution Proposals for Scotland and Wales" followed the 1973 recommendations of the Royal Commission on the Constitution (the Kilbrandon Report) by suggesting that separate Welsh and Scottish Assemblies be established by 1977.

The hope at Westminster is that such elected assemblies will constitute a "firebreak" against the spread of nationalism. England and Scotland already have different systems of law, a different judiciary, different educational systems, different national churches, and, for most domestic matters, different government departments. But Westminster holds the purse strings and therein lies the current problem.

* Issue of July 26, 1975.
** Cited by Richard Rose, professor of politics at the University of Strathclyde, Glasgow, in *The New Republic*, Sept. 20, 1975.

## Terrorism in Britain

For centuries there has been fighting between British soldiers and Irish civilians,* but only in the past year have terrorists brought widespread violence to English soil. Last year 41 English men and women were killed by bomb blasts in various public places.

The bombings have been attributed either officially or in the public mind to the provisional wing of the underground Irish Republican Army. After an unofficial cease-fire in February 1975, terrorism resumed in central London on Aug. 4. A bomb exploded in the lobby of the Hilton Hotel, killing two persons and injuring 62 others.

In Ulster itself, more than 1,300 persons have lost their lives and 10 times that number have been injured in the sectarian fighting between the Catholic and Protestant communities. There is no end in sight to the bloodshed. Politicians in Ulster seem united only in their despair.

A constitutional convention called by the British is now deadlocked. The two main political blocs at the convention, the United Ulster Unionist Council (Protestant) and the Social Democratic and Labor Party (Catholic), remain unreconciled on the central issue of how to share power. Meanwhile, the British government continues to pay an annual economic subsidy of almost $900 million to Ulster and spends an additional $100 million to maintain 14,000 troops there.

* See "Religious Divisions in Northern Ireland," *E.R.R.*, 1970 Vol. I, pp. 121-137.

The primary issue next year, Peter Jay of *The Times* has written, is "simply how long and how far the Chancellor [of the Exchequer] can resist pressures for reflation." There is general public agreement that while this Labor government may have wider support from the union movement than the Tory government, any sign of weakness, any crack in its pay policy would open the flood gates of inflation. "The prospects of our country if we were to fail would be grim indeed," Harold Wilson told the nation on Aug. 20.

### Chances of a National Coalition in Next Cabinet

Addressing the leaders of the mine workers in July, Wilson said that the time had come for them to show loyalty to the nation by not pursuing large pay demands. The alternative was the prospect of a breakdown of constitutional democracy in Britain. "The issue now is not whether this or any other democratic socialist government can survive and lead the nation to full employment and a greater measure of social justice. It is whether any government so constituted, so dedicated to the principles of consent and consensus within our democracy, can lead this nation."

Jack Jones warned the TUC conference that "out of the despair and confusion that is already present" could come a national coalition. Wilson has rejected all talk of coalition government and Mrs. Thatcher seems agreed with him on the inefficacy of such a government. However, Labor is, in effect, receiving coalition support for those policies which command a fair measure of consensus in Parliament and in the country. The Tories are in no hurry to assume control, *The Economist* wrote, "because they want it to be a Labor government that at least shows that an elected British Parliament can stand up to a blackmailing strike and prevail."

---

*"The next year is crucial."*

Prime Minister Harold Wilson,
national broadcast, Aug. 20, 1975

---

If the economic crisis comes to a boil late this winter, the leadership of the Labor Party may then decide that one-party government is no longer viable. In a situation of national disaster, a strongman might possibly emerge. Enoch Powell is widely seen as such a figure because "his cross-party support makes it easier to imagine him as the head of a hypothetical government of national unity," wrote Richard Bourne in *The Nation.*[11] Many political analysts—Professor Hugh Clegg and commentator Ronald Butt are two—are pessimistic about Britain's long-term chances of remaining a democratic society. "The trouble is that where socialism diminishes personal responsibility, it may prove to be impossible to enjoy responsible government in the long run without state sanctions which would be inimical to our whole tradition of freedom," Butt has written. In Britain's welfare state the odds being placed on the survival of parliamentary democracy have never been lower.

---

[11]Richard Bourne, "Recession, EEC and Mrs. Thatcher," *The Nation*, March 8, 1975.

# Selected Bibliography

## Books

Erickson, Arvel B. and Martin J. Havran, *England*, Anchor Books, 1968.
Hechter, Michael, *Internal Colonialism: The Celtic Fringe in British National Development 1536-1966*, Routledge, Kegan Paul, 1975.
Levin, Bernard, *The Pendulum Years*, Jonathan Cape, 1970.
Sampson, Anthony, *The New Anatomy of Britain*, Hodder & Stoughton, 1971.
Taylor, A.J.P., *English History 1914-1945*, Oxford University Press, 1965.

## Articles

Bourne, Richard, "Recession, EEC and Mrs. Thatcher," *The Nation*, March 8, 1975.
Chapman, Colin, "The Multi-Million Pound Handout," *Sunday Times*, May 25, 1975.
Day, Alan, "Our Best Hope of Pulling Through," *The Observer*, July 6, 1975.
Elliott, John, "Guidelines for the new pay package's survival," *Financial Times*, July 14, 1975.
Jay, Peter, "Latest Instalment of a Dilemma," *The Times*, Sept. 2, 1975 (annual financial and economic review).
Rose, Richard, "Oil Based Scottish Nationalism," *The New Republic*, Sept. 20, 1975.
Sewill, Brendon, "Is the right to strike in the wrong?" *The Guardian*, May 12, 1975.
"Upstairs/Downstairs at the Factory," *Time*, Sept. 15, 1975.
Shawcross, "Who are the Masters Now?" *Encounter*, September 1975.
*The Economist*, selected issues.
*The Guardian*, "The Crisis of Capitalism," July 1, 1975, a special report.
"Why Nothing Works in Britain," *Business Week*, Feb. 10, 1975.

## Studies and Reports

"Attack on Inflation: A Policy for Survival: A guide to the Government's Programme," HMSO, August 1975.
*Britain 1975: An Official Handbook*, Central Office of Information.
Editorial Research Reports, "Britain in the 1960's: Descent From Power," 1967 Vol. II, p. 699; "British Election, 1970," 1970 Vol. I, p. 425.

# SOUTHERN AFRICA IN TRANSITION

by

## Yorick Blumenfeld

## 1 9 7 5
## Apr. 4

# SOUTHERN AFRICA IN TRANSITION

OUTLINES of a peaceful resolution of the tense social, political and economic problems besetting the white and black societies in the southern tier of African states are beginning to appear. Replacing hostile confrontation is the prospect of new economic cooperation for this huge area, more than half the size of the United States but populated by only some 50-60 million people. In Rhodesia, which is now one key to peace in the region, guerrillas who want to wage "chimurenga" (armed struggle for liberation of the state, which they call Zimbabwe) have observed a cease-fire since December. Despite many obstacles, preparations continue for a constitutional conference to determine that country's future.

A potentially decisive development occurred during the last week of March when the government of Zambia, led by its highly respected President Kenneth D. Kaunda, arrested about 50 leaders of the Zimbabwe African National Union (ZANU). ZANU has actively opposed the cease-fire in Rhodesia and has objected to negotiations with the white minority government of Prime Minister Ian Smith. "News of the Zambian crackdown on the Zimbabwe African National Union hit southern Africa like a bombshell, so unexpected and far-reaching in its implications was the action," wrote David B. Ottaway in *The Washington Post* (March 29, 1975). "It immediately raised hopes that the stalled talks between white and black leaders for a settlement of the Rhodesia problem may soon be resumed."

The revolution in Portugal in April 1974 broke the stalemate which had existed for the past decade between the army and guerrillas in Portugal's African colonies. Mozambique is to become independent on June 25, 1975. And Angola, barring an upset in the schedule caused by persisting differences among rival liberation movements, will celebrate its independence on Nov. 11, 1975.[1] These developments in Portuguese-speaking Africa have been welcomed as a giant stride toward decolonization of the continent. The carefully structured "white buffer zone" around the Republic of South Africa now seems pointless.

[1] The Portuguese Cape Verde islands, farther north off West Africa, are to gain their independence July 5, 1975.

As a result, John Vorster, South Africa's prime minister, has launched an unprecedented effort to adapt to the changing circumstances. Attempts are being made to resolve Pretoria's lengthy and illegal wardship of South West Africa (Namibia). South Africa's foreign minister, Hilgard Muller, has said that dramatic moves now under way could lead to "southern Africa taking on a completely different appearance." Vorster asserted last November that people "will be amazed at where the country stands in 6 to 12 months' time."

## Vorster's New Attempts to Promote Coexistence

After a long period of isolation, South Africa is leading a breakthrough into black Africa. "We are as much part of Africa as any other African country and this is being accepted by more and more African countries," Vorster said on March 3. He was the first South African prime minister to confer with black leaders at home and abroad. Last September he flew secretly to the Ivory Coast as a member of a team to see President Felix Houphouet-Boigny and President Leopold Senghor of Senegal. In November 1974 he met President Kenneth Kaunda of Zambia and most recently, on Feb. 11, he paid a call on President William Tolbert of Liberia.

The South African prime minister told a press conference in Capetown on Feb. 20 that he had dedicated himself to the normalization of relations between his country and the other states on the continent. He is convinced that if South Africa can resolve the remaining "colonial" issues and bring about a peaceful settlement in Rhodesia, it will win time to solve its own domestic racial problems through "separate development." "Separate development" means continued apartheid, for Vorster himself has said that "in white South Africa the whites will rule—and let there be no mistake about that."[2]

Vorster's "peace offensive" nevertheless seems viable because it has concentrated on immediate objectives in which both black and white leaders have a shared interest. Vorster has skillfully balanced South Africa's economic and financial supremacy against the political demands of the blacks. Two of the southern African states, Zambia and Malawi, must have new outlets to the sea and all of them need economic and technological assistance from elsewhere. To attain these objectives, they are ready for détente. The economic linking of South Africa, Zambia, Rhodesia (Zimbabwe), Mozambique, Angola, Malawi, Lesotho, Botswana and Swaziland holds great appeal for Presi-

---

[2] Vorster, who is 58, faces no immediate challenge to his leadership because of his sudden change of tack. In the April 1974 elections Vorster polled more votes than any other candidate and received a clear 5-year mandate. His personal prestige has consequently never been higher, despite misgivings of the extreme right wing.

dent Kenneth D. Kaunda of Zambia.[3] However, this plan of
"normalization" or even of cooperation between South Africa
and the black African states conflicts with efforts of the Afro-
Asian block to ostracize South Africa because of its racial
policies.

### Pressures to Resolve the Rhodesian Deadlock

Prime Minister Vorster's efforts to promote a non-violent
settlement in Rhodesia are the key to his strategy for defusing
the threat of black African nationalists to his own country.
What is novel in this situation is that, together with the British
and the Zambian governments, Vorster is pushing the Rhodesian Front Party, led by Prime Minister Ian Smith, to accept a
negotiated transition to majority rule in Rhodesia. Because
Rhodesia's regime has depended on South African support for
its survival, Vorster's withdrawal of more than 2,000 South
African police, who had been involved in counter-insurgency
border duty, could force Smith into a settlement.

[3] Kaunda is scheduled to confer with President Ford on April 19 during an official visit to
the United States.

The *Guardian* said in an editorial on Feb. 13, 1975: "That control of events in Rhodesia is no longer in Mr. Ian Smith's hands is now obvious to almost everyone except Mr. Smith." In the past, United Nations trade sanctions against Rhodesia failed because Portugal and South Africa were willing to supply the landlocked state. However, that situation has been reversed since the talks between Vorster and Kaunda in which Zambia pledged to halt all guerrilla activity in southern Africa if an agreement acceptable to the nationalist movements in Rhodesia could be reached. James Callaghan, the British foreign secretary, made a tour of the region in January and concluded that the only options open to Rhodesia were a peaceful transition to independence through a negotiated settlement or the resumption of a violent struggle on a much more intense scale than before.

The basis for the proposed Rhodesian conference, discussed in Lusaka, Zambia, last fall, was that majority rule would be attained in Rhodesia after the life of one post-conference parliament. This body would be elected on a qualified franchise which would give the vote to all Africans with seven years of primary education and one year of secondary education. The leaders of the African National Council (ANC) felt able to accept this proposal because they estimated that between 150,000 and 300,000 Africans would qualify to vote for the interim parliament. As there are only 84,500 white voters in Rhodesia, the black leaders were confident they could achieve the immediate parliamentary majority they had been demanding.

However, Charles Mohr of *The New York Times* reported on Dec. 17, 1974, that Rhodesian government statistics did not bear out the optimism of the ANC. According to Rhodesian records, only about 64,000 blacks enrolled in the first year of secondary schools between 1952 and 1969 and not all of them finished their first year of schooling. The formula worked out in Lusaka would thus permit Ian Smith to argue to the wary 270,000 white Rhodesians that he would be continuing the policy of "maintaining civilized standards" because only educated Africans would be allowed to vote for the interim legislature, which would, in effect, continue to be ruled by the Rhodesian Front Party.

The Rhodesian Front has placed limited trust in Smith to preclude the possibility of his granting far-reaching concessions on the crucial franchise issue. Smith has indicated he would "readily" stand down as prime minister. "I have been in this game for quite a while now and I can assure you that there would be no tears shed if I had to leave now," he has said. Smith has repeatedly asserted that while his government believes in a constitutional settlement, it will only settle on terms that will be

## Countries of Southern Africa

| Present Name | Former Name | Area (sq. miles) | Estimated Population (in millions, mid-1974)* |
|---|---|---|---|
| Angola | same | 481,351 | 6.0 |
| Botswana | Bechuanaland | 219,815 | 0.7 |
| Lesotho, Kingdom of | Basutoland | 11,600 | 1.0 |
| Malawi | Nyasaland | 45,747 | 4.9 |
| Mozambique | same | 297,731 | 9.0 |
| Namibia | South West Africa | 318,261 | 0.7 |
| Rhodesia (Zimbabwe) | Southern Rhodesia | 150,333 | 6.1 |
| South Africa, Republic of | Union of So. Africa | 471,982 | 24.3 |
| Swaziland, Kingdom of | same | 6,704 | 0.5 |
| Zambia | Northern Rhodesia | 290,586 | 4.7 |

* World Population Estimates prepared by the Environmental Fund.

beneficial to the white community. Cornered between Vorster's yearning for a settlement and the hostility to concessions from his own party, Smith is expected to stall for time by any means available.

For their part, the nearly six million blacks in Rhodesia are becoming increasingly impatient. A minority is pushing for direct and violent confrontation. Robert Mugabe, the former general secretary of the Zimbabwe African National Union (ZANU) said upon his release from detention in December: "We want majority rule as a fact. We will deal with the mechanics of a transfer of power after that fact has been accepted. It is majority rule now. We are tired of minority rule—we have had it too long."

### Coming Independence of Angola and Mozambique

Although a provisional government was installed in the Angolan capital of Luanda on Feb. 1, 1975, and the former colony is to gain its independence on Nov. 11, the process of decolonization has proved troublesome. The three national movements, which together with the Portuguese administrators have an equal share in the transitional movement, are already fighting for popular support in the referendum scheduled to be held in the autumn. As correspondent John Borrell reported in *The Observer* (Feb. 2, 1975), the three competing groups feel that whoever wins the first round in the elections for a constituent assembly is going to govern the country permanently because there are generally no second elections in Africa.

Holden Roberto's National Front for the Liberation of Angola, Dr. Agostinho Neto's Popular Movement for the Liberation of Angola (MPLA) and Dr. Jona Savimbi's Union for the Total Liberation of Angola (UNITA) are the three main movements contesting the ability of the nationalists to substitute democracy for revolution. However, one faction of the MPLA, headed by Daniel Chipenda, has threatened to plunge the country into civil war. Chipenda, who heads a tribal army of 3,000 men near the town of Luso in eastern Angola, has demanded to be included in the interpartite governing circle. In late March 1975, reports from Luanda, Angola's tense capital, said there had been renewed fighting between rival guerrilla forces. The number of casualties was officially set at 50, but Angolan sources said that at least 100 and perhaps 500 people had been killed. Neighboring Zaire, which is thought to have designs on Angolan territory, was reported to be backing one guerrilla group. There are 24,000 Portuguese troops still in Angola, and an official on a peace-keeping mission there said the situation was like "dynamite."

Mozambique, which gains its independence June 25, is having no such political problems because the president-designate, Samoral Machel, has already selected his Frelimo government. Soon after the Frelimo (Front for the Liberation of Mozambique) took over the provisional government last September, the prime minister, Joaquim Chissano, pledged non-interference in the policies of Mozambique's two neighbors, South Africa and Rhodesia. Confrontation is not currently in the interest of the country's nine million people divided into more than 80 ethnic groups and speaking more than 20 different dialects.[4]

Mozambique faces a threat of widespread starvation unless it receives substantial aid from Portugal, South Africa, and the United Nations. Even now, Mozambique would be experiencing famine were it not for food shipments from South Africa. About 100,000 of Mozambique's blacks work in South African mines and Pretoria has been paying 25 per cent of their wages in gold at a subsidized price of $42.22 an ounce. Prime Minister Vorster has warned that should the Frelimo make its territory available for terrorist action, South Africa not only would cut all subsidies but also would take military action against Mozambique. Moreover, Mozambique must sell electricity from the great Caborra Bassa dam to South Africa to keep that hydroelectric project in operation.

## Continuing Efforts to End Impasse Over Namibia

South Africa has controlled the huge territory of South West Africa, twice the size of California, since it seized the former

---

[4] See "Tribalism vs. Nationalism in African Development," *E.R.R.*, 1960 Vol. II, pp. 805-821.

German protectorate in 1915. First, the area was ruled under martial law, then under a League of Nations mandate. After World War II, South Africa rejected U.N. trusteeship of South West Africa, now called Namibia, and in 1971 it ignored a 13-2 advisory ruling by the International Court of Justice at The Hague that South Africa's administration of Namibia was illegal and should be terminated immediately. Finally, on Dec. 17, 1974, the U.N. Security Council unanimously adopted a resolution calling on South Africa to make a "solemn declaration" of its intention to relinquish control of Namibia by May 30, 1975. If this deadline is not met, the Council will consider "appropriate measures."

For its part, Pretoria, which has administered the territory as an integral part of South Africa, claims it would be "pleased" to be rid of Namibia. The *Star* of Johannesburg commented editorially that "real and rapid disengagement from South West Africa is a key component of the current détente bargain in southern Africa." In talks with President Tolbert of Liberia, Vorster is reported to have said that "My government in the last 10 to 15 years has spent millions of rands on development in South West Africa. We do not want an inch of South West Africa's territory, and I would only be too pleased to get South West Africa off our backs."

The Security Council has demanded that this sparsely populated territory, which has only 700,000 inhabitants, be granted independence as a unitary state under the leadership of the South West Africa People's Organization (SWAPO). South Africa, on the other hand, is intent on dividing the area into several independent tribal states. The "homelands" would include Ovamboland, which would have about half the total population, Basterland with 16,000 tribesmen, Tswanaland with 17,000 natives, Kaokoland with 18,000 and Caprivi with 25,000. The South African government insists that each of these ethnic groups is entitled to independence.

The South African case received considerable support in January when the chief of the Kerero people, Clemens Kapuuo, who had been petitioning the U.N. for an independent and unitary Namibia for a decade, changed his mind and wrote to Secretary General Kurt Waldheim suggesting that Ovamboland be granted separate independence. Ovamboland is the political stronghold of the SWAPO movement and Chief Kapuuo was expressing a widely held fear that the Ovambo tribe would dominate the whole country.

SWAPO has also had its troubles. In January 1975, close to 55 per cent of the Ovambo people cast their ballots in an election held by South Africa although SWAPO had called for a total boycott. This would suggest that the SWAPO militants, who come from the northern strip of South West Africa, are neither as powerful nor as representative as they would have the United Nations believe. South African officials said that the elections showed that "all options are open" for Namibians to choose their own destiny. However, most observers agree that South West Africa, most of which is desert, could not be self-supporting as a state.

## Traditions of the White Colonizers

EUROPEANS have lived in southern Africa since the 15th century. Concalo de Sousa was sent there as a representative of the King of Portugal in 1490, accompanied by the first missionaries. In 1534 a cathedral was built at Sao Salvador in Angola and in 1575 Luanda was founded. After that date, the sovereignty of Portugal over Angola was undisputed.

Although Bartholomew Diaz, a Portuguese, first rounded the Cape of Good Hope in 1488, it was not until the mid-17th century that the Dutch Boers (farmers) established the first settlements on the Cape for the Dutch East India Company. The Cape, about midway on the trade route to India, was an ideal supply station. The first act of the Dutch settlers was to kill, enslave or expel the native Hottentots.

The Dutch soon were joined by Germans and refugee French Huguenots seeking a livelihood. In those days of slow travel and communication over the wide spaces of a sparsely populated land, the settlers developed a culture of their own and a language to express it.[5] They began to call themselves Afrikaners and were later to argue that Africa had welded them into a distinct new nation. Their isolation encouraged a sense of separateness that was to have profound political consequences.

After several unsuccessful attempts, the British took over the original Cape Province in 1806 and the first contingent of 5,000 British settlers arrived in 1820. Many of the Boers, unwilling to accommodate themselves to the new and more liberal British policy toward the natives, migrated from the Cape to the interior in the 1830s, in what became known as the great Trek, to found the republics of Transvaal and the Orange Free State.

[5] Margaret Ballinger, *From Union to Apartheid* (1969), p. 16.

Persisting tension between the Afrikaners and the British led finally to the Boer War of 1899-1902. Britain's victory in that conflict was followed by establishment of the Union of South Africa in 1910.

The position of the Boer population was recognized by continuing the Roman Dutch Law, but the status of the native blacks was sharply limited.[6] Although outnumbered by more than four to one, the whites maintained supremacy through increasingly rigorous legislation. Afrikaners often justified this course by citing scripture as interpreted by the Dutch Reformed Church. According to these Afrikaners, God made men of two colors and the dark descendants of Ham were destined forever to be hewers of wood and drawers of water. But an equally deep cause for resentment between the races could be traced to the bloody wars which the 19th century Afrikaners fought with the native populations as they battled their way northward.

## Intensification of Segregation in South Africa

At the end of World War II, although South Africa was a founding member of the United Nations, it refused to sign the U.N. Declaration of Human Rights. In the elections of 1948 the South African Nationalists, under Daniel Mahan, won a parliamentary majority over the United South African party headed by Jan Christiaan Smuts because they promised much harsher restriction of the black and colored populations. The 2.3 million colored (persons of mixed European and African or Malayan descent) were disenfranchised soon after the Nationalists took over.

In 1950 Prof. F. R. Tomlinson was appointed to investigate the practical steps needed to separate the races. The Tomlinson report eventually recommended that the 264 existing scattered Bantu (native) areas should be consolidated into eight reservations or homelands for the principal races. The Zulu, Zhosa and Tswana homelands would become miniature states, each with its own government. Although criticized as representing a revival of tribalism, the Bantu Authorities Act of 1951 provided for merger among different tribes and at least gave the blacks some measure of autonomy. However, because the areas allotted to the 15 million blacks consisted of only 13 per cent of the total land surface of the republic, they could not provide sufficient employment or food. The Bantu reservations were to be kept deliberately underdeveloped so that if and when employers in the white areas needed extra labor, the blacks would be waiting to provide it.

---

[6] The Native Administration Act of 1927, for example, empowered the government to rule Africans by decree and to order the removal or banishment of any African or group of Africans.

In the late 1950s, as a consequence of the ever more rigidly enforced segregation laws, the black and colored residents were evicted from Johannesburg to separate quarters outside the city. The Promotion of Self-Government Act of 1959 finally did away with white representation for Africans in Parliament as the Bantus were henceforth to be self-governing in their homelands. Tension became particularly pronounced in many rural areas where the tribesmen revoted against those chiefs who enforced government policy.[7]

## Hostility Engendered by the Policy of Apartheid

The tension raised by the "pass laws," which restricted the movement of blacks, broke out in rioting at Sharpeville in 1960. White police, determined to put down the rioters, killed 69 Africans and wounded 178 more. The government reacted by declaring a state of emergency throughout the country. The army was used to surround certain African residential areas and thousands of people were arrested and detained without trial. The government also banned the African National Congress and the Pan Africanist Congress. In spite of mounting international protest, South Africa withdrew from the Commonwealth rather than modify its racial policies. On May 31, 1961, it proclaimed itself a republic.

To carry out separate development, the country in effect was partitioned into two areas. The Bantus and the whites were each to control their own affairs and eventually achieve equality in their respective modes of living. However, apartheid involved a huge displacement of people. At least two million Bantus were uprooted and "consolidated" into the homelands. The Transkei, whose Xhosa people were granted self-government in December 1963, is scheduled to become at least nominally independent within the next few years. However, the other Bantus refused such "independence" because they feel it would cut them off from claims on the wealth of South Africa and would make a mockery of their true status.

The system of apartheid restricts the blacks to designated living areas, circumscribes their rights to own property or engage in trade and prevents them from entering white urban areas unless they are required to go there to serve white employers.[8] The blacks, moreover, are excluded from most skilled jobs and are not allowed to join registered trade unions. It is estimated that 1.3 million workers, constituting 51 per cent of the black labor force, are now regular migrants shifting between their city jobs and their Bantu homelands.

[7] Albie Sachs,"South Africa: The Violence of Apartheid" (1969), p. 6.
[8] Donald B. Easum, "Southern Africa Five Years after the Lusaka Manifesto," *Department of State Bulletin,* Dec. 16, 1974, p. 838.

Initially, the leaders of the Bantu governments were considered government stooges. But lately, primarily because of the example of Chief Gatsha Buthelezi, the Zulu leader, they have become outspoken in expressing black frustrations and demands. *The Economist* reported that last January the chiefs presented Premier John Vorster with a number of unprecedented demands, including permanent citizenship rights for blacks, full trade union rights, equal job opportunities, equal pay, the Africanization of black universities and the release of political prisoners.[9] At the end of this unruly meeting, Chief Buthelezi handed copies of a memorandum to the press saying that unless there were meaningful changes in South Africa's race policies, "civil disobedience and disruption of services" would come as a "logical alternative."

## Unyielding Separatism of Rhodesia's Whites

It was the flamboyant developer, Cecil Rhodes, who obtained mineral rights in Rhodesia from several Matabele chiefs in the 1880s. Chief Lobengula, a Matabele leader, signed a treaty in 1888 making his territory a British sphere of influence. The British South Africa Company, organized by Rhodes, occupied the territory in 1890 and granted land to the British settlers. Several native rebellions were crushed during the first decade. In 1922 the white Rhodesians voted against joining the Union of South Africa and the next year, on the partititon of Rhodesia, the southern half of the country became a self-governing colony with its own parliament and its own police force and army.[10] Although British policy was to work through the Salisbury government for a gradual transition to majority rule, it was a policy that was successfully sabotaged by the whites.

---

*"The Rhodesian white man fears racial discrimination and humiliation in reverse."*

Rev. Ndabiningi Sithole
African National Council

---

The persistent intent of the white settlers was to keep the black Rhodesians disenfranciced. There was never a racial exclusion act as such, but the literacy and property qualifications for voting fixed by the 1898 constitution had the effect of barring from the polls all but the top stratum of blacks. In 1912 the property and income qualifications were doubled, and a policy of periodically raising the requirements for voting was continued. By 1939 only 70 of the 28,000 voters in Rhodesia were black.

[9] "Louder Voices," *The Economist*, Feb. 1, 1975, p. 38.
[10] Martin Loney, *Rhodesia* (1975), p. 15.

Demonstrations by the Rhodesian blacks against racial discrimination led in the 1950s to a policy of "racial partnership." The 1961 constitution allocated 15 seats out of a total of 65 to Africans. The British government professed a desire to achieve an accommodation with the moderate black politicians and looked to changes in the constitution as a means of effecting a stable transition to black rule within 15 years. However, this prospect gravely disturbed the white settlers and precipitated a Unilateral Declaration of Independence (UDI) in 1965.[11] Although the United Kingdom never recognized the declaration, and the United Nations imposed economic sanctions against the illegal regime, aid from both Portugal and South Africa helped Rhodesia to maintain its stand.

After UDI, the whites under the leadership of Ian Smith passed a Law and Order Act which enabled the Rhodesian Front government to prohibit meetings, imprison many of the nationalist leaders, and take other action leading to such comprehensive repression and intimidation that the African population was left with no legal channel for organized expression of its discontent. The discrimination by the whites was carried so far that communication between the races was virtually halted. As the ANC leader Ndabiningi Sithole wrote in *The Times* of London (Feb. 11, 1975): "The thought of African rule in Rhodesia scares the European out of his senses....He fears that the African might treat the European as the European has treated the African during the past 80 years. In other words, the Rhodesian white man fears racial discrimination and humiliation in reverse."

---

# Prospects for Peaceful Transition

---

THE RAPID decolonization of Africa in the late 1950s and early 1960s was generally peaceful. Only in the Portuguese colonies of Angola and Mozambique were there prolonged guerrilla struggles. Now, as independence comes to Portuguese Africa, conditions in Rhodesia and South Africa will attract more attention in the United Nations and in Afro-Asian councils. However, as *The Economist* has pointed out, the very size of the white population in South Africa (3,751,000 in 1970) will have to be taken into account. Either the whites there will be offered a

[11] C. Palley, *The Constitutional History and Law of Southern Rhodesia (1886-1965)*, p. 316. Northern Rhodesia or Zambia, under the leadership of Kenneth D. Kaunda, had become an independent republic within the British Commonwealth in 1964.

prospect of change gradual enough to persuade them of the benefits of cooperation, or there will be risk of armed conflict that might spread to all of southern Africa.

Although South Africa with its apartheid policies may be regarded by the rest of the world as an unjust society, economically and militarily the republic towers over its neighbors. It produces about three-fourths of the entire industrial product of the African continent. And while the overwhelming power of its white population will inevitably be a nagging problem to the black states, it is in the context of that strength that the region's relations may well have to be resolved.[12]

## Political Challenge by South African Reformers

Alan Paton, the South African novelist, has remarked that the only hope for evolutionary change in South Africa would seem to lie with the Afrikaner community. While the determination of the white supremacists to retain power is clear, the republic is not the monolith that it often appears to be from the outside. Among the nationalist majority are the *verkramptes* (or narrow ones), who believe that one concession can only lead to another and is thus to be avoided, and the *verligtes* (or enlightened ones) who would like to institute those changes which in the long run would give the whites a reasonable chance to survive as a culturally distinct and separate group. The *verligtes* insist that ways must be found to ameliorate the situation of the urban black population outside the homelands.

There is a growing movement under way to soften the impact of the most oppressive aspects of apartheid, which include widespread search without a warrant, the lack of judicial review, indefinite detention without trial, and reversal of the onus of proof under which the accused must prove himself innocent.[13] Foreign Minister Hilgard Muller has said that "The government will not hesitate to do away with humiliating measures and practices which harm good relations between white and non-white and which have nothing to do with the maintenance of our own identity and sovereignty." The South African army announced on Dec. 9, 1974, that it was opening its ranks to black soldiers; they would be allowed to carry arms and would be paid the same as white soldiers.

In Capetown the Nico Malan Theater complex has been opened to blacks and coloreds as well as whites since last January 1975.

---

[12] According to the International Institute for Strategic Studies, South Africa has a defense budget of $750 million, an air force of about 100 combat fighters, 120 tanks and 1,050 armored cars. See *The Military Balance 1974-75*, p. 41. According to *The Washington Post* (March 30, 1975), the government's proposed 1975-76 defense budget is $1.5 billion.

[13] Alan Cook, "South Africa, the Imprisoned Society" (1974), p. 4.

In Pretoria the city council has agreed to allow blacks to drive municipal tractors and in Pietmaritzburg the city council has decided to invite representatives of the disenfranchised colored citizens to sit as non-voting members on the council and its standing committees. Black passengers traveling on South Africa's two luxury express trains may now use the dining cars and bars along with the whites. And while the Immorality Act still prohibits sexual intercourse between whites and members of other races, it is now very lightly enforced.[14]

It is thought that in order to quiet domestic and international protests over the next few years, the government will ease the hated pass-law system, may give leasehold rights to urban blacks, and might generally ease the restrictions applying to non-whites in urban areas. Black Africans will most likely be given the right to belong to trade unions and there will probably be a review of the status of political prisoners.

Chief M. Gatsha Buthelezi, the Zulu leader, wrote in the *Los Angeles Times*, March 27, 1975: "South Africa faces two critical choices now. The black areas can be properly consolidated, which would provide the basis for equitable federation with white South Africa. Or the black people can be given representation in Parliament as full participants in a single South Africa. I feel it is my moral duty to point out that these are the only logical alternatives we have if we do not want our people to resort to civil disobedience and disruption of services in this land."

### Blacks' Struggle for Majority Rule in Rhodesia

The Rhodesian settlement issue was placed in jeopardy on March 4, 1975, when Ndabaningi Sithole was arrested on charges of having planned the assassination of his opponents. The African National Council called off all further constitutional talks with the Rhodesian government until his release. Robert Mugabe, the secretary general of ZANU, said that Sithole's arrest had shattered the so-called détente. Mugabe said ZANU would "do nothing to interfere with the progress of guerrilla warfare in Rhodesia."

Last December the three black nationalist groups agreed to merge their differences in order to present a unified negotiating team for dealing with Ian Smith. However, the in-fighting within the new ANC was barely submerged. The ZANU militants have been pushing for "chimurenga"—armed confrontation. As *The Economist* said on Feb. 22: "Zanu's sights are firmly fixed on the leadership of Zimbabwe after independence, and it is

---

[14] Charles Mohr, "Government in South Africa Continues to Tighten Its Control over the People," *The New York Times*, Nov. 18, 1974 (part of a series which ran Nov. 17-20, 1974).

probably right in maintaining that the movement which fights for and succeeds in winning independence will gain the allegiance of the people."[15]

For the ANC, the new constitution for Zimbabwe must embrace swift progress to majority rule. The ZANU militants have demanded immediate majority rule as well as a socialist government with dramatic and radical changes including sweeping land reforms. "We do not want to just replace white faces with black faces. The system itself is unjust and needs to be changed," says Edison Zvogbo, the co-founder of ZANU.

Rhodesian whites are concerned that a timetable be organized which will foster an orderly transition of power. The president of the Centre Party, Pat Bashford, has asked that the ANC speak to whites about their future. "We know the ANC seeks political power," said Bashford, "but we have not the faintest idea of what they are going to do when they get it."[16]

Sithole, before being jailed, asserted that "African leaders on all levels accept the basic proposition that Zimbabwe is as much the white man's home as it is that of the black man." Sithole pointed out that without the diversified skills of the whites, Zimbabwe would be a much poorer country. From the African leader's point of view the glaring weakness of the present governmental structure is that Rhodesia's civil service is all white and that the blacks have had little experience with government. Some whites, such as Sir Roy Welensky, believe that blacks must be brought into the executive without delay so as to prepare them for the responsibilities of government. But this is clearly not the view of the majority of Rhodesian whites.

## Growing Economic Predominance of South Africa

South Africa is by far the richest state on the African continent. Its standard of living and its wages are higher than in any other African country. The average white wage is close to $600 a month and the average black wage is $100. South Africa has an immense potential for development. The *Swiss Review of World Affairs* has suggested that the country's economic growth should continue to blossom at a rate of up to 8 per cent a year.[17] With close to 75 per cent of the world's reserve of chromium, 60 per cent of all diamonds, 70 per cent of all platinum, and 30 per cent of the uranium discovered thus far, the republic has become an expansionist economic power.

---

[15] One of the difficulties facing the ANC is that the Chinese, who have supported ZANU with arms, training and money do not want to see the other groups, who have had Soviet backing, in power. Sino-Soviet rivalry has undoubtedly played a role in keeping the factions apart.

[16] David B. Ottaway, *The Washington Post*, Feb. 2, 1975.

[17] Peter Seidlitz, "South Africa's Lonely Economic Boom," *Swiss Review of World Affairs*, July 1974, p. 16.

The Republic of South Africa accounts for 80 per cent of the inter-regional trade in the vast section of Africa below the Zambesi River. A large part of Pretoria's interest in détente with its black neighbors concerns the threat to the labor supplies on which the operation of the mines depends. With its gold output alone worth close to $5 billion last year, the republic needs a guarantee of steady labor. Last year Malawi supplied 117,743 miners, Mozambique 84,752, and Lesotho 74,761. With South Africans currently making up only one-fourth of the pit workers, the threat to the republic's economy is clear.

---

*"The hopes and expectations of our people have been raised. This is the time to deliver the goods if we are to avert disaster for all of us."*

Chief M. Gatsha Buthelezi
Zulu leader

---

Although the Arab states have given vocal backing to black Africa, they have been primarily responsible for the gold boom, because much of the extra money flowing to them from the crude oil price increases has been invested in gold bullion from South Africa. Dr. Jan Marais, chairman of the board of the Trust Bank of Africa, has even said that "The Arabs have done us an enormous favour." South Africa is less dependent on oil imports than other industrial nations because it relies on coal-powered thermal reactors for much of its energy.

### Risks in a Failure of Black-White Negotiations

Whether there will be peaceful or revolutionary change in southern Africa to a great extent depends on South Africa's John Vorster and his effort to force his views on Rhodesia. If Pretoria could pressure the Rhodesian whites into accepting majority rule, *The Times* of London has commented, then "the black states might feel much more ready to deal with the Republic as a member, however aberrant, of the African community, and to accept the Afrikaners as a 'tribe' in African terms." But Sir Seretse Khama, the president of Botswana, said last November in opening his parliament: "Before there can be any prospect of a peaceful solution to the problems of this region... the white-ruled states should first demonstrate positively a willingness to change their racial policies. Without such commitment to change, violence will remain the only way to bring about change in white-ruled southern Africa."

American policy towards South Africa has been to encourage any positive developments and to work toward a non-violent resolution of the republic's racial problems. Private American firms, which have an investment of over $1 billion in South Africa, are being encouraged to maintain or expand enlightened employment practices. Since 1962 the United States has maintained a strict embargo on the sale or shipment of arms or military equipment to South Africa, and visits by the U.S. Navy have been banned.

In Rhodesia it is reported that Ian Smith may call South Africa's bluff by ignoring its threat to cut off aid and supplies. Smith is gambling on the fact that internal opposition in South Africa would prevent Vorster from following up on his threats. Neal Ascherson, reporting for *The Observer* from Salisbury on March 2, wrote that if the proposed constitutional conference fails or is called off, Smith is prepared to put forward a scheme to "provincialize" Rhodesia on the Swiss canton model. Rhodesia would be split into three "separate development" areas, two black and one white, under a nominated federal parliament.

However, events are almost certain to overtake any such division. The Rhodesian army and police, despite the recruitment of mercenaries abroad, are desperately short of manpower and it is known that both the army leaders and Smith's intelligence services are pressing him to a settlement. As difficult as eventual negotiations might be, there is a realization that if progress is not made, "the alternative," in Vorster's words, "is too ghastly to contemplate."

# Selected Bibliography

## Books

Ballinger, Margaret, *From Union to Apartheid*, Bailey Brothers & Swinfen, 1969.

Carson, Joel, *No Neutral Ground*, Crowell, 1974.

First, Ruth, Jonathan Steele and Christable Gurney, *The South African Connection*, The Penguin African Library, 1973.

Heribert, Adam, *Modernizing Racial Domination*, University of California Press, 1974.

Loney, Martin, *Rhodesia*, The Penguin African Library, 1975.

Sachs, Albie, *Justice in South Africa*, University of California Press, 1974.

Selby, John, *A Short History of South Africa*, George Allen & Unwin, 1973.

## Articles

"Angola: Free at Last," *Newsweek* (International Edition), Jan. 27, 1975.

Ascherson, Neal, "The Isolation of Ian Smith," *The Observer*, March 2, 1975.

Cotter, William R., "How Africa Is Short-Changed," *African Report*, November 1974.

Guelke, Adrian, "Vorster's Rhodesian Betrayal," *The New Statesman*, Jan. 24, 1975.

"Rhodesia: Infighting," *The Economist*, Feb. 22, 1975.

Seidlitz, Peter, "South Africa's Lonely Economic Boom," *Swiss Review of World Affairs*, July 1974.

Uys, Stanley, "Southern Africa—The Whirlwind of Change," *The Guardian*, Dec. 28, 1974.

"Vorster Can See It," *The Economist*, Dec. 21, 1974.

Younghusband, Peter, "The Afrikaner Spirit," *Newsweek*, April 29, 1974.

## Studies and Reports

Denver University, "Portugal and Africa: A New Day Dawns," Fall 1974.

*Editorial Research Reports*, "African Nation Building," 1973 Vol. I, pp. 355-372; "Political Turmoil in Southern Africa," 1963 Vol. I, pp. 385-403; "White Outposts in Southern Africa," 1966 Vol. II, pp. 805-824.

International Defense and Aid Fund: Cook, Allen, "South Africa, the Imprisoned Society" (1974); Sachs, Albie, "South Africa: the Violence of Apartheid" (1969); Sprack, John, "Rhodesia, South Africa's Sixth Province" (1974).

# ETHIOPIA IN TURMOIL

by

## David Boorstin

**1 9 7 4**
**Dec. 6**

# ETHIOPIA IN TURMOIL

T HE WORLD'S OLDEST Christian monarchy has come to an end. On Sept. 12, His Imperial Majesty Haile Selassie I, "Conquering Lion of the Tribe of Judah, Elect of God and King of the Kings of Ethiopia," was taken from his palace in a blue Volkswagen and put into army custody. The military decree that formally deposed him ended more than half a century of personal rule; it was the coda for three thousand years of Ethiopian history.

The creeping revolutionary coup by an anonymous group of low-ranking army officers began in February *(see chronology, p. 911)*. In fact, however, it was observed that the troubles began in October 1973, "when the full scale of the country's disastrous drought became apparent, followed by indisputable evidence that the old government was too corrupt and inefficient to save at least 100,000 Ethiopians from starving to death."[1] The drought brought starving refugees to the cities and inflated food prices, creating an economic and social crisis which led to demonstrations and prepared the way for militant action.

On Nov. 23, 59 former ministers, bureaucrats and intimates of the Emperor were executed, ostensibly for their role in the disaster. At least 140 others are expected to go on trial for their lives before a military tribunal from which there is no appeal. The 120-man Provisional Administrative Council now ruling the country under a shroud of secrecy named Brig. Gen. Tafari Benti as its chairman and figurehead ruler Nov. 28—just five days after his predecessor, the popular Lt. Gen. Aman Michael Andom, was killed at his home in a gun battle with troops sent to arrest him. The executions and the arrest of Gen. Aman[2] were said to have been instigated by 35-year-old Maj. Mengiste Haile Mariam, vice-chairman of the military government (or Dirg, as it is known in Ethiopia).

Major Mengiste, who received military training in the United States, was officially identified Nov. 17 as the man behind the

---

[1] Martin Walker, columnist for *The Guardian* specializing in African affairs, writing in *The New York Times,* May 19, 1974.

[2] Ethiopians are known by their first name; second and third names are usually those of the father.

163

coup. Yet very little is known about him, about the military council or about their plans for Ethiopia or for the 82-year-old Emperor who until recently personified his country. Reports in Lebanese newspapers on Nov. 27 that Haile Selassie's execution was imminent provoked an international storm of protest, in which the Organization for African Unity (OAU) joined. Haile Selassie was a founder of the OAU, and his personal style of diplomacy made him a world figure. He has since agreed to turn over his personal fortune abroad—reportedly in exchange for his life.

## Uncertain Course of the New Military Regime

Most observers had assumed all along that the armed forces held the key to Ethiopia's political future. But many had also assumed that Haile Selassie would retain virtually absolute powers until his death. What was surprising was the ease with which he was ousted. "Whatever happened to the bloodbath most diplomats had predicted? Where was the rioting by people who were said to be ready to fight tooth and nail to defend their divinely appointed monarch?" asked a correspondent for the Paris daily *Le Monde*.[3] Over a period of weeks and months the military had skillfully used radio, television and the press to destroy the popular image of Haile Selassie. They charged that he had tolerated and even fostered corruption in the interests of maintaining his authority and stashed away billions of dollars in foreign banks while peasants died of starvation.

Although speculation persists that Haile Selassie may make a comeback, the critical question is not whether he can regain power, but what course the military rulers will take. Having pulled down a regime whose foundations were deeply imbedded in Ethiopia's history and its culture, they appear uncertain what to put in its place. Showing that opposition will not be tolerated, they have moved against labor leaders, students and rival officers who pressed for a rapid return to civilian government. The military men have pledged to modernize their ancient country, but whether this goal can be achieved, and by what means, remains to be seen. Opinions within the Provisional Administrative Council range from those favoring the establishment of a military junta to those seeking the establishment of a People's Republic on the Chinese model. Haile Selassie had skillfully practiced the art of divide-and-rule, and the divisions within the military reflect those in the nation it now leads.

Whatever form the new government may take, the greatest challenge it faces is revising Ethiopia's archaic system of land

---

[3] Jean-Claude Guillebaud, *Le Monde* correspondent, in *The Manchester Guardian Weekly*, Sept. 28, 1974.

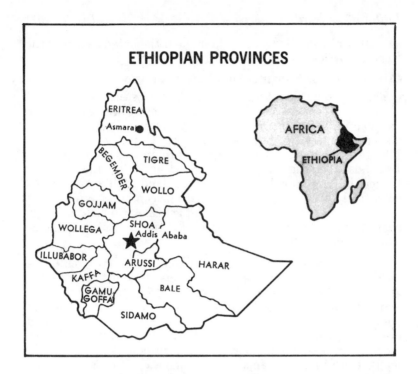

**ETHIOPIAN PROVINCES**

tenure. It has been said "The land tenure system is the foundation of Ethiopian society and the fundamental cause of its underdevelopment."[4] More than 85 per cent of Ethiopia's 25 million people are subsistence farmers. Their per capita income is extremely low even by the standards of other developing countries.[5] Agriculture accounts for about 55 to 60 per cent of the nation's Gross Domestic Product, one of the highest proportions in any country in the world.

Thus "even very rapid development of other sectors of the economy—industry, tourism, natural resources, 'commercial' agriculture—can have only a marginal effect for many years on the bulk of the Ethiopian population.... Dramatic national improvement cannot take place so long as an enormous and stagnant peasant agricultural sector is barely able to feed the country."[6] The modernization of Ethiopian agriculture is a prerequisite for national economic development and of importance to its neighbors as well, for Ethiopia has a rich

---

[4] John M. Cohen, "Ethiopia After Haile Selassie: The Government Land Factor," *African Affairs*, October 1973, p. 380.

[5] According to the World Bank, the Ethiopian figure of $80 a year makes it one of the world's 25 poorest nations and puts it on a par with Bangladesh, the Somali Republic, Zaire and Burma, and well below Nigeria ($140), Kenya ($160) and Algeria ($360). John M. Cohen reported that the annual growth rate in the agricultural sector is 2.4 per cent a year, "probably less than the overall population growth...."

[6] Harrison C. Dunning, "Land Reform in Ethiopia: A Case Study in Non-Development," UCLA *Law Review*, December 1970, pp. 294-295. Dunning spent several years teaching law at Haile Selassie I University, Addis Ababa.

agricultural potential that could make it the bread basket of the Horn of Africa and the Middle East.

## Crucial Issue of Bringing About Land Reform

The land tenure system is a formidable obstacle to change. It is one of the most complex in the world, so intricate and so variable in different areas as to defy systematic classification. Generally speaking, however, land rights fall geographically into two categories. The northern provinces (Eritrea, Tigre, Begemder, Gojjam, and parts of Shoa and Wollo) are characterized by communal tenures where land rights are shared collectively by residents of the parish or community. The right to a parcel of land often depends on genealogical claims of descent from a common ancestor. In the southern regions, sharecropping is the rule.

Agricultural tenancy exists throughout the country, but in the south it is more pronounced and onerous. Tenant farmers must give from one-third to one-half of their crops to the landowner and they also pay taxes. Since there is an overabundance of potential tenants, landowners are able to rent their land profitably and go to live in Addis Ababa, the capital.[7] Those landowners who remain have virtual autonomy on their own lands, controlling the appointment of local officials and often using retainers as private armies to enforce their control. Apart from moral questions raised by such an exploitative system, it creates serious economic problems.

Since farmers do not own their land under either communal or tenant systems, they cannot qualify for development loans requiring collateral. They rarely have any written agreement with those who own the land, and the general insecurity of their tenure is compounded by a lack of reliable land surveys and land records. The boundaries for their small holdings are uncertain, and they fear that an accurate survey might lead the state to seize any surplus. The prevalence of land litigation, in part the inevitable consequence of inadequate land records but also an activity valued for its own sake, is a further source of insecurity.[8]

It is frequently noted that the sharecropping system discourages innovation, since the Ethiopian peasant knows that to

---

[7] The proportion of total area held by absentee landlords in the southern provinces ranges from 12 to 48 per cent, and about half of the farmers are tenants. In Illubabor province, the proportion of tenants runs as high as 73 per cent.

[8] According to the official English-language paper, *The Ethiopian Herald,* July 21, 1974, "no less than four million Ethiopians crowd the nation's courts." Donald N. Levine noted in his book *Wax and Gold* (1965) the psychological and social importance of litigation among the Ethiopian people. He pointed out that while 27 high court judges were sufficient to handle the litigation for all of England and Wales, the corresponding number in Ethiopia was 118.

# Chronology of the Coup, 1974

**February**

18-24  Rioting and demonstrations in Addis Ababa over inflation, unemployment, and mismanagement of drought relief.

26  Army's 10,000-man 2nd Division seizes Asmara, nation's second largest city, to press demands for better pay and conditions and demand cabinet resignations.

27  Premier Akilou Habte Wold and 19 other ministers resign.

28  Haile Selassie names former U.N. Ambassador Endalkachew Makonnen new Prime Minister and raises army pay.

**March**

5  Haile Selassie agrees to call constitutional convention, seen as leading to creation of constitutional monarchy.

7  Confederation of Ethiopian Labor Unions (CELU), representing 80,000 to 100,000 members, calls nation's first general strike over wages and benefits.

11  Government agrees to act on CELU demands, ending strike; military mutiny continued by air force; riot police break up student demonstration.

**April**

8  Government announces program of reform, but military mutinies continue; strikes and protests multiply; and growing unrest, sometimes violent, spreads to countryside.

18  Acceding to Army pressure, Premier Endalkachew agrees to place under arrest former Cabinet ministers, pending trial for their role in the famine.

20  Fifty thousand Moslems demonstrate in Addis Ababa, demanding an end to religious discrimination.

26  Following Emperor's refusal to permit the arrests, police and armed forces units begin a series of raids, arresting more than 200 civilian and military officers.

**June**

15  Many officials banned from traveling abroad.

28  Army's 4th Division seizes virtual control of Addis Ababa and begins a new round of arrests of prominent persons.

**July**

9  Arrests continue, including some of Emperor's closest associates. Military issues manifesto reiterating its pledge of loyalty to the Emperor but calling for implementation of new constitution reducing him to a constitutional monarch.

12  Powerful Ras Mesfin Sileshi surrenders, removing important threat to revolutionaries.

17  Governor of Eritrea and mayor of its capital, Asmara, arrested; troops seize control.

24  Premier Endalkachew ousted by military, Michael Imru recalled from U.N. mission in Geneva to head new government.

**August**

1  Army announces arrest of ex-Premier Endalkachew and nine other prominent figures.

16  Armed forces stage impromptu military parade including some members of Imperial Bodyguard. Armed Forces Coordinating Committee abolishes Crown Council, Court of Justice and military committee. Newspapers publish unprecedented calls for

abolition of monarchy, and more of Emperor's closest associates are arrested.

24  Premier Imru accedes to AFCC demand for cabinet reshuffle.
25  AFCC announces nationalization of Emperor's residence in capital and other estates throughout the country.
27  Haile Selassie placed under house arrest; report by special civilian commission implicates him in cover-up of drought disaster.

**September**
 2  First public demonstrations against the Emperor; others follow Sept. 8.
11  Church Patriarch Abuna Twoflos abandons Haile Selassie, does not mention him in New Year's message, asking instead God's blessing on the revolutionary movement. AFCC denounces Emperor, charging in broadcasts that he secreted billions of dollars in foreign banks in the names of his two children; arrests Emperor's daughter and seizes her palace.
12  Haile Selassie peacefully deposed, removed from palace. Provisional military government announced under Lt. Gen. Aman Michael Andom, designated spokesman for AFCC. Parliament dissolved, constitution suspended, strikes and demonstrations banned.

**October**
 7  Rival military factions clash in capital.

**November**
17  Leader of coup named as Maj. Mengiste Haile Mariam; reports of power struggle within military.
22  Gen. Aman ousted from leadership of military government, put under house arrest.
23  Fifty-nine former high-ranking military and civilian officials executed; Gen. Aman killed in gun battle at his house.
27  Reports of pending execution of Haile Selassie; U.N. and many countries urge African nations to intercede with Ethiopian junta to save his life on humanitarian grounds.
28  Amid signs of increased fighting in Eritrea, the military government names Brig. Gen. Tafari Banti as chairman and figurehead.

**December**
 2  Bombs explode in Addis Ababa; though officially attributed to followers of old regime, suspected to be work of ELF terrorists responding to military's new hard line.

---

increase production is merely to increase his payments to the landowner. Ironically, projects aimed at increasing agricultural productivity through modern farming techniques have made many tenants worse off than before. The CADU[9] project in Chilalo sponsored by the Swedish government has shown formerly tradition-minded landowners that agriculture can be made profitable through modern methods. Consequently, they have evicted about 6,000 of their small tenants in order to engage in large-scale commercial farming or to rent their land

---

[9] Chilalo Agricultural Development Unit.

on long-term contracts with fixed high rents to other commercial farmers or to urban investors. The remaining tenants,
though able to produce more, are also charged higher rents.[10]

## Haile Selassie's Gifts of Land to Stabilize Power

Although there have been changes in land tenure, they rarely
have been reforms aimed at promoting economic development
and social justice. More often they were intended to improve
government tax resources or to reward various groups for
loyalty and support. As his predecessors had done, Haile
Selassie allocated government land to supporters who, in turn,
acquired a vested interest in maintaining the status quo. "The
story is one of studies, plans, and new governmental agencies,
not one of implementation."[11] Legislation was defeated in the
Ethiopian parliament, most of whose members were conservative local nobles and landowners.

The landholding families, together with the Ethiopian Orthodox Church and the imperial family, own a majority of the land
in Ethiopia—by one "reasonable estimate," 55 per cent.[12] The
government owns most of the rest. Estimates of government-
held lands vary, but according to one study these amount to 46.6
per cent of the total area of Ethiopia and 11.8 per cent of the
arable land. This means as many as 25 million acres of arable
government land are available for granting to private individuals—an area roughly the size of Kentucky.[13]

In a country where land represents not only livelihood but
social and political power, this huge land bank amounts to a formidable weapon. Haile Selassie used it skillfully, increasing his
gifts of land as his need for political support grew. Even when
his land grants took the form of social programs aimed at helping landless peasants, the complexities of administering the land
grant system tended to ensure that those who received land were
gentry, civil servants and influential military or police officers.

Hence, the problem of land reform in Ethiopia is much more
than simply redistributing a national resource. In recent years
an increasing number of military and bureaucratic personnel
have been tied into the system through government land grants,
and since social and political power and land-ownership have
long been inextricably connected, land reforms are bound to be
vigorously resisted by those in a position to implement them.

---

[10] John M. Cohen, "Land Reform in Ethiopia," paper presented at the 16th Annual
Conference of the African Studies Association, at Syracuse University in 1973.

[11] Dunning, *op. cit.*, p. 271.

[12] Patrick Gilkes, "The Coming Struggle for Ethiopia," *Africa Report*, May-June 1974, p.
33.

[13] The figures are from studies done for the Ethiopian Ministry of Land Reform and Administration, cited by Cohen in "Ethiopia After Haile Selassie," pp. 371-372.

Even if the central government commits itself to a definite program of peasant land grants and tenancy reforms, implementing and enforcing such a program throughout the countryside will remain an awesome task.

## Armed Forces as Catalyst of Change in Society

While the army was crucial in upholding the old regime, few observers were surprised it was also the instrument of the downfall. "The army has already seized power in some dozen African states, most of them with much smaller military establishments than Ethiopia's," Christopher Clapham noted in 1969. "The possibility of an army takeover is therefore at least a very strong one...and many officers in the armed forces seem to be aware of its potentialities."[14] The military provided the only serious threats to Haile Selassie's power after a 1960 coup attempt, and the success of their demands for higher pay in 1961 and 1964 demonstrated their political power. Income has long been a source of dissatisfaction among enlisted personnel, although the Emperor tried to ensure the loyalty of their superiors by granting them substantial salaries, favors and gifts.

Ethiopians have a strong military tradition, and the armed forces have enjoyed heightened prestige as a result of their efforts to defend the country and later liberate it from the Italians, and more recently to protect it from Somali incursions *(see p. 923)*. Through contact with European and American military instructors in Ethiopia, and through training abroad and service with the United Nations military missions in Korea and the Congo, the Ethiopian armed forces have had exposure to Western influences.[15] Relative to the church, the nobility and the provincial landowners, military officers represent a more educated and socially mobile elite: for several years in the late 1950s and early 1960s the top secondary-school graduates were conscripted directly into the Harar Military Academy, Ethiopia's West Point.

Yet the armed forces are anything but unified. They suffer from the divisive forces of conflicting family, regional and educational loyalties at work in Ethiopian society as a whole. As he did with other powerful groups, the emperor skillfully fostered these differences and played factions against each other to secure his own position. The older and more senior officers who fought the Italians or went into exile during the late 1930s are generally more conservative, and many of them are substan-

---

[14] Christopher Clapham, *Haile-Selassie's Government* (1969), p. 191.
[15] The preponderant foreign influence has been American and Israeli. The United States has equipped the army, and Israel has helped especially with counter-insurgency training. British, Indian, Swedish and Norwegian missions have also been involved with military programs in Ethiopia.

tial landowners. They are not trusted by the junior officers (majors and below) who now form the provisional military government. The killing of General Aman and some of his supporters was the result of a power struggle in which senior officers were reportedly trying to supplant the subalterns who engineered the actual deposition of the Emperor.

Dissension within the armed forces, and more particularly the Provisional Administrative Council, now centers on the question of how Ethiopia should be ruled. The air force is thought to take the most radical stance. Its 2,250 men (compared with the army's 41,000) are an elite group due to their long contact with foreign personnel and their high levels of education and technological expertise. They also have had contact with students at Haile Selassie I University where air force personnel attend courses.

The students, though similarly divided, are reported generally to be assuming an increasingly anti-military tone. This is partially in response to a military ruling that some university students and teachers be sent to the provinces to help carry out a national program of education and social reform. Some view this as an excuse to get "radical" students—those favoring a quick return to civilian government—out of the capital. It could, however, have a significant effect if the students were to succeed in persuading peasants to defy their landlords when the crops are in and rent is due.

---

# Rise and Rule of Ethiopia's Empire

---

THE ROYAL LINE which was deposed Sept. 12 goes back, at least in legend, to biblical times. The story of the Queen of Sheba's visit to the court of Solomon in Jerusalem is referred to in the First Book of Kings (X, 1-13) and is repeated in the Second Book of Chronicles (IX, 1-12). According to Ethiopian legend, Solomon tricked her into sleeping with him, and the offspring was a son who became Menelik I, first king in the Solomonid line from which the world's oldest Christian monarchy is descended.[16]

Even discounting such legendary beginnings, the Ethiopian state can be traced back some 2,000 years to the time when Semitic peoples from Southern Arabia, who had settled trading

---

[16] Article 2 of the revised Constitution of Ethiopia published in 1955 stipulated: "The Imperial Dignity shall remain perpetually attached to the line of Haile Selassie I,...whose line descends without interruption from the dynasty of Menelik I, son of the Queen of Ethiopia, the Queen of Sheba, and King Solomon of Jerusalem." Thus legal endorsement was given to a myth which had played an important part throughout Ethiopian history.

posts along the Red Sea coast of what is now Eritrea, spread inland and asserted their rule over the local people. These immigrants were of diverse origin: one group, the Yemeni Habashat (Arabic Habashah) gave the country its ancient name Abyssinia; another group gave its name to the ancient language Geez, still used as the liturgical language of the Ethiopian Orthodox Church and the root of modern Amharic, the country's first language today.[17] The various immigrant groups, each with its own prince *(negash)*, were gradually federated under the ruler of Aksum, who styled himself *negusa nagasht,* or "king of kings." He was the first Ethiopian Emperor.

This highland city-state grew to dominate the whole north, and even controlled part of southern Arabia. Its Red Sea ports lay along the route from India to the Mediterranean and Aksum flourished, thanks to its strategic importance to both the Roman (later Byzantine) and Persian empires. The height of its glory was reflected in the mammoth stelae (cylindrical pillars) erected in the 3rd or 4th century A.D.[18] At about that time two Syrian youths, both Christians, were shipwrecked on the Ethiopian coast and were taken to the Aksumite king. Through him they spread their faith among the ruling classes. One of the two, later St. Frumentius, was consecrated by the Bishop of Alexandria and became the first Archbishop of Aksum around 350 A.D. Thus Ethiopia was one of the first Christian countries, a fact which has had considerable importance in its relations with the West.

The Aksumite empire ebbed in the 6th and 7th centuries, as trade declined with the expansion of Persian influence and later, more significantly, with the rise of Islam and its holy wars. Cut off from the Red Sea, the Ethiopian state turned south toward the African interior, from the Aksumite heartland of Tigre to Gojjam, Shoa (now the nation's center) and beyond. For almost a thousand years the isolated Ethiopian state periodically flourished and declined, its fortunes tied to the varying strengths of its central rulers and incursions by Galla tribesmen from the south and Moslems from the north and east. With Portugese help the Moslems were defeated but, exhausted by the struggle and by internecine rivalries, the state did not recover until the late 19th century. The Emperors Tewodros II and Yohannes IV then overthrew the Galla chiefs and began to reassert their central power over the feudal princes.

---

[17] Many languages are used in Ethiopia, including about 70 different dialects of Semitic, Hamitic, Nilotic and Bantu origin. As in other African countries this situation contributes to the nation's disunity. The Ethiopian Broadcasting Services, which claim to reach over 9.6 million Ethiopians, broadcasts in nine languages including English (the second official language, used in higher education), French and Arabic.

[18] They rose to a hundred feet and weighed four to five hundred tons. Some of them still stand.

The foundations of the modern Ethiopian state were laid by Emperor Menelik II, crowned in 1889. He faced a new external threat, for the opening of the Suez Canal in 1869 had reestablished the importance of the Red Sea route to India and the European powers were competing for strategic footholds there. Britain and France established themselves in Somaliland, and Italy soon came into conflict with Ethiopia. By decisively defeating the Italians at the Battle of Adowa in 1896 Menelik preserved his country's independence during the European "Scramble for Africa." Apart from Eritrea, which was left to Italy, the country's borders were made virtually what they are today.

## Expansion and Avoidance of Colonial Domination

Like a predecessor, Tewodros II, Menelik sought to modernize his country and succeeded in more than doubling its area. The ancient territory of Abyssinia covered the present-day provinces of Tigre, Begemder, Gojjam, and parts of Shoa and Wollo. Menelik's conquests (which began even before he became emperor, as he expanded the southern kingdom Shoa of which he was *negus*) added the remaining provinces of Wollega, Harar, Gemu Goffa, Bale, Arussi, Illubabor, Kaffa and Sidamo, as well as parts of Shoa and Wollo. The imperial capital was moved south to Menelik's new seat in Shoa, Addis Ababa.

This process of expansion led to many of Ethiopia's present problems, for the conquering Abyssinians were of two geographical and linguistic groups, the Amhara and the Tigre. Those conquered included a number of groups, most importantly the Galla. "What happened in the process of territorial expansion is that the Amhara and Tigre people became at the same time a minority group and the holders of suzerainty over a vast collection of peoples who did not share the Abyssinians' living tradition and who were not Christians but pagans or Moslems."[19] Colonization took place not under a Western power but under the Abyssinians, and in particular the Amhara, who sought to impose their language and culture throughout the country and to this day have largely maintained their elite status.

These conquests also led to the establishment of the onerous system of land tenure which now blocks Ethiopia's development. Conquered territory was confiscated by the crown and divided along feudal lines among local chiefs, the church, and powerful northerners who irresponsibly ruled both the land and people.[20]

---

[19] John M. Cohen, "Peasant Production in Ethiopia," paper presented to the Colloquium on Ethiopia, State Department, Washington, D.C., 1974.

[20] Menelik's expansionist policy remains a political issue today, especially in the Somali Republic which disputes the Ethiopian borders. He is still sometimes labeled a "black imperialist."

By preserving and extending the territories of ancient Ethiopia, by restoring order and imposing his rule—however imperfectly—over the local nobles, Menelik laid the foundations of a modern unitary state. Yet his policies also created obstacles to further development which, it is now clear, outlasted the Ethiopian monarchy.

### Haile Selassie's Path to Power Six Decades Ago

Haile Selassie himself deposed a ruler—although unlike the recent coup, his had many precedents in Ethiopian history. In August 1907 the Emperor Menelik II suffered a stroke; by 1909 he was a helpless invalid and remained so until his death in 1913. Having no sons, he named as heir his grandson Lij Eyasu, son of the ruler of Wollo, Ras Mikael. A former Moslem, Ras Mikael had support from the leaders of other northern privinces as well as the allegiance of many of the vast number of Galla and Moslem subjects in the newly expanded empire. The Shoan noblemen feared Eyasu's ascendancy, for through his father's connections he was capable of uniting the Moslem and Galla peoples and returning power to the north. The powerful Ethiopian Church also feared his religious leanings towards Islam, and the Italian, French and British governments viewed with alarm a possible Ethiopian alliance with Moslem Turkey and its German ally.

Discontent grew as Eyasu built mosques and made a series of matrimonial alliances with influential Moslem leaders. At the urging of Shoan noblemen and after some hesitation, Archbishop Abune Mattheos, on Sept. 27, 1916, excommunicated Lij Eyasu and confirmed their proclamation making Menelik II's daughter Zauditu the new Empress and young Tafari Makonnen, son of the Duke of Harar, Regent of Ethiopia with the title of Ras. It was not the first or last time that the church played a deciding role in the nation's power struggles. After a period of fierce fighting, Zauditu was crowned Empress on Feb. 11, 1917. Ras Tafari Makonnen, later to become Emperor Haile Selassie I, became Regent of Ethiopia and heir presumptive to the throne at the age of 25. By then he had already served as governor-general of two provinces where he had established a reputation as a progressive.[21]

Tafari's youth and modernistic tendencies did not sit well with many of those in authority, and he had to rule in concert with several elder statesmen. He gradually secured his position, however, and by 1924 was confident enough to take an extensive foreign tour through Europe and the Middle East. He created a sensation, not only because of the style in which he traveled (his

---

[21] See Richard Greenfield's *Ethiopia: A New Political History* (1965).

entourage included a private zoo) but because he stressed Ethiopia's need for modernization with European help. While his concerns were real, it has been noted that this trip also laid the foundations for the Western view of him as a committed reformer, a view which persisted long after it was justified by the facts.

In 1926 the death of two powerful figures, the archbishop and the minister of war, enabled Tafari to further tighten his control and take command of the imperial armed forces. The conservative nobles, uneasy at his attempts to curb their powers and slave traffic,[22] staged an unsuccessful coup. Having repulsed his foes, Tafari was strong enough to demand the title of Negus (king) from Empress Zauditu and assume complete control over the central government. He was crowned in October 1928. In the spring of 1930, the 54-year-old empress died unexpectedly—and rather mysteriously, although accounts differ. The regent assumed power and was crowned emperor amid sumptuous celebrations on Nov. 2, 1930, taking the name Haile Selassie, meaning "Power of the Trinity."

As emperor he continued to pursue the twin policies of centralization and modernization in the face of considerable opposition from the provincial lords. One of his first actions in 1931 was to grant the people their first constitution, although its importance, like that of the Senate and Chamber of Deputies it established, was more symbolic than practical. Progress was achieved in customs and tax administration, public works and organization of the police and military.

## Italian Conquest, Restoration and 1960 Uprising

Soon afterward fascist Italy began to eye Ethiopia as a suitable country for conquest. Haile Selassie appealed to the rest of the world for help but none was forthcoming. The Italian invasion took place in 1935 without a formal declaration of war. Ethiopians united against the invaders but were overwhelmed by superior weapons and poison gas. Haile Selassie went into exile in May 1936, stopping at Geneva to deliver to the League of Nations a remonstrance and an unforgettable warning: "It is us today. It will be you tomorrow."

During the Italian occupation (1936-41) Ethiopia was annexed and joined to Eritrea and Italian Somaliland to form Italian East Africa. This brief period was the only portion of recorded Ethiopian history during which the country lost its independence. Early in World War II British armies routed Italian forces in North Africa, and Haile Selassie re-entered Addis

---

[22] The latter in cooperation with the League of Nations which Ethiopia had joined in 1923.

Ababa on May 5, 1941—five years to the day after Italian troops had marched into the city. Little had changed in his absence. "Overall, the effects of the occupation on the central government seem to have been surprisingly slight. The emperor continued, more or less, where he had left off in 1936, with the same personal supremacy, very similar gradually modernizing policies, and much the same group of officials...."[23] In the postwar period he skillfully achieved his goal of undermining the authority of provincial lords and centralizing government. By modernizing the military, the tax system, and provincial administration he stripped the nobility of their most important powers.[24]

Haile Selassie succeeded in creating a "new nobility" of high-level bureaucrats who were responsible to him and whose powers were in direct ratio to their access to his ear. Although many of these new dignitaries were members of the old nobility who were absorbed into the new political organization, others were recruited according to their loyalty and ability. Some were from the lower classes, or collaborators whose past made them dependent on his good will. He prevented this new elite from gaining autonomous power by the process of *shum-shir*—periodically reshuffling assignments to prevent any official from acquiring a significant following. He further forestalled challenges to his own authority by creating a calculated balance of disunities. In addition to fostering traditional divisions, he played on the rivalries between those who had fought in the resistance and those who had collaborated.

These political machinations, however, appear to have had only a marginal effect on the condition of most of the Ethiopian people. "The two decades which followed the Restoration in Ethiopia saw Haile Selassie's personal power much enhanced but they will probably be remembered more for what did not happen than for what did."[25] Conditions were growing ripe for political change, however.

Haile Selassie had encouraged the growth of secular education at home and abroad in order to train his new elite of bureaucrats, but the effect proved revolutionary. American-educated intellectual Girmame Neway, together with his brother Mengistu who commanded the Imperial Bodyguard, organized a coup d'etat in December 1960 when the emperor was

---

[23] Clapham, *op. cit.*, p. 20.
[24] Donald N. Levine, *Wax and Gold* (1965), p. 180. In the armed forces as in other powerful institutions, however, the nobility continued to play an important role: a recent survey showed that 21 per cent of the cadets at Harar Military Academy were from aristocratic families. Provincial authorities, although employees of the central government, frequently remained the noblemen who had traditionally ruled the same area.
[25] Greenfield, *op. cit.*, p. 312.

on a state visit to Brazil. The coup failed in a matter of days, at an estimated cost of 1,000 lives, and Haile Selassie returned to a tumultuous welcome. The attempt and the causes of its failure were significant, however: the regime had underestimated the forces of change, and the revolutionaries underestimated the abiding power of traditional authority.[26] Girmame Neway committed suicide, but his brother Mengistu, sentenced to be hanged, said: "I go to tell the others that the seed we set has taken root."

The palace revolution, which sought not merely to displace a ruler but to remold the whole system and motivation of government, was a landmark in Ethiopian history. It "gave a short and violent jolt to the even uneventfulness of Ethiopian politics, and left a drastically changed situation in its wake."[27] It showed that although Haile Selassie had been the procreator of much of the demand for modernization, this demand had become self-sustaining in at least a small segment of the population.

# Problems and Prospects of a New State

ETHIOPIA'S NEW rulers will have to cope with the problems of the present as well as those of the past. They must quell dissidence among the nation's 18,000 teachers and 3,000 university students who at first cheered the coup but now fear the establishment of a military regime as authoritative as the one that has been displaced. And while the drought which triggered the recent events has eased, the government has said that additional food aid is needed this year.

Relief efforts in Eritrea province have been hindered by a continuing insurgency there. Discontent in Eritrea is the new regime's most pressing problem. Since 1889, Eritrea has been successively an Italian colony, a British-administered territory, a U.N.-sponsored semi-autonomous federated state and, beginning in 1962, a province of Ethiopia. Their distinct history has led some Eritreans to see themselves as a separate and culturally superior group. "From the eighth century down to the present, wars of religion have seen Eritrea pass back and forth between Ethiopian Christian and Arab Moslem rule....The 1.6

---

[26] According to eyewitness accounts cited in *The New York Times*, soldiers of the Imperial Bodyguard "fell to their knees when they saw the old monarch, kissed his shoes and, in tears, surrendered their sub-machine guns to him."

[27] Clapham, *op. cit.*, p. 25. In the closing moments of the coup the rebels machine-gunned a group of Cabinet ministers, thus offering a grisly precedent for the Nov. 23 killings.

## America's Interest in Ethiopia

Ethiopia's lack of colonial ties to European countries made   an early favorite of President Truman's Point Four program. Since 1952, the United States has spent some $350 million on economic assistance and $200 million on military assistance to Ethiopia. An important U.S. Army communications base in Asmara, Eritrea, was established during World War II and gave the United States a strategic interest in Ethiopian affairs. With the development of communication satellites, the base's significance has recently decreased. According to the State Department, fewer than 100 Americans are now stationed at the base.

In 1974, Ethiopia received about $20 million in non-military assistance and $17 million in drought relief, mostly food grain. Projected 1975 figures are approximately $30 million in economic assistance and non-food aid, and about $4 million in food assistance. Military aid in 1974 took the form of an $11.3 million grant and $11 million in credit sales of military equipment. In addition, $4 million to $5 million in military equipment was purchased for cash. Requested but not yet appropriated for 1975 are $11 million in a military aid grant and $5 million in credit. State Department has announced that all aid programs are now under review.

million inhabitants of the province are Christian and Moslem in nearly equal proportion, and Arab nationalisms have sought to detach the Moslem half of the province from Ethiopian loyalties."[28]

For the last four years a state of emergency has existed. The predominantly Moslem Eritrean Liberation Front (ELF), with about 4,000 men trained in Arab countries, has been waging guerrilla war against the government and the armed forces. The former governor of Tigre province, Ras Mengasha, one of the few surviving members of the nobility, is reported to have fled to Sudan and held talks with Eritrean guerrilla leaders. It is possible that Mengasha, who some Ethiopians believe has a better claim to the throne than Haile Selassie, may attempt to form an alliance with the ELF and challenge the military regime.[29]

In his brief period in power General Aman, an Eritrean himself, had suggested negotiations with the ELF. His ouster was seen as a sign that the military government now intends to take a hard line against the rebels. The ELF calls for nothing less than total independence for Eritrea, while the government is

---

[28] John Franklin Campbell, "Rumblings Along the Red Sea: The Eritrean Question," *Foreign Affairs*, April 1970, p. 539.
[29] *The New York Times*, Nov. 29, 1974.

clearly unwilling to allow the country's coast line and its two ports to disappear.[30]

Another long-standing territorial dispute exists with the Somali Republic, which claims sovereignty over the nomadic Somalis who populate much of eastern Ethiopia. Tensions caused by ill-defined boundaries in the arid eastern regions have been exacerbated recently by exploration for oil there. In the past Ethiopia has voiced fears of an invasion by the Somali Republic in making requests for increased amounts of U.S. military aid. At the moment the Somali Republic seems to be content to let events in Ethiopia take their course, and its restraint at a time when the Ethiopian armed forces are in a low state of combat-readiness has led to skepticism in diplomatic circles about the alleged threat.

## Continuing Significance of the Ethiopian Church

The Ethiopian Orthodox Church has been at the center of the nation's life since the fourth century. Since 1959 it has been fully independent from the Coptic church in Egypt from which it had always taken its archbishop; that year the Ethiopian archbishopric was raised to a patriarchate. Although the Ethiopian Church shares the general characteristics of Eastern churches, it also observes several customs of Jewish origin: circumcision is universally practiced, the Sabbath is kept, and the ark is an essential feature in every church. It is generally estimated that 35 to 40 per cent of the population is Christian, at least an equal number is Moslem, and the rest animist. As the established state religion the church has been reluctant to allow religious data to be collected, but its hold is said to have declined in recent years while the power of Islam and spirit-possession cults has grown.

The church has maintained a strong conservative influence, especially in the provinces. It owns about 5 per cent of the country's total land and 20 per cent of the arable land, from which it is entitled to draw considerable income and tax revenue. Its strong support of the traditional foundations of Ethiopian society made the patriarch's abandonment of Haile Selassie in his Sept. 11 New Year's message[31] *(see chronology)* all the more striking. Though the church has not played kingmaker, it has several times in Ethiopian history played the scarcely less important role of king-confirmer.

The Eritrean problem and the complaints of Moslem Ethiopians are far from being the only disunifying factors that

---

[30] As in other guerrilla wars, the Eritrean conflict has prompted reports of atrocities on both sides. The Eritrean deputies in the Ethiopian parliament resigned en masse on Aug. 16 in protest of an alleged massacre of civilians by Ethiopian troops in July.

[31] The Ethiopian calendar is based on the old Julian calendar.

will hinder attempts to modernize the country. In the long term, the southern Galla groups, who constitute about half of the population, may present an even more serious threat.

It is said that even among student activists, ethnicity often provokes disunity. In this respect the absence of foreign colonial rule has been portrayed as a source of difficulty for Ethiopia in its quest for modernity. Colonial rulers provided some other countries with the basis for modern government. In addition to building up communications and importing institutions to facilitate their own rule, colonialists often broke down traditional social groups and ways of life and provoked national unity through native efforts to drive them out. Although the new rulers can hope to take advantage of Ethiopia's claim to being Africa's oldest and most independent unitary state, they must also overcome the geographically and culturally centrifugal forces which have for so long made progressive government an impossibility.

## Selected Bibliography

### Books

Clapham, Christopher, *Haile-Selassie's Government*, Longmans, Green & Co. Ltd., 1969.
Greenfield, Richard, *Ethiopia: A New Political History*, Praeger, 1965.
Levine, Donald N., *Wax and Gold: Tradition and Innovation in Ethiopian Culture*, University of Chicago Press, 1965.

### Articles

Campbell, John Franklin, "Rumblings Along the Red Sea: The Eritrean Question," *Foreign Affairs*, April 1970.
Cohen, John M., "Ethiopia After Haile Selassie: The Government Land Factor," *African Affairs*, October 1973.
Dimbleby, Jonathan, "The End of the Lion's Empire," *The New Statesman*, Oct. 18, 1974.
Dunning, Harrison C., "Land Reform in Ethiopia: A Case Study in Non-Development," UCLA *Law Review*, December 1970.
*The Ethiopian Herald*, selected issues.
Gilkes, Patrick, "The Coming Struggle for Ethiopia," *Africa Report*, May-June 1974.

### Studies and Reports

Cohen, John M., "Pleasant Production in Ethiopia: Social and Institutional Constraints to Rural Change," paper presented to the Colloquium on Ethiopia, U.S. State Department, 1974.
Editorial Research Reports, "African Nation Building," 1973 Vol. I, p. 355.
Koehn, Peter, "Forecast for Political Change in Ethiopia: An Urban Perspective," paper presented to the 16th Annual Conference of the African Studies Association, Syracuse University, 1973.

# INDIA UNDER AUTHORITARIAN RULE

by

## Marc Leepson

**June 11**
**1 9 7 6**

# INDIA UNDER AUTHORITARIAN RULE

A YEAR AGO, on June 26, 1975, Prime Minister Indira Gandhi of India declared a state of internal emergency during the height of an intense political crisis. In so doing, she ordered the arrest of hundreds of Indian citizens, suspended civil liberties and imposed strict censorship on the press. Although Mrs. Gandhi in her official message to the nation expressed hope that a speedy improvement of "internal conditions" would allow her to revoke the emergency proclamation "as soon as possible," the decree remains in effect today.

The measures enacted under the emergency have markedly changed the system of government in the world's largest democracy, and they raised questions as to whether the word "democracy" still applies. There are two basic—and conflicting—explanations of the reasons for the emergency proclamation. There is Prime Minister Gandhi's. She said she invoked national emergency powers—powers granted to the government under the Indian constitution—to preserve internal order and save the nation from chaos. Then there are her critics who say she took the step not to save India but to save her own political life.

Mrs. Gandhi faced a deepening political crisis on the eve of the emergency proclamation. The night before it was announced, 72-year-old Jaya Prakash Narayan, a widely respected opposition leader and a former close associate of national heroes Mohandas K. Gandhi (no relation to Mrs. Gandhi) and Jawaharlal Nehru (Mrs. Gandhi's father), addressed thousands at a rally in New Delhi. J. P., as Narayan is known in India, called for a "total revolution" against Mrs. Gandhi, and demanded her resignation. The coalescing of opposition strength behind J. P. started in 1974 during a period of economic and political troubles throughout India.

## Events Leading to Full Government Control

The immediate events that led to the emergency proclamation began on June 12, 1975, when Mrs. Gandhi was found guilty by the state High Court of Allahabad of "corrupt practices" during her campaign for parliamentary re-election in 1971. The specific offense was relatively minor: that on two occasions she used government workers to help in her campaign, constructing stages and setting up loudspeakers at a political rally in her home city of Allahabad.[1] Judge Jag Mohan Lal Sinha ordered Mrs. Gandhi to be barred from holding public office or from seeking office for six years. Execution of the order was delayed 20 days to give her time to appeal the decision to the Indian Supreme Court.

Mrs. Gandhi was cleared of 12 other charges including allegations that she exceeded the limit of campaign spending, that she used an Indian Air Force plane in her campaign, and that her supporters bribed voters. But her conviction on the two minor charges led opposition leaders and some members of Mrs. Gandhi's Congress Party to call publicly for her resignation. S. K. Patil, a former member of the Congress Party, said, "At long last, Mrs. Gandhi has met her Watergate. I am...delighted to see that law and justice have prevailed."[2]

But the Prime Minister did not resign. Instead, she took her case to the Supreme Court. Mrs. Gandhi presented her appeal to only one justice, V. R. Krishna Iyer, since the court was not in session at the time. Justice Iyer, whom she had appointed to the court, ruled on June 24, 1975, that she could remain in office, but he refused to allow her to participate in debates of Parliament. This decision, only a partial victory for Mrs. Gandhi, did not totally clear her of the charges, and her political opponents renewed their outcry for her immediate resignation.

## Western Reaction to Arrests and Censorship

The declaration of the emergency roused worldwide reaction. In the West, almost all of the public response was negative. Headlines and editorial comment decrying "the end of democracy" greeted the initial news and that which followed. On June 26, the government announced 676 arrests and the imposition of what a *New York Times* correspondent termed "the toughest press censorship in the 28 years since independence.[3]

Reports of the numbers arrested varied widely. By June 28, the government officially listed around 1,100 arrests. Those arrested were described as right-wing political opponents of Mrs. Gandhi, members of the Congress Party who opposed her, journalists, university students and teachers. Lewis M. Simons of *The Washington Post* reported that informed sources said the arrest total had reached 4,000.[4] Early in July the censored

---

[1] Mrs. Gandhi defeated her opponent, Socialist leader Raj Narain, by a vote of 183,309 to 71,499.

[2] Quoted in *The Washington Post*, June 13, 1975.

[3] James M. Markham in *The New York Times*, June 28, 1975.

[4] In *The Washington Post*, June 29, 1975. Simons, a resident correspondent in India for three years, was ordered to leave the country by the government on June 30, 1975, for his refusal to abide by the censorship regulations. He was the first foreign journalist expelled.

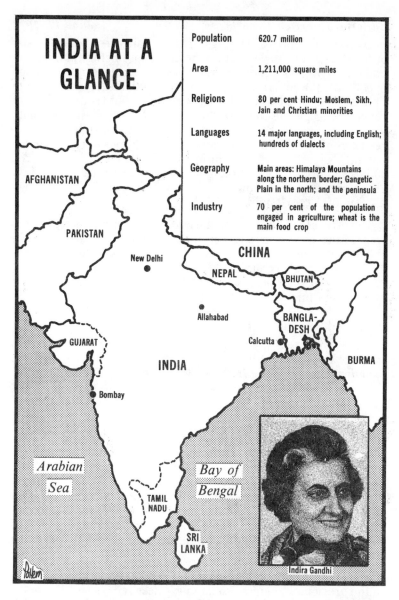

## INDIA AT A GLANCE

| | |
|---|---|
| Population | 620.7 million |
| Area | 1,211,000 square miles |
| Religions | 80 per cent Hindu; Moslem, Sikh, Jain and Christian minorities |
| Languages | 14 major languages, including English; hundreds of dialects |
| Geography | Main areas: Himalaya Mountains along the northern border; Gangetic Plain in the north; and the peninsula |
| Industry | 70 per cent of the population engaged in agriculture; wheat is the main food crop |

Indira Gandhi

Indian press reported more than 5,000 had been arrested, including 1,200 political opponents of the Gandhi administration. Mrs. Gandhi, addressing a group of business and labor leaders in New Delhi on July 12, said that three-fourths of those arrested were common criminals, smugglers, profiteers and hoarders. She termed the number of arrests "very meager" compared to India's population of over 600 million.

Once the emergency was decreed, foreign journalists were told to submit all stories to censorship except those based on two daily government press briefings. The Indian press was initially ordered to clear stories with official censors before publication and later was issued press "guidelines" by the government. Then on July 21, the government distributed guidelines for the foreign press. The new rules ended prior censorship but required foreign reporters to pledge they would not, among other things, quote opposition remarks in Parliament. At least three correspondents[5] refused to sign the pledge and were deported. Kuldip Nayer, a senior editor of the *Indian Express*, the country's largest English-language daily, was arrested on July 25, presumably for failing to comply with the rules. He had been a critic of Mrs. Gandhi.

The official explanation of the crackdown on the foreign press was that some newspapers continually distorted the situation in India, ignoring the achievements of the government and exaggerating its shortcomings. Mrs. Gandhi said in an interview: "A section of the world press has always belittled India and her actions and misrepresented what is done here."[6]

## Improved Services and Economic Conditions

There were scattered protests against the emergency edicts mostly in states where opposition parties were strong. Demonstrations and violence were brought under control quickly. According to the observations of Westerners in India, Mrs. Gandhi remains popular, especially in the thousands of small villages where 80 per cent of the people live.

One reason is that India's fortunes have taken an upturn. Most reports from India since the emergency note that the Indian civil service, which was known for its inefficiency, developed a new spirit of punctuality, hard work and cleanliness. Moreover, economic conditions have improved. The inflation rate of 30 per cent in 1974 dropped to near zero by September 1975 and is relatively stable today. Prices in New Delhi's restaurants were lowered last summer and a tax cut was given to middle-income groups.

The International Monetary Fund reported in April 1976 that in the previous 12 months consumer prices fell 5.6 per cent in India—the largest drop in any country. The price of rice, which had been rising rapidly, was stabilized by the government, and sugar and bread prices declined. India's economy has also been aided by the benefits of last summer's good monsoon season—the rains were the best in years. Farmers harvested record grain crops, making food relatively plentiful.

---

[5] Loren Jenkins of *Newsweek*, Peter Hazelhurst of *The Times* of London and Peter Gill of the *Daily Telegraph* of London.
[6] *Saturday Review*, Aug. 9, 1975.

## Chronology of an Emergency

**1975**

**June 12.** Prime Minister Indira Gandhi found guilty by state court of "corrupt" practices during 1971 election.

**June 24.** Supreme Court Justice partially clears Mrs. Gandhi but rules she is ineligible to participate in parliamentary debates.

**June 25.** Opposition Leader J. P. Narayan addresses thousands at rally in New Delhi; calls for Mrs. Gandhi to resign.

**June 26.** Emergency proclaimed; political figures including Narayan arrested, censorship imposed.

**July 4.** Twenty-six political parties banned.

**July 22.** Upper house of Parliament approves emergency decree; opposition leaders walk out.

**July 23.** Lower house ratifies upper house action.

**July 24.** Parliament bars courts from overturning the decree.

**Nov. 7.** Supreme Court reverses conviction of Mrs. Gandhi.

**Nov. 12.** Narayan, critically ill, released from prison.

**1976**

**Jan. 29.** Lower house makes censorship permanent.

**March 12.** National government takes control of the state government of Gujarat—the last state ruled by opposition.

**April 28.** Supreme Court upholds government's right to imprison political opponents without court hearings.

**May 15.** Asoka Mahta, a leading opponent of Mrs. Gandhi, is released from jail.

Some of the favorable economic factors are attributed to the discipline of Mrs. Gandhi's authoritarian control rather than to any new policy embodied in a 20-point program she outlined to the nation at the time she declared the emergency. Two of the 20 points were intended to liquidate rural indebtedness and to speed the distribution of surplus land among the peasants.

## Impending Changes in Foreign Policy

The Soviet Union has generally supported Mrs. Gandhi's emergency. The United States, on the other hand, has refused to comment officially, but U.S.-India relations can be characterized as chilly. Moscow's support, which had been unconditional at the onset of the emergency, is beginning to ebb, however. The Russians are concerned that Mrs. Gandhi's emergency rule is turning steadily to the right. The Communist Party of India (CPI)—a pro-Russia party and the only Communist party not outlawed in India—is reported to be growing restive under the state of emergency, objecting particularly to the ban on strikes. Nevertheless, Soviet leaders gave Mrs. Gandhi a warm welcome when she arrived in Moscow for an official visit on June 8.

Mrs. Gandhi has continued to denounce the United States for alleged influence of the Central Intelligence Agency in India's internal affairs and to criticize American newspapers for their treatment of the emergency. Her criticism prompted the Ford administration to drop a proposed $65-million economic aid package for India in fiscal year 1976. But Congress is considering President Ford's request for $197.3-million in economic and food aid for India during fiscal year 1977.

There was no public response by Moscow or the CPI to India's unwelcome announcement on April 15 that it was restoring diplomatic relations with China. These ties had been broken since 1962 when the two countries went to war over a boundary dispute. Relations were strained further by China's continuing support for Pakistan, India's traditional enemy. But now there is an attempt to end the enmity with Pakistan. Four days after announcing it would send an ambassador to Peking, the New Delhi government made public a letter from Mrs. Gandhi to Pakistani Prime Minister Zulfikar Ali Bhutto offering to "discuss measures for the restoration of diplomatic relations."

---

# Ten Years Under Indira Gandhi

---

T HE YEARS SINCE Indira Gandhi was sworn in as India's third Prime Minister on Jan. 24, 1966, have witnessed a series of political, social, economic and military traumas, culminating in the 1975 emergency proclamation. The first nine years of Mrs. Gandhi's leadership could be divided into three phases.[7] The first phase lasted until a tumultuous split of the Congress Party in 1969. Following that schism, Mrs. Gandhi cemented her power in a recreated Congress Party and reduced her party opponents nearly to powerlessness. The second phase covers the years 1969-73 when Mrs. Gandhi reached the peak of popularity and political strength. The final phase began in 1974 with the recovery of opposition strength and the floundering of the Indian economy, and it continues to the present time.

The fact that Indira Gandhi was the daughter of Jawaharlal Nehru is important to her political success. But there are other significant factors. An intelligent, widely traveled and politically astute woman, she gained prominence during her father's tenure as the first Prime Minister of India, in 1947-64. Nehru's only child, she went to live in her widowed father's home soon after he assumed the office.[8] Mrs. Gandhi took on the duties of

---

[7] See Neville Maxwell, "Woman on a White Horse: India 1975," *Round Table*, October 1975.

[8] Mrs. Gandhi's marriage to Feroze Gandhi was disintegrating at the time. Feroze Gandhi died in 1960, years after the marriage had broken up.

official hostess. She soon became her father's closest adviser and was identified with him throughout India.

There were others—veterans of the fight against the British—who rivaled Mrs. Gandhi for the Congress Party's leadership. When Nehru died in 1964, Lal Bahadur Shastri, a trusted Nehru aide, was chosen by party leaders to become Prime Minister. Mrs. Gandhi was selected to join the Shastri government as minister for information and broadcasting. But Shastri died unexpectedly on Jan. 11, 1966, and the party was once again faced with the succession question.

Morarji Desai, who had narrowly lost to Shastri two years earlier, pushed hard to win the Congress Party's blessing. But the party bosses balked at giving power to Desai, who many thought would be an authoritarian, uncontrollable leader. Especially active against Desai was Congress Party President Kamaraj Nadar, who marshalled party strength behind Mrs. Gandhi. Kamaraj and the other party leaders considered her the perfect candidate—strong enough to win the election, yet weak enough to be managed by the party hierarchy. Mrs. Gandhi was popular throughout India, especially among Hindi-speaking people.[9] She overwhelmingly defeated Desai for the leadership post, thus assuring herself the prime ministership.

### Initial Political Support and Election Setback

Within a year of her elevation to the office, Mrs. Gandhi began to assert her independence of other Congress Party leaders. As she became stronger, Kamaraj and his colleagues—the "syndicate"—decided to replace her after the 1967 general election. But the 1967 contest brought stunning losses to the party. Opposition parties gained power in several states, and the Congress Party retained only a small majority in Parliament.[10] The move to unseat Mrs. Gandhi was put off until Karamaj and the syndicate could regroup and regain the political power they lost in the election.

The losses could be attributed to economic and social turbulence in India. A devastating drought in 1965 led to food shortages the following year, and war with Pakistan in 1965 depleted India's fiscal resources. The United States halted economic aid to India during the war and inflation soared. Adding to the economic troubles were old problems of intense regional and linguistic rivalries. Riots erupted early in 1966 over the issue of

---

[9] Indira Gandhi's mother, a devout Hindu, raised her daughter to speak vernacular Hindi. Mrs. Gandhi used this ability to political advantage while serving under her father to appeal to the Hindu masses.

[10] India's 22 states have strong governments, although the federal government exercises centralized control. Each state has a highly developed administrative structure that extends to the districts, towns and village.

## The Language Question

India's constitution designates Hindi the country's official language. But 13 other languages are formally recognized. These include English, the inheritance of British rule which is the language of India's upper classes. Legislation was enacted in 1967 to protect local languages in each of India's regions, while at the same time making English an official language in addition to Hindi. Communications in government departments, Parliament, state-owned businesses and between the central and state governments are required to be conducted in Hindi and English. Since 1967 several states have made local languages the official tongue in those states.

choosing India's official language,[11] creating a "scene of decline, confusion and incipient collapse"[12] as Mrs. Gandhi took office in January of that year.

Despite the fact that her administration did little to relieve the pressing economic problems of 1966, Mrs. Gandhi held onto her position in the party and the government. After the 1967 election, she began to assert her independence even more vigorously, giving her supporters and confidants important posts in the government and shoving aside Desai's adherents. Mrs. Gandhi now began to benefit from three straight years (1967-69) of favorable monsoon rains that led to better harvests, more food, a drop in inflation and a general upswing in industrial performance.

### Personal Popularity Amid Split in the Party

In November 1969 came the Congress Party split. She dismissed Desai, her leading rival, as deputy prime minister and nationalized 14 major banks—two acts that won her wide support among the Indian people. She was now perceived as a fighter for their rights against the conservative, old guard politicians. The next political test was the 1971 general election. With the Congress Party divided, Mrs. Gandhi's followers gained only 43.6 per cent of the popular vote. But the opposition was so deeply divided that her wing of the party had a comfortable majority in Parliament.

India's military triumph over Pakistan also came in 1971. India, with Russian support, aided a victorious uprising in East Pakistan which created the new state of Bangladesh.[13] Mrs. Gandhi reached her pinnacle of popularity after the victory. In

---

[11] Although English is used by most government officials, business executives and intellectuals, India has 13 other major languages and hundreds of dialects. *See box above.*

[12] So described by Zareer Masani in *Indira Gandhi, A Biography* (1976), p. 148.

[13] See "East Pakistan's Civil War," *E.R.R.*, 1971 Vol. II, pp. 567-584.

the February 1972 state elections her party won huge majorities in nearly every Indian state. She was supreme in the government, the party and among the people. Indeed, she was widely thought of by the masses as *Durga*, the Hindu goddess of war.

Then how did Mrs. Gandhi's popularity shrink to the point that she was in political danger three years later? The answer lies in what happened to India's economy and society when the effects of the 1971 war effort in Pakistan began to be felt. The resultant high rate of inflation and industrial recession deeply hurt millions of Indians, 40 per cent of whom (by government calculations) live below the poverty line of 40 rupees—around five dollars—a month.

Hoarding, black market profiteering, smuggling and speculation became blatant and widespread, and the ruling Congress Party was nearly powerless to deal with it. The party was plagued by inefficiency, graft and corruption, in both the national and state governments. The public distribution of consumer goods, including food, became one of the government's most difficult tasks.

## Attempt to Deal With Nation's Overpopulation

Central to any discussion of India's social and economic problems is that country's burgeoning population. India's population is currently estimated[14] to total 620.7 million, second only to China's. The population increases by around 13 million annually and is projected to reach or exceed one billion by the year 2000. There have been government campaigns to lower the birth rate but, aside from bureaucratic ineptitude, the basic barrier to population control arises from Indian society. The Hindu religion greatly emphasizes the birth of sons. And the largely uneducated masses of Hindu and Moslem people have resisted most of the government's efforts to introduce contraception—sometimes with violence.

In a country where only around 5 per cent of the married couples use conventional birth control devices, the government introduced a new birth-control program on April 16, 1976. Among other things, it raised the minimum marriage age for men (from 18 to 21) and women (from 15 to 18) and authorized payment[15] to a married man or woman who voluntarily undergoes sterilization. Several of the state governments are also considering stringent birth-control laws. One state, Maharashtra, has under study a law to make sterilization compulsory for parents of three or more children.

---

[14] By the Population Reference Bureau in Washington, D.C.

[15] From $8 to $15—the fewer the children a couple already has, the higher the payment.

The expanding population puts an enormous strain on India's economy. A writer noted recently: "India has made economic progress since independence, doubling her food production and tripling her industrial output. Yet, because of the population explosion...[India] seems to stand still."[16] From 1973 through 1975 the economic situation in India deteriorated rapidly and was accompanied by sometimes violent mass protests. These were led by members of the extremist, ultra-conservative Jan Sangh, a Hindu party, and the Maoist Naxalite Party. Although her Congress Party still controlled Parliament, Mrs. Gandhi's popularity declined markedly. The Arab oil embargo in 1973-74, together with the higher costs of oil and other imported materials, hit India hard.

The climate of disenchantment in 1974 led the 72-year-old Narayan, "probably the most respected person in India,"[17] to come out of political retirement and challenge Mrs. Gandhi. He called for a campaign against corruption and for reforms in education, elections and politics. J. P., frail and in poor health, drew support from students, workers and intellectuals from the middle classes. They were joined by opponents of Mrs. Gandhi from the left and right. Throughout the year, this movement picked up strength and influence around the country. That November Mrs. Gandhi met with him, an old and close friend of her father, but nothing came of this attempt at reconcilation. Instead, the gulf widened and J. P. was among the first arrested when the emergency was proclaimed. Because of his deteriorating health, he was released from jail in November 1975.

---

# Survival of Democracy in India

---

IN THE YEAR since the promulgation of the emergency declaration, Mrs. Gandhi has been widely accused of destroying India's democracy. But the Prime Minister continues to claim that, on the contrary, what she has done has been to safeguard democracy. On a visit to the United States in August 1975, she said she remained committed to democracy—"not merely because it is a good idea but because, for a country of India's vast size and great diversity, I think democracy—that is, the people's participation—is the only way to make it function."[18]

It has been observed that Mrs. Gandhi was brought up in the

[16] Paul Kurtz, "The End of Indian Democracy?" *Freedom at Issue,* March-April 1976, p. 25.
[17] So described by Norman D. Palmer in "The Crisis in India," *Orbis,* summer 1975, p. 388.
[18] "Meet the Press" (NBC-TV) interview, Aug. 24, 1975.

## Proclaiming an Emergency

The emergency proclamation of June 26, 1975, invoked Clause I of Article 352 of India's constitution. The clause states in full: "If the President is satisfied that a grave emergency exists whereby the security of India or any part of the territory is threatened, whether by war or external aggression or internal disturbances, he may, by Proclamation, make a declaration to that effect."

India's President, upon whom this power is bestowed, is virtually a figurehead in politics; real power rests with the Prime Minister. The June 26 proclamation was declared by President Fakruhhin Ali Ahmed at Mrs. Gandhi's behest.

India technically has been under a state of emergency since December 1971 during its latest war with Pakistan. That emergency, which was never lifted, granted the government extra-parliamentary powers. The June 1975 proclamation declared a second, simultaneous state of emergency.

democratic tradition under her father and helped him guide India's fledgling democratic state. She also learned the art of political survival from her father. And she has proven to be adept at wielding the considerable powers of her office to suit her purposes. Regardless of her professed belief in democracy, India under the emergency has witnessed an expansion of authoritarian powers and an erosion of democratic rights.

The Indian constitution was modeled basically on the British and American systems of democratic government. In its application to a land so vastly different from Britain and America, though, Indian democracy has taken its own peculiar form. An Indian writer described his country's constitution as partly "a sheer act of faith." Poverty, illiteracy and underdevelopment, he said, "present a daily warning to the working of democracy, and it has needed a heroic leadership to give content and continuing nurture to it."[19]

For centuries, the largely illiterate, destitute masses had been ruled by authoritarian despots. Indians learned about democracy during the years of British rule but were not allowed to practice it until independence came in 1947. "Heroic leadership" came from Nehru, who molded the Indian government to fit the needs of his nation. The overwhelming power and popularity of the Congress Party led to a democratic but essentially one-party system of government under powerful prime ministers. It has been said the government has "the air of a monarchy with local satrapies dispensing patronage and favors."[20]

---

[19] Nayantara Sahgal, "The Making of Mrs. Gandhi," *South Asian Review*, April 1975, p. 209.

[20] Ved Mehta, "Democracy in a Poor Country," *The New Yorker*, March 22, 1976, p. 92.

The Indian democracy was far from perfect. From the start it was marred by corruption, especially on the state level. But it endured, keeping the religious, racial, regional and linguistic groups united under one central government. The people were granted freedom of speech and political expression, two of democracy's fundamental rights. Although the Congress Party clearly held political control, many minority representatives were elected to state and national legislatures.

India's constitution significantly differs from those of the Western democracies in its preventive detention provisions, designed to preserve order by suspending civil rights during emergencies. These laws were used by Britain during colonial days and were put into India's constitution only after heated debate. India was faced with Communist-led rebellions when the constitution was drawn up in February 1950 and the decision to adopt preventive detention has been called a triumph of "necessity...over due process."[21] The laws were invoked for the first time for an internal emergency in 1975 by Indira Gandhi. Thus far, Mrs. Gandhi has kept within the letter of the law (and the constitution) with the measures she has had invoked since the emergency was proclaimed.

## Tightening of Controls Since the Emergency

The Gandhi government has imposed a series of laws and regulations that have broadened the scope of the emergency rules. The original proclamation suspended the freedoms of speech, expression, assembly and association. Since then, the rights to move around the country, to acquire property and to choose any profession have been suspended. In addition, those arrested no longer have the right to know the charges against them or to have court hearings.

Parliament passed a bill in January to retain the press censorship permanently, even after the emergency is lifted. Parliamentary elections, which were scheduled for March 1976, have been postponed for a year. At least 26 small, extremist political parties have been banned, as have protest marches, rallies, public demonstrations and a number of anti-government publications. Thousands have been arrested, although the actual number is impossible to determine; the government refuses to disclose any recent figures.[22]

Leaders of four remaining parties, including J. P. Narayan, said at a press conference in Bombay on May 25 they had made plans to form a single party so that their opposition could be more effective. They hoped to have the new fusion party func-

---

[21] A. H. Hanson and Janet Douglas, *India's Democracy* (1972), p. 63.

[22] *The New York Times* reported on April 17, 1976, that "the most reliable estimates of those now in jail vary between 30,000 and 75,000."

tioning by June 26. The party will comprise members of the Jan Sangh, Socialist, Opposition Congress and Bharatiya Lok Dal parties. The declared goal of this group is to restore civil liberties, freedom of press and speech, an independent judiciary and to establish an egalitarian social order.

It has been argued that the only way India can be administered effectively is through strong, authoritarian government, either from the right or left. And Mrs. Gandhi's apparent success in bringing discipline to India would seem to bear out that proposition. All of India's neighbors—China, Pakistan, Bangladesh, Burma, Nepal, Sri Lanka—are ruled by powerful, non-democratic governments. In this respect, the tightening of Mrs. Gandhi's control and the limiting of civil rights in India can be seen as part of a movement in South Asia, and in much of the Third World, toward authoritarianism in lands where poverty and illiteracy are the main social problems.

Mrs. Gandhi is vague about when she will lift the emergency. She has said only that the emergency is "temporary" and will be ended when internal order is restored. There is some evidence that all the emergency powers may be made permanent. Parliament has already approved two constitutional amendments that, in effect, write some of the emergency restrictions into the main body of law.

### Scenarios for India's Future Political Course

There is speculation that Mrs. Gandhi, at age 58, may be preparing to turn over her political power to Sanjay Gandhi, her youngest son. Sanjay, 29, has been named to the executive committee of the Congress Party's youth wing and has made speeches throughout India in support of his mother's programs. In addition, the censored Indian press has been allowed to portray Sanjay as "his mother's constant companion, her super-adviser and crown prince."[23] The prospect of a "Nehru dynasty" does not appear farfetched.

In neighboring Bangladesh, President Sheik Mujibar Rahman and most of his immediate family were assassinated in a military takeover of the government last summer. But thus far in India, it appears that the military has stood firmly behind Mrs. Gandhi. How the military would react in the event of a rebellion arising from the dozens of splinter groups throughout India is largely conjectural. There is no evidence that any such uprising is imminent, but violence among India's disparate minority groups has occurred repeatedly in modern Indian history. One reason for the emergency decree was that sections of the country feel less than totally committed to the Indian Union.

---

[23] See Werner Adam, "Gandhi & Son," *Swiss Review of World Affairs*, March 1976, p. 7.

# Selected Bibliography

## Books

Bhatia, Krishan, *Indira: A Biography of Prime Minister Gandhi*, Praeger, 1974.

Brecher, Michael, *Nehru's Mantle: The Politics of Succession in India*, Praeger, 1966.

Das, Durga, *India: From Curzon to Nehru and After*, John Day, 1970.

Galbraith, John Kenneth, *Ambassador's Journal: A Personal Account of the Kennedy Years*, Houghton Mifflin, 1969.

Hanson, A. H. and Janet Douglas, *India's Democracy*, W. W. Norton, 1972.

Masani, Zareer, *Indira Gandhi, A Biography*, Crowell, 1976.

Morris-Jones, W. H., *The Government and Politics of India*, Hutchinson, 1967.

Nossiter, Bernard D., *Soft State: A Newspaperman's Chronicle of India*, Harper & Row, 1970.

## Articles

Adam, Werner, "Gandhi & Son," *Swiss Review of World Affairs*, March 1976.

Bowring, Philip and Lawrence Lifschultz, "India: Farmers Await an Emergency Transfusion," *Far Eastern Economic Review*, Oct. 24, 1975.

Fallaci, Oriana, "Indira's Coup," *New York Review of Books*, Sept. 18, 1975.

Gandelman, Joe, "How a 'Democracy of Convenience' Came to Die," *The Progressive*, October 1975.

*India News* (publication of the Information Service, Embassy of India), selected issues.

Kurtz, Paul, "The End of Indian Democracy?" *Freedom At Issue*, March-April 1976.

Lukas, J. Anthony, "India Is as Indira Does," *The New York Times Magazine*, April 4, 1976.

Maxwell, Neville, "Woman on a White Horse: India 1975," *Round Table*, October 1975.

Mehta, Ved, "Democracy in a Poor Country," *The New Yorker*, March 22, 1976.

Palmer, Norman D., "The Crisis of Indian Democracy," *Orbis*, summer 1975.

## Reports and Studies

Editorial Research Reports, "India's Election and Economic Prospects," 1967 Vol. I, p. 43; "India 1971: Strained Democracy," 1971 Vol. I, p. 123.

Population Reference Bureau Inc., "Intercom, the International Newsletter on Population," April 1976.

# INDEX

## A

# INDEX

# INDEX

# INDEX

# INDEX

## N

**Nadar, Kamaraj** - 189
**Namibia**
  South Africa's control - 148
**Narayan, Jaya Prakash**
  Challenge to Gandhi - 183, 192, 194
**National Front for the Liberation of Angola** - 148
**National Security.** See Defense and National Security.
**Nehru, Jawaharlal** - 183, 188, 193
**Netherlands**
  Lockheed scandal - 14
**Neto, Agostinho**
  Angolan independence - 148

## O

**Orfila, Alejandro**
  Panama Canal negotiations - 78
**Organization for African Unity**
  Selassie's execution protested - 164
**Organization of American States (OAS)**
  Panama Canal issue - 67

## P

**Pakistan**
  Relations with India - 188
**Panama**
  Canal controversy origins - 71
  Canal Zone map - 65
  Negotiations with U.S. - 64
  Panama Canal at a glance (box) - 70
  Panama Canal chronology (box) - 75
**People's Republic of China**
  Arms transfers of major suppliers, 1965-74 (box) - 8
  India's diplomatic relations - 188
  Sino-Soviet tensions - 56
**Philippines**
  Church opposition to political arrests - 87
  Communist guerrillas' resistance - 89
  Development under U.S. tutelage - 94
  Diplomatic initiatives with Communists - 99
  Government, land, people (box) - 93
  Internal problems after independence - 96
  Issues facing Marcos - 97
  Land reform plan - 98

Map - 85
Muslim struggle for independence - 88, 97
"New Society" - 84
Population growth - 99
U.S. interest in the Philippines (box) - 90
U.S.-Philippine links - 91
World War II devastation - 95
**Poland**
  Arms transfers of major suppliers, 1965-74 (box) - 8
**Politics**
  Angola, Mozambique independence - 147, 148
  Britain's arena of political struggle - 131
  Britain's trade union movement - 132
  British Labor Party challenges - 134
  Coalition governments, popular front era - 32
  Ethiopian coup chronology, 1974 - 167
  Ethiopian military regime's course - 164
  India's future political course - 195
  India under authoritarian rule - 181-196
  Labor governments in Britain since 1945 (box) - 133
  Marxism definition disputes - 28
  Philippines under martial law - 83
  Portuguese Communists' failure - 24-28
  Portuguese moderates' victory - 26
  Postwar leftist coalitions, France and Italy - 33
  Rhodesian blacks' struggle for majority rule - 156
  Rhodesian Front Party - 145, 146
  South African reformers' challenges - 155
  25th Soviet Party Congress - 41-60
  Western European Communism - 21-40
**Popular Movement for the Liberation of Angola (MPLA)** - 148
**Portugal**
  Angolan independence - 147
  Communist involvement in overthrow - 25
  Communist role reassessed - 27
  Communists' failure - 24
  Moderates' victory - 26
  Mozambique independence - 148
**Proxmire, William (D Wis.)**
  Bribery of foreign officials - 18

## Q, R

**Race Relations**
  Apartheid tensions - 152
  Rhodesian blacks' struggle for majority rule - 156

# INDEX

# INDEX